Morality

Morality

Restoring the Common Good in Divided Times

Jonathan Sacks

HODDER &
STOUGHTON

First published in Great Britain in 2020 by Hodder & Stoughton
An Hachette UK company

1

Copyright © Jonathan Sacks, 2020

The right of Jonathan Sacks to be identified as the Author of the Work has been
asserted by him in accordance with the Copyright, Designs and Patents Act 1988.

All Scripture references are taken from the author's own translation.

A CIP catalogue record for this title is available from the British Library

Hardback ISBN 978 1 473 61731 5
Trade Paperback ISBN 978 1 529 34263 5
eBook ISBN 978 1 473 61732 2

Typeset in Sabon MT by Hewer Text UK Ltd, Edinburgh
Printed and bound in Great Britain by Clays Ltd, Elcograf S.p.A.

Hodder & Stoughton policy is to use papers that are natural, renewable
and recyclable products and made from wood grown in sustainable
forests. The logging and manufacturing processes are expected to
conform to the environmental regulations of the country of origin.

Hodder & Stoughton Ltd
Carmelite House
50 Victoria Embankment
London EC4Y 0DZ

www.hodder.co.uk

To our grandchildren:
Noa, Ari, Elisha, Gedalya, Zev,
Ariella, Natan, Talya and Noam

הַמַּלְאָךְ הַגֹּאֵל אֹתִי מִכָּל־רָע יְבָרֵךְ אֶת־הַנְּעָרִים
וְיִקָּרֵא בָהֶם שְׁמִי וְשֵׁם אֲבֹתַי אַבְרָהָם וְיִצְחָק
וְיִדְגּוּ לָרֹב בְּקֶרֶב הָאָרֶץ:
(Gen. 48:16)

May all you do be blessed

Contents

Preface and Acknowledgements

The journey of which this book is the culmination began more than fifty years ago. Although I have spent much of my adult life as a religious leader, my first love, long before I decided to become a rabbi, was moral philosophy, which I studied at both Cambridge and Oxford. I was incredibly blessed to have as my tutors three of the greatest philosophical minds of our time. My third-year undergraduate tutor was Roger Scruton. My doctoral supervisor at Cambridge was Bernard Williams and at Oxford, Philippa Foot.

They were outstanding. But the state of moral philosophy in general was not. It was clever but not wise. A.J. Ayer told us, in a famous chapter of *Language, Truth and Logic*, that moral judgements, being unverifiable, were meaningless, the mere expression of emotion. Another philosopher told us that ethics was a matter of inventing right and wrong. Morality – so went the popular view – was either subjective or relative, and there was little in academic philosophy of the time to say otherwise. James Q. Wilson, the great Harvard political scientist, discovered, while teaching a class on Nazi Germany, that there was no general agreement that those guilty of the Holocaust had committed a moral horror. 'It all depends on your perspective,' one student said.[1]

All three of my teachers knew that there was something wrong with all of this. It was superficial, philistine and irresponsible. Each found a way out, though it took time. Bernard Williams told me in 1970 that he did not know how to write moral philosophy – though he quickly recovered and produced his first book, called, like this one, *Morality*, in 1971. I had meanwhile decided that the best place to begin was within my own tradition of Judaism, which has had an almost unbroken conversation on the nature of a good society since the days when Abraham was charged to teach his children 'the way of the Lord by doing what is right and just' (Gen. 18:19).

There were others who could see what was going wrong. Philip Rieff said that 'Culture is another name for a design of motives directing the self outward, toward those communal purposes in which alone the self can be realised and satisfied', and that this was now being systematically abandoned in pursuit of what he called 'the triumph of the therapeutic'.[2] Joan Didion, in her book *The White Album*, wrote, 'I have trouble maintaining the basic notion that keeping promises matters in a world where everything I was taught seems beside the point.'[3]

For me, the most persuasive was Alasdair MacIntyre and his masterwork, *After Virtue*, in which he argued that though we continue to use moral language, 'we have – very largely, if not entirely – lost our comprehension, both theoretical and practical, of morality'.[4] All we possess, he said, is disconnected fragments of what was once a coherent view of the world and our place within it. He ended the book with a warning of 'the coming ages of barbarism and darkness'. That book, despite its pessimism, brought me back to moral philosophy. MacIntyre has been one of the great influences on my life, though there is this obvious difference between us: being Jewish, I am disinclined to pessimism.[5] I prefer hope.

Love your neighbour. Love the stranger. Hear the cry of the otherwise unheard. Liberate the poor from their poverty. Care for the dignity of all. Let those who have more than they need share their blessings with those who have less. Feed the hungry, house the homeless, and heal the sick in body and mind. Fight injustice, whoever it is done by and whoever it is done against. And do these things because, being human, we are bound by a covenant of human solidarity, whatever our colour or culture, class or creed.

These are moral principles, not economic or political ones. They have to do with conscience, not wealth or power. But without them, freedom will not survive. The free market and liberal democratic state together will not save liberty, because liberty can never be built by self-interest alone. I-based societies all eventually die. Ibn Khaldun showed this in the fourteenth century, Giambattista Vico in the eighteenth and Bertrand Russell in the twentieth. Other-based societies survive.

Morality is not an option. It's an essential.

*

The book is structured as follows: in Part One, 'The Solitary Self', I look at the impact of the move from 'We' to 'I' on personal happiness and well-being, in terms of human loneliness, the over-emphasis on self-help, the impact of social media and the partial breakdown of the family.

Part Two, 'Consequences', is about how the loss of a shared morality has serious negative consequences for both the market and the state. This section begins with a chapter, 'From "We" to "I"', that is a brief intellectual history of the growth of individualism. It ends with a chapter, 'Time and Consequence', that attempts to explain why decisions that seem sound in the short term can be disastrous in the long term.

Part Three, 'Can We Still Reason Together?', is about the progressive loss of respect for truth and civility in the public conversation. It has become very difficult to talk and listen across divides. Is truth still of value in politics? Is the collaborative pursuit of truth still the purpose of a university? How have social media affected the tone and tenor of our relationships with one another? What does all this do for trust, an essential precondition of the good society?

In Part Four, 'Being Human', I look at the connection between morality, human dignity and a meaningful life. I also look at why morality is necessary, the different forms it can take, and the connection between it and religion.

Finally, in Part Five, 'The Way Forward', I set out my own credo as to why morality matters, and then suggest ways in which we can strengthen it in the future.

*

This book is about the power of 'We', and it is a delight to say that it took shape through three encounters with remarkable groups of people.

The first was the ceremony on my receipt of the Templeton Prize in 2016.[6] That was when I first set out my argument about the outsourcing of morality. It was a memorable evening, and I want to express my thanks to the Templeton family for the occasion itself and for the great work they do through the John Templeton Foundation. It was a great sadness that Dr John (Jack) Templeton had died a year earlier, and another that his wife Dr Josephine (Pina) passed away just before I could send her a draft of this book. I miss them both. They were wonderful people whose lives were lifted on the wings of high ideals. My thanks to their daughters, Heather Templeton Dill and Jennifer Templeton Simpson, for their friendship and their great work – and to all involved at the John Templeton Foundation, which funds some of the most visionary research into the impact of altruism and positive emotions like joy, hope and forgiveness on society and on physical and emotional health.

The second occasion was my TED Talk in Vancouver in April 2017.[7] This was the first time I had spoken at TED and it was the most nerve-wracking speech I think I have ever given. Chris Anderson, the curator of TED, and his team have lifted the communication of ideas to a new plane, and it was inspirational if daunting simply to be in their company. Because they are the best listeners in the world, they bring out the best in their speakers. The topic of the 2017 conference was 'The Future You', so I argued that for the sake of the future 'You', we should strengthen the future 'Us'. I said that ours is an age in which there is too much 'I' and too little 'We'. I spoke about the 'We' of relationship, the 'We' of identity and the 'We' of responsibility, and I suggested that we perform a search-and-replace operation on our mind. Wherever we encounter the word 'self', we should substitute the word 'other'. So instead of self-help, other-help; instead of self-esteem, other-esteem. That, I argued, would transform us and begin to transform our world.

The third was the five-part series, *Morality in the 21st Century*, that I did for BBC Radio 4 in September 2018.[8] I've always enjoyed working with the BBC. For more than thirty years I have done 'Thought for the Day' on the *Today* programme on Radio 4, and for twenty-two years I produced television programmes each year for BBC One. Religion and ethics are and must remain a central part of the BBC's remit as a public service broadcaster and as one of the most influential shapers of British culture as a whole. That role becomes all the more important when, in the unregulated chaos of online information, misinformation and disinformation, we find it ever harder to identify trustworthy sources of the truth. So it was a great delight to make this series, made all the more so by the active involvement of Christine Morgan, series editor, and head of radio religion and ethics, and Dan Tierney, the series producer. I don't think I have ever enjoyed programme-making so much.

The eleven expert participants in the programmes, drawn from Britain, the United States and Canada, were outstanding, as I fully expected them to be. They were: Nick Bostrom, Professor of Applied Ethics at the University of Oxford; David Brooks, *New York Times* columnist and author; Melinda Gates, co-chair of the Bill & Melinda Gates Foundation and philanthropist; Jonathan Haidt, Professor of Ethical Leadership at New York University; Noreena Hertz, Honorary Professor at University College London; Jordan Peterson, Professor of Psychology at the University of Toronto; Steven Pinker, Professor of Psychology at Harvard University; Robert Putnam, Professor of Public Policy at Harvard University; Michael Sandel, Professor of Political Philosophy at Harvard University; Mustafa Suleyman, co-founder and Head of Applied AI at DeepMind; and Jean Twenge, Professor of Psychology at San Diego State University. Their influence on my thought is evident throughout this book. No less significant is the encouragement I received from having studied their work, in some cases over many years, and realising that I was not alone.

The stars of the programmes, however, were undoubtedly the students from four secondary schools who joined me in the studio to discuss the responses of our experts. They came from Manchester High School for Girls, Manchester Grammar School for Boys, Graveney School in Tooting, and Queens' School in Bushey. They were intelligent, engaged, had the confidence to challenge some of the experts' views, and had a delightful sense of humour also. Almost everyone who commented on the programmes singled them out for praise, and they are a compelling source of hope for the future.

I might have guessed in advance that a book seeking to re-prioritise the 'We' over the 'I' would turn out to be a thoroughly collaborative endeavour. But never could I have suspected how true this would be. Here my heartfelt thanks go to my editor, Ian Metcalfe, and the team at Hodder. Never have I been as thoroughly edited as I was on this occasion by Ian, who went through every line of every page of several drafts with a critical focus and willingness to challenge that I've never encountered before. The good things in this book are largely due to him. I take credit for the mistakes and the infelicities. This was real teamsmanship.

As always, Louise Greenberg, my literary agent, has shown a faith in me that I find humbling and largely undeserved. Louise produced my first foray into this territory, the 1990 Reith Lectures on 'The Persistence of Faith'.[9] Her help and understanding this time were exceptional. Thanks to Justin McLaren and D-J Collins, Dayan Ivan Binstock and David Frei who offered helpful and insightful comments on the book.

For the 'We' dimension of my working life, I am blessed with the best team in the world: Joanna Benarroch, Dan Sacker and Debby Ifield, who have made everything I do possible. What makes them special is not just their total dedication, professionalism and enthusiasm. It is their unremittingly high moral standards. They care about doing the right thing in the right way. They live by the values of loyalty, integrity, responsibility and humility, and I have become a better person because of them. Dan on this occasion did much of the research for the book, and made many suggestions concerning substance and style.

The most important person in my life is my wife Elaine. This year we will celebrate our golden wedding. I tried to explain in my TED Talk what drew me to Elaine in the first place: the fact that she was as unlike me as possible. I was earning graduate qualifications in self-doubt and existential angst. She was radiating joy. Hence my theory, which is a summary of the book: namely, *It's the people not like us who make us grow*.

Finally, I have dedicated this book to our grandchildren. It was for the sake of their future that I wrote it.

INTRODUCTION

Cultural Climate Change

A free society is a moral achievement.

Over the past fifty years in the West this truth has been forgotten, ignored or denied. That is why today liberal democracy is at risk.

Societal freedom cannot be sustained by market economics and liberal democratic politics alone. It needs a third element: morality, a concern for the welfare of others, an active commitment to justice and compassion, a willingness to ask not just what is good for me but what is good for all-of-us-together. It is about 'Us', not 'Me'; about 'We', not 'I'.

If we focus on the 'I' and lose the 'We', if we act on self-interest without a commitment to the common good, if we focus on self-esteem and lose our care for others, we will lose much else. Nations will cease to have societies and instead have identity groups. We will lose our feeling of collective responsibility and find in its place a culture of competitive victimhood. In an age of unprecedented possibilities, people will feel vulnerable and alone.

The market will be merciless. Politics will be deceiving, divisive, confrontational and extreme. People will feel anxious, uncertain, fearful, aggressive, unstable, unrooted and unloved. They will focus on promoting themselves instead of the one thing that will give them lasting happiness: making life better for others. People will be, by historic standards, financially rich but emotionally poor. Freedom itself will be at risk from the far right and the far left, the far right dreaming of a golden age that never was, the far left dreaming of a utopia that will never be.

Liberal democracy is at risk in Britain, Europe and the United States. So is everything that these democracies represent in terms of freedom, dignity, compassion and rights. The most technologically advanced societies the world has ever known have forgotten just this: we are not machines, we are people, and people survive by caring for one another, not only by competing with one another. Market economics and liberal politics will fail if they are not undergirded by a moral sense that puts our shared humanity first. Economic inequalities will grow. Politics will continue to disappoint our expectations. There will be a rising tide of anger and resentment, and that, historically, is a danger signal for the future of freedom.

I believe that we are undergoing the cultural equivalent of climate change, and only when we realise this will we understand the strange things that have been happening in the twenty-first century in the realms of politics and economics, the deterioration of public standards of truth and civil debate, and the threat to freedom of speech at British and American universities. It also underlies more personal phenomena like loneliness, depression and drug abuse. All these things are related. If we see this, we will already have taken the first step to a solution.

*

Warnings of the threat to liberal democracy are today being sounded by political leaders. On 8 November 2019, the thirtieth anniversary of the fall of the Berlin Wall, the German Chancellor Angela Merkel warned that 'the values on which Europe is founded – freedom, democracy, equality, rule of law, human rights – they are anything but self-evident.' Days earlier the French president Emmanuel Macron declared that we were experiencing 'the brain death of NATO'. Europe, he said, stands on 'the edge of a precipice'. Speaking in London on 13 November 2019, Hillary Clinton spoke about the women MPs who were leaving politics because of the abuse and threats they receive from extremists. Britain, she warned, may be 'on the path to authoritarianism, that is the path to fascism'.[1] Giving weight to such concerns, in June 2019 a combative Vladimir Putin declared that 'Liberalism is obsolete.'[2] These are not normal times.

Thirty years ago, with the collapse of communism and end of the Cold War, the West seemed part of another narrative altogether. It was called 'the end of history', and it seemed that the free market and liberal democracy would gradually and painlessly conquer the world. People everywhere wanted the wealth the market created and the freedom liberalism bestowed. For a while that seemed plausible, but today, to its adversaries, the West looks jaded, enervated, divided and weak.

Few people in recent years can have escaped the feeling that strange and unprecedented things are happening. The world has not been proceeding calmly along its accustomed course. The international political arena has not recovered equilibrium since 11 September 2001. The global economy has not reconfigured itself since the crash of 2007/8. The rising tide of drug abuse in the United States and the United Kingdom suggests that not all is well in many people's lives. The tenor of debate, whether in politics or academia, has become angrier and more vituperative. Some deep and destabilising transformation is taking place in the twenty-first century, but it is hard to say what. In an age of information overload, when so much of the news comes to us in such small, disconnected slices, we live in a world of desiccated soundbites, which increases our sense of not knowing where we are. This can lead to feelings of powerlessness, anxiety and fear, and a desperate desire to find people who will resolve the dissonance for us.

*

One of the most important symptoms of this culture-shift is the changing face of politics. Since 2016 and the Brexit referendum, British politics has, for much of the time, been reduced to fiasco and farce by the Yes–No, Hard–Soft, Deal–No Deal drama of Britain's withdrawal from the European Union. The government, for much of that time, has failed to present a united front, while the main opposition party showed itself unwilling or unable to confront the highly documented presence of antisemitism in its ranks. Both of these phenomena marked new lows in post-Second World War British political history.

Elsewhere in Europe, during the same period, there have been riots in France, Germany, Italy, Spain and Sweden. A seasoned observer of French politics, John Lichfield, said about the *Gilets jaunes* ('yellow jacket') riots in Paris in 2018/19 that he had never seen 'such wanton destruction . . . such random, hysterical hatred, directed not just towards the riot police but at shrines to the French republic beyond itself, such as the Arc de Triomphe'. The battle, he said, 'went beyond violent protest, beyond rioting, to the point of insurrection, even civil war'.[3]

In January 2019, thirty writers, historians and Nobel laureates, among them Simon Schama, Ian McEwan and Salman Rushdie, warned in a manifesto that 'Europe as an idea is falling apart before our eyes'. They spoke of 'the populist forces washing over the continent'. The European ideal, they said, 'remains the one force today virtuous enough to ward off the new signs of totalitarianism that drag in their wake the old miseries of the dark ages'.[4]

In the United States, the 2016 presidential election was one of the most divisive on record. According to a Reuters/Ipsos survey, 15 per cent of Americans had stopped talking to a relative or close friend as a result of the election. There was demonisation on both sides. It was a clear case of the kind of politics the late Bernard Lewis once encapsulated as, 'I'm right. You're wrong. Go to Hell.' Three years later, Peggy Noonan, one of the most eloquent voices in American politics, wrote in the *Wall Street Journal* that 'People are proud of their bitterness now.' The polarisation feeds on itself, becomes ever more acute: 'America isn't making fewer of the lonely, angry and unaffiliated, it's making more every day.'[5]

One term in particular has surfaced in many descriptions of the new politics, namely *populism*. This is not an easy term to define and is sometimes used very loosely as an insult rather than as a precise description. In general, though, the term is used to describe a form of politics that occurs when people see unacceptable gaps opening up in wealth and opportunity, when they sense assaults on their values either from an *avant garde* or from outsiders, when they feel that the establishment elites are working against them, not for them, and that the government is not addressing their problems. This leads to a call for strong leaders, and to relative indifference to the democratic process. A 2017 study of the rise of populism in the major developed countries showed that votes for populist parties were at their highest level since the 1930s, with a massive increase since 2013.[6]

Throughout the West there has been a loss of trust in public institutions and leaders, a rise of extremism in politics and a notable failure of governments to address fundamental problems such as climate change and the discontents of the global economy. A new phenomenon has begun to emerge: of 'identity politics' – that is, political campaigning focused not on the nation as a whole but on a series of self-identifying minorities, leading to the counter-politics of populism on behalf of a beleaguered and enraged native-born population who see themselves sidelined by the elites and passed over in favour of the minorities.

Meanwhile the very principles of political discourse have been damaged to the point where there has been a serious breakdown in trust. The manipulative use of social media, the distortions that have gone by the name of post-truth, alternative facts and fake news, and the mining of personal data that should never have been available for such purposes, have led to widespread cynicism concerning the political process. The sheer number of books with titles like *The Strange Death of Europe, How Democracies Die, The Retreat of Western Liberalism, The Suicide of the West* and the like suggest that an unusually large number of analysts have concluded that liberty itself, as we have known it in recent centuries, is at risk.

'Demoralised, decadent, deflating, demographically challenged, divided, disintegrating, dysfunctional, declining' is how

Bill Emmett describes the state of the West today, as seen through many Western eyes as well as those of its detractors.[7] Or as the famous Jewish saying puts it, 'Start worrying. Details to follow.'

*

A second set of phenomena relates to personal happiness – or lack of it. Living standards for most of us in the West have reached levels our ancestors could not have contemplated. We have access to goods, delivered to our door, from almost every place on Earth. We can choose more widely, travel more extensively, and we enjoy more personal freedom than any previous generation. The Internet and social media have brought the world to us and us to the world. We hold more computing power in our hands than was to be found in entire scientific departments fifty years ago. Never have we had wider access to knowledge. Never have we had more immediate contact with people throughout the world. This is in many respects the world of which our ancestors could only dream. Poverty, hunger, illiteracy, premature death, all of these things have been addressed with monumental success. Life expectancy has grown between two and three years every decade for the past century. On the face of it, we could not be in a better place.

Yet there are signs that this is far from the case. For example, in the United States, more than 70,200 Americans died from drug overdose in 2017, a doubling of the figure in a single decade, and a tripling in twenty years. This is truly an area in which America leads the world. Death rates from drug overdose are almost four times higher than in seventeen other wealthy nations, and for the first time in recent history, life expectancy in the United States is actually falling. Alcoholism is killing more people and more younger people. Suicide rates are up 33 per cent in less than twenty years.

In Britain, a 2018 report revealed that the number of people aged fifty and above who have received hospital treatment for drug abuse has more than quadrupled in a single decade, up from 1,380 to 7,800. The good news is that there has been a 6 per cent fall in the number of younger people seeking treatment. However, adult drug abuse still has an effect on the youth population because of the numbers of young children being recruited by drug gangs to distribute cocaine and heroin.[8]

Drug abuse is often related to the wider phenomenon of depression, and rates of depression among American teenagers are also rapidly rising. In a recent poll survey by the Pew Research Center, 70 per cent of young Americans, aged between thirteen and seventeen, say that anxiety and depression are serious issues among their peers; it tops what they see as their generation's concerns.[9] In 2017, 13 per cent of American teenagers said they had experienced at least one major depressive incident in the past year, up from 8 per cent in 2007 – a 59 per cent increase in a single decade.[10] Meanwhile, a 2018 report by the Children's Society in Britain came up with the shocking statistic that 20 per cent of fourteen-year-old girls in Britain had deliberately self-harmed in the previous year.[11]

In 2018 Jean Twenge, one of the participants in my BBC radio series on morality, wrote a definitive study of *iGen*, her term for young people born in 1995 or after. In it she documents the dramatic rise in suicides, attempted suicides and depressive illnesses among American teenagers, along with an equally dramatic fall in their self-reported accounts of life satisfaction. They are, it seems, a very anxious generation – iGeners, she says, 'are scared, maybe even terrified'. They are 'both the physically safest generation and the most mentally fragile'.[12]

This is more than a conundrum. It raises a fundamental question about where we are going in the market-economic, liberal democratic West. We may have won the battle for life and liberty, but the pursuit of happiness still eludes us. We keep chasing it, but it keeps running faster than we can.

*

A third dimension of our contemporary unease has to do with the economics of inequality. The most conspicuous example is the ever-widening disparity between chief executive pay and the rest. One example: in 2018 the chief executive of Disney, Bob Iger, received a total payment for the year of $65.6 million (£50 million), provoking outrage from Abigail Disney, granddaughter of Roy and grandniece of Walt Disney. She called it 'naked indecency'. It represented 1,424 times the median pay of a Disney worker. It is time, she said, 'to call out the men and women who lead us . . . about how low we are prepared to let hard-working people sink while top management takes home ever-more outrageous sums of money'. Expecting corporate boards to do so is, she said, unreasonable because 'they are almost universally made up of CEOs, former CEOs, and people who long to be CEOs'.[13]

This tendency, highlighted at the time of the financial crash in 2007/8, has been growing for a long time. In America in 1965 the ratio of chief executives' to workers' pay was 20:1. Today it is 312:1.[14] There might be less raising of eyebrows if the chief executives were entrepreneurs, creating their own business, taking their own risks, investing their own personal savings. But they were not. They were risking their shareholders' money and their employees' future. It is hard to avoid the conclusion that a small elite of executives, board members and major shareholders has allowed this to happen at the cost of a more equitable distribution of the company's success.

This, though, is only part of a much wider problem: the disconnection between economics and society that has grown as manufacturing and trade have become globalised. In a bounded economy, economic growth tends to benefit the nation as a whole, even though the rewards are not distributed equally. That is not the case when production can be outsourced to low-wage economies in some other part of the world such as Southeast Asia. This tends to concentrate economic activity in the West to urban trading centres, leaving vast swathes of the country – former mining and manufacturing areas, for example – depressed and deprived

Cultural Climate Change

with high rates of unemployment, drug taking and crime, low social capital, poor schools, and few chances for children growing up there.

Even California, in the 1960s the epitome of the American dream, is suffering. Today it faces a massive crisis of homelessness: though it contains an eighth of the national population, it has a quarter of the nation's homeless. It is economically deeply stratified, between the super-rich of Silicon Valley and the entertainment industry, a middle class of the state bureaucracy, academics and people in the media, and at the bottom what Gerald Baker of *The Times* calls the 'modern serfs', who have 'few assets, no stake in their economy, and thanks to prohibitive housing costs, limited mobility'.[15] Utopia has become dystopia.

Former International Monetary Fund economist Raghuram Rajan, in his book *The Third Pillar* (2019), argues that the human webs of connection, the relations, values and norms that bind us to one another, are being torn apart by technological innovation. The result, as we are seeing, is social unrest, violence and populism. Rajan argues that markets must re-establish their connection with the web of human relations and become socio-economics, that is, concerned not only with profits but also with social impact.

The widespread use of artificial intelligence will have a major impact on employment. Current estimates suggest that between 20 and 50 per cent of jobs will be affected. We do not know whether an equal number of new jobs will be created, or whether there will be a rise in unemployment, or some other adjustment, such as a reduction in working hours. But the economies of the West are on the cusp of massive technology-driven change. It would be foolish to suppose that economic growth can be pursued indefinitely as an abstract exercise in profit maximisation without regard to the impact on human beings and the communities in which they live.

*

9

A fourth phenomenon is the assault on free speech taking place on university campuses in Britain and America, giving rise to new phenomena like safe spaces, trigger warnings, micro-aggressions, and no-platforming, all designed to limit or ban the expression of sentiments that might offend some students, even if their banning offends others. To an ever greater extent, mob rule is taking the place of what was once the sacred mission of the university, namely the collaborative pursuit of truth. The idea that certain views, and people holding them, might be banned merely because they might upset someone, which is what is happening in many academic circles today, is astonishing. It is the new intolerance.

During 2019, I had the shock of seeing one of the participants in my BBC Radio 4 series on morality, Jordan Peterson, the University of Toronto psychologist, denied a research fellowship at the Cambridge University Divinity School on the grounds that a photograph had been taken of him alongside an individual wearing a T-shirt with an offensive message. There was no suggestion that Peterson had registered the offensive message, let alone endorsed it – the incident took place after a lecture, hundreds had paid to have their photograph taken with him, and he only had a few seconds with each. What, I wondered, was the role in a Divinity School of ideas like faith, truth, justice, generosity and forgiveness? Had they heard of the saying, 'Judge not that ye be not judged'? Would Abraham, Moses, Amos or Jeremiah, each of whom challenged the received wisdom of their day, have found a platform under such ill-conceived censoriousness?

This is only one example of a much wider problem. A 2017 report by *Spiked* magazine found that, of 115 universities and student unions in Britain, 63.5 per cent were 'severely' restrictive of free speech, with more than 30 per cent somewhat restrictive. The leading human rights and free speech advocate Peter Tatchell, commenting on the report, said: 'Universities used to be bastions of free speech and open debate. As this report shows, they are increasingly hedging free speech with all kinds of qualifications, making it no longer free.'[16]

A November 2019 report by Policy Exchange in Britain showed that a plurality of students supported a ban on Jordan Peterson (41 per cent) and feminist Germaine Greer (44 per cent), whose presence at a university was protested against on the grounds that she was 'transphobic'. Some 40 per cent of students said they felt uncomfortable at expressing aloud attitudes that conflicted with the views of their fellow students. The report warned that 'instead of being places of robust debate and free discovery' Britain's universities were 'being stifled by a culture of conformity'.[17]

Although the universities and students are at the opposite end of the political spectrum from Vladimir Putin, they seem to be veering close to his view that liberalism – of which free speech is an essential component – is obsolete. Only someone lacking in historical knowledge of what happened in French and German universities in the 1920s and 1930s could fail to find this first step to lead down a very dangerous path indeed.

Campus witch-hunting is itself only one of a cluster of new phenomena that are having a corrosive effect on tolerance and truth. We have seen the return of public shaming and vigilante justice via social media campaigns. There is post-truth, the term that came to prominence during the 2016 American presidential election, signalling that veracity is taking second place to the mass manipulation of emotion. There is the loss of civility in public discourse. Social media have given everyone a voice, and often it is a shrill one. All these things undermine the sense of belonging together as a single community that reasons respectfully together.

*

These and the other phenomena I discuss in the book are not unrelated. They are the multiple consequences of a single underlying shift in the ethos of the West. Climate change has many causes and symptoms: greenhouse gases, toxic emissions, the loss of tropical rainforests, rising sea levels, the melting of ice caps and glaciers, the proliferation of extreme weather conditions, the extinction of species of plant and animal life and the threat to many more. Different though these are, they are all part of a single phenomenon: global warming.

Likewise, divisive politics, inequitable economics, the loss of openness in universities, and the growth of depression and drug abuse are the result of what I call cultural climate change. They are the long-term consequences of the unprecedented experiment embarked on throughout the West a half-century ago: *the move from 'We' to 'I'*.

All countries and cultures have three basic institutions. There is the *economy*, which is about the creation and distribution of wealth. There is the *state*, which is about the legitimisation and distribution of power. And there is the *moral system*, which is the voice of society within the self; the 'We' within the 'I'; the common good that limits and directs our pursuit of private gain. It is the voice that says No to the individual 'Me' for the sake of the collective 'Us'. Some call it conscience. Freud called it the superego. Others speak of it as custom and tradition. Yet others call it natural law. Many people in the West spoke of it as the will and word of God.

Whatever its source, morality is what allows us to get on with one another, without endless recourse to economics or politics. There are times when we seek to get other people to do something we want or need them to do. We can pay them to do so: that is economics. We can force them to do so: that is politics. Or we can persuade them to do so because they and we are part of the same framework of virtues and values, rules and responsibilities, codes and customs, conventions and constraints: that is morality.

Morality is what broadens our perspective beyond the self and its desires. It places us in the midst of a collective social order. Morality has always been about the first-person plural, about 'We'. 'Society', said Lord Devlin, 'means a community of ideas; without shared ideas on politics, morals, and ethics, no society can exist.'[18] *Society is constituted by a shared morality*. Although

Nietzsche challenged this view as early as the 1880s, it remained the prevailing public opinion until the 1960s. To be a member of society was to be socialised, to internalise the norms of those around you, to act for the good of others, not just yourself. The assumption was that you must be part of something larger than yourself before you can be yourself.

Morality achieves something almost miraculous, and fundamental to human achievement and liberty. It creates trust. It means that to the extent that we belong to the same moral community, we can work together without constantly being on guard against violence, betrayal, exploitation or deception. The stronger the bonds of community, the more powerful the force of trust, and the more we can achieve together.

Friedrich Hayek put it well. We get along with one another, he says, because 'most of the time, members of our civilization conform to unconscious patterns of conduct'.[19] Without these habits of heart and deed, there would be severe limits on what we could do together. Freedom, he says, has never worked 'without deeply ingrained moral beliefs, and coercion can be reduced to a minimum only where individuals can be expected as a rule to conform voluntarily to certain principles'.

Morality is essential to freedom. That is what John Locke meant when he contrasted *liberty*, the freedom to do what we ought, with *licence*, the freedom to do what we want. It is what Adam Smith signalled when, before he wrote *The Wealth of Nations*, he wrote *The Theory of Moral Sentiments*. It is what George Washington meant when he said, 'Human rights can only be assured among a virtuous people.' And Benjamin Franklin when he said, 'Only a virtuous people are capable of freedom.' Or Thomas Jefferson when he said, 'A nation as a society forms a moral person, and every member of it is personally responsible for his society.' Lose morality, and eventually you will lose liberty.

That was the received wisdom for centuries. How did it change? It began with relatively abstract ideas. There was a long period of reflection on the nature of the individual and the self, starting with the Reformation, continuing through the Enlightenment and culminating in the nineteenth-century radicalism of Kierkegaard and Nietzsche. Between the 1930s and 1960s came the existentialists in France and the emotivists in Britain and America, who argued that there was no such thing as an objective moral order: there are only private choices based on subjective emotions. But these new ideas did not dislodge the assumption that society was built on the foundation of a shared morality.

Starting in the 1960s, that changed. First came the *liberal revolution*: it is not the task of law to enforce a shared morality. Morality gave way to autonomy, with the sole proviso that we did not do harm to others. Then, in the 1980s, came the *economic revolution*: states should minimally interfere with markets. Then, in the 1990s and gathering pace ever since, came the *technological revolution*: the Internet, tablets, smartphones and their impact on the global economy and the way we communicate with one another. Social media in particular has changed the nature of interpersonal encounter.

Each of these developments has tended to place not society but the self at the heart of the moral life. It is not that people became immoral or amoral. That is palpably not so. We care about others. We volunteer. We give to charity. We have compassion. We have a moral sense. But our moral vocabulary switched to a host of new concepts and ideas: autonomy, authenticity, individualism, self-actualisation, self-expression, self-esteem.

A Google Ngram search (measuring the frequency with which a word occurs in printed texts over a given historical period) reveals that words that used to be commonplace have become rarer since the 1960s, particularly respect, authority, duty, ought, conscience and honour; though the biggest fall was between 1960 and 2000. Since then, some have recovered their salience. Other subtle shifts have taken place, however: regret has tended to displace remorse, and shame has become more common than guilt. One of the most striking findings is that, while talk of responsibilities has remained more or less stable, since 1960 there has been a sharp rise in the use of the word 'rights'. We may still moralise, but we are reluctant to express guilt, remorse or responsibility.

*

I believe that underlying much of what has happened has been the misapplication to morality of the economic principle of *outsourcing*. The idea goes back to Adam Smith's division of labour and David Ricardo's theory of comparative advantage that says, even if you are better than me at everything, still we both gain if you do what you're best at and I do what I'm best at and we trade. The question is: are there limits? *Are there things we can't or shouldn't outsource?*

One example happened in the years prior to the financial crash in 2007/8. The banks began to *outsource risk*, lending far beyond their capacities in the belief that either property prices would go on rising forever, or more significantly, if they crashed, it would be someone else's problem, not theirs. The crash proved that in a highly interconnected financial system you can't outsource risk on that scale. Not only does it fail to protect you from risk; it also prevents you from knowing what is happening until it is too late and disaster has become inescapable.

Another recent example, almost unnoticed, is the outsourcing of *memory*. Smartphones and tablets have developed ever larger memories, while ours and those of our children have become smaller and smaller. Why bother to remember anything if you can look it up in a microsecond on Google or Wikipedia? But this confuses *history* and *memory*, which are not the same thing at all. History is an answer to the question, 'What happened?' Memory is an answer to the question, 'Who am I?' History is about facts, memory is about identity. History is about something that happened to someone else, not me. Memory is my story, the past that made me who I am, of whose legacy I am the guardian for the sake of generations yet to come. Without memory, there is no identity, and without identity, we are mere dust on the surface of infinity.

Something similar happened to morality. When I went as an undergraduate to Cambridge University in the late 1960s, the philosophy course was called Moral Sciences, meaning that just like the natural sciences, morality was objective, real, part of the external world. I soon discovered, though, that almost no one believed this any more. Morality was held to be no more than the expression of emotion, or subjective feeling, or private intuition, or autonomous choice. It is whatever I choose it to be. To me, this seemed less like civilisation than the breakdown of a civilisation.

The result was that, in effect, morality was split in two and outsourced to other institutions. There are moral choices and there are the consequences of those choices. The market gives us choices, and morality itself is just a set of choices in which right or wrong have no meaning beyond the satisfaction or frustration of desire. The result is that we find it increasingly hard to understand why there might be things we want to do, can afford to do, and have a legal right to do, that nonetheless we should not do because they are unjust or dishonourable or disloyal or demeaning: in a word, unethical. Ethics is reduced to economics.

As for the consequences of our choices, these have been outsourced to the state. Bad choices lead to bad outcomes: failed relationships, neglected children, depressive illness, wasted lives. But the government would deal with it. Marriage was no longer needed as a sacred bond between husband and wife, and the state would take responsibility for any negative consequences. Welfare was outsourced to government agencies, so there was less need for local community volunteering. As for conscience, which once played so large a part in the moral life, that could be outsourced to regulatory bodies. So, having reduced moral choice to economics, we transferred the consequences of our choices to politics.

All of this was done with the highest of intentions, but it overlooked one of the most important lessons to have emerged from the wars of religion in the sixteenth and seventeenth centuries and the new birth of freedom that followed. A free society is a moral achievement, and it is made by us and our habits of thought, speech and deed. *Morality cannot be outsourced because it depends on each of us.* Without self-restraint, without the capacity to defer the gratification of instinct, and without the habits of heart and deed that we call virtues, we will eventually lose our freedom.

*

The long experiment that began in the 1960s had many causes. There was the exhaustion brought about by two world wars. In Britain there was the threefold promise of the welfare state: the National Health Service, retirement provision and social care. There was the emergence of a distinct youth culture. There was the birth control pill and the sexual revolution. It was an extraordinary coming together of many factors that led people to believe that we were entering an endless summer of experiment and fun with no bill to pay for our transgressions. No one who lived through the sixties will ever forget them.

But now our children and grandchildren are paying the price of abandoning a shared moral code: divided societies, dysfunctional politics, high rates of drug abuse and suicide, increasingly unequal economies, a loss of respect for truth and the protocols of reasoning together, and the many other incivilities of contemporary life.

When morality is outsourced to either the market or the state, society has no substance, only systems. And systems are not enough. The market and the state are about wealth and power, and they are hugely beneficial to the wealthy and the powerful, but not always to the poor and the powerless. The rich and strong will use their power to exploit the rest, financially, politically and, as we know after the rise of the #MeToo movement, sexually also. Thucydides tells us that the Athenians told the Melians: 'the strong do what they want, while the weak suffer what they must'. The same, it often seems, is true today.

When there is no shared morality, there is no society. Instead, there are subgroups, and hence identity politics. In the absence of shared ideals, many conclude that the best way of campaigning is to damage your opponent by *ad hominem* attacks. The result is division, cynicism and a breakdown of trust. The world is divided into the people like us and the people not like us, and what is lost is the notion of the common good. When the 'I' takes precedence over the 'We', the result is weakened relationships, marriages, families, communities, neighbourhoods, congregations, charities, regions and entire societies.

What has become chillingly clear is the insight Émile Durkheim articulated in the 1890s, that in a society in which there was *anomie* – the absence of a shared moral code – there would be a rise in the rate of suicides. We cannot live without a structure, whether consciously learned or unconsciously absorbed, to guide us through what is otherwise unstructured chaos. This has surely been a factor in the upsurge of depression, stress-related syndromes, drug and alcohol abuse, and attempted and actual suicides especially among young people, teenage girls most of all.

The reason we cannot outsource morality to the market or the state is that they operate on completely different principles. The simplest way of seeing this is by a thought experiment. Imagine you have £1,000 and you decide to share it with nine others; you are left with a tenth of what you had at the beginning. Imagine you have total power, say a 100 per cent share in a company, and then decide to share 90 per cent of it between nine others; you have a tenth of the power you had before. Wealth and power operate by division. The more we share, the less we have.

Imagine now that you have a certain measure of influence, or friendship, or knowledge or love and you decide to share that with nine others: you do not have less. You may have more. That is because these are social goods: *goods that exist by sharing*. These are goods that have a moral or spiritual dimension, and they have this rare quality that the more we share, the more we have.

That is why the market and the state, the fields of economics and politics, are arenas of competition, while morality is the arena of cooperation. A society with only competition and very limited cooperation will be abrasive and ruthless, with glittering prizes for the winners and no consolation for the losers. It will be a low-trust environment, in which lawyers play a large role and mutual confidence a very limited one.

A society with a strong, shared moral code is a high-trust place, where the winners set an example of caring for the losers – indeed, where they do not speak of them as losers but as fellow citizens. High-trust societies are those in which the 'We' resonates more loudly than the 'I', where CEOs care for the team not just for themselves, where politicians act for the good of all, especially the marginal and disadvantaged, and where people in distress find comfort in community rather than being left to suffer on their own. We need to recover the sense of 'all-of-us-together'.

*

This is not a work of cultural pessimism. I am hopeful for the future. Two of the participants in my BBC radio series on morality, David Brooks and Jean Twenge, have noted that Generation Z (or Gen-Z for short), those born in or after 1995, are more moral and altruistic than the preceding generations, Generation X and Millennials. I had the lively experience during the recording of our morality programmes of sitting with teenagers from four British secondary schools, discussing moral challenges of our time, and despite the fact that the other participants were among the greatest experts in their field in the world, the teenagers emerged as the stars of the show. They were committed, insightful, thoughtful and wise. Our Google Ngram searches showed that moral language has been used increasingly since the turn of the millennium. My own experience of lecturing in Britain and America these past few years has convinced me that there is a genuine interest in recovering a moral framework to guide us in some of the formidable challenges facing us, from climate change to artificial intelligence to mass immigration to economic inequality. The G7 has signed up to an engagement with impact economics, an approach to business that quantifies social impact as well as profit. (I say something about this in the last chapter.) These are positive signs.

There are those who believe that the loss of a shared moral framework is irreparable. Some have even spoken of a descent into the dark ages.[20] Wittgenstein said that trying to salvage damaged traditions by wilful effort is like trying with one's bare hands to repair a broken spider's web. I do not share these views.

Hope is to be found in a remarkable passage in Steven Pinker's *The Language Instinct*. He tells the story of linguists who studied pidgin English, originally used by slaves. (Prince Philip, for example, was delighted to discover on a visit to New Guinea that he was referred to as *fella belong Mrs Queen*.) A pidgin has words but no grammar, vocabulary but no syntax. What the linguists discovered, to their amazement, is that the children of pidgin speakers had created their own new language, called a *creole*, which is pidgin plus grammar. Their parents had been robbed of a language, but they, without even knowing what they were doing, had simply invented one.[21]

There exists, within nature and humanity, an astonishing range of powers to heal what has been harmed and mend what has been broken. These powers are embedded within life itself, with its creativity and capacity for self-renewal. That is the empirical basis of hope. Nature favours species able to recover, and history favours cultures that can do so.

Once, when undergoing a medical check-up, the doctor put me on a treadmill. 'What are you measuring?' I asked him. 'How fast I can go, or how long?'

'Neither,' he replied. 'What I want to measure is, when you get off the machine, how long it takes your pulse to return to normal.' I realised that health is not a matter of never being ill. It is the ability to recover.

Recovering liberal democratic freedom will involve emphasising responsibilities as well as rights, shared rules, not just individual choices, caring for others as well as for ourselves, and making space not just for self-interest but also for the common good. Morality is an essential feature of our human environment, as important as the market and the state but outsourceable to neither. Morality humanises the competition for wealth and power. It is the redemption of our solitude.

When we move from the politics of 'Me' to the politics of 'Us', we rediscover those life-transforming, counterintuitive truths: that a nation is strong when it cares for the weak, that it becomes rich when it cares for the poor, that it becomes invulnerable when it cares about the vulnerable. If we care for the future of democracy we must recover that sense of shared morality that binds us to one another in a bond of mutual compassion and care. There is no liberty without morality, no freedom without responsibility, no viable 'I' without the sustaining 'We'.

PART ONE

The Solitary Self

I

Loneliness

Harvard sociology professor Robert Putnam has done more than anyone in our time to document the loss, in contemporary America, of social capital, the bonds that join us to one another in relationships of mutual responsibility and trust. In a famous 2000 book he gave the phenomenon a name. Noting that more people than ever were going ten-pin bowling, but fewer than ever were joining teams, he called it *Bowling Alone*. This became a metaphor for the decline in membership of clubs, movements and voluntary associations, the attenuation of community life and the decline of marriage as an institution. In many areas of life, what people used to do together, they now do alone.

As part of my radio series on morality for the BBC, I sought his opinions on current trends. In his office in the John F. Kennedy Center at Harvard he spoke with passion about how society had moved since the 1960s from the 'We' society of 'We're all in this together' to the 'I' society of 'I'm free to be myself.' The loss of community has many consequences, one of which is social isolation. As we will see, this has proved deeply damaging for our physical and psychological health.

One of the hypotheses he has tested is that the use of language, measured over time, shows that we have moved in the past half-century from a 'We' culture to an 'I' culture.[1] As his full findings have not yet been published, I asked Dan Sacker, who helped me with research for this book, to use a Google Ngram search to chart the frequencies of the words 'We' and 'I' in all English and American books, year by year, from 1900 to 2008. The two graphs are quite different. The use of 'We' is relatively stable over time, but the use of 'I' falls steadily from 1900 to 1965, at which point it begins a precipitate rise. From then on, the first-person singular dominates.

A similar, though more restricted, test was carried out in 2011 by Nathan DeWall of the University of Kentucky. He studied the lyrics of top-ten pop songs between 1980 and 2007, and discovered that the use of first-person plural pronouns – we, us, our – had declined, while first-person singular – I, me, mine – had increased. Words that expressed anger or aggression – hate, kill, damn – also increased, while words for social interactions – talking, sharing – became less common, as did those conveying positive emotions.[2] DeWall's view is that pop lyrics are a mirror of social and attitudinal change, and that the shift from 'We' to 'I' is reflective of the wider culture.

In another context, *Prospect* magazine commissioned a linguistic analysis of the angry Brexit debate in the House of Commons on 25 September 2019, during which Prime Minister Boris Johnson used terms like 'traitors', 'betrayal' and 'surrender' of his opponents. The analysis noted that, on average, the Prime Minister used a word from Harvard University's list of semantic-ally hostile terms every twenty-eight words, roughly every one and a half sentences – an unusual level of aggression. More rele-vant here is the fact that he used the word 'I' 340 times – far more frequently than normal.[3] Political discourse, especially when used by prime ministers and presidents, has historically tended to the inclusive, even royal, 'We'. Increased use of the word 'I' suggests that politics has become more about personalities than policies, and about the leader rather than the nation he or she seeks to lead.

Admittedly, there are limits to what you can infer from pronouns.[4] But the linguistic shift does seem to reflect this deep move from the structures of togetherness to the solitary self, the assertive 'I': cultural climate change. The whole of this book will be about the consequences in different areas, but this chapter is about the disastrous impact on our sense of connectedness to others. When 'I' prevails over 'We', loneliness follows.

For any social institution to exist, we must be prepared to make sacrifices for the sake of the relationship or the group. That is true of marriage, parenthood, membership in a community or citizenship in a nation. In these environments we enter a world of We-consciousness, in which we ask, not what is best for me but what is best for all-of-us-together.

A football team of the most brilliant players in the world will not succeed if each acts like a diva. An orchestra of dazzling musicians, each of whom feels entitled to give their own interpretation of a symphony, will produce not music but noise. A political party in which each member of parliament publicly delivers his or her judgement as to what policy should be will be a shambles. A government in which ministers publicly contradict one another will be a disgrace.

A Jewish joke puts it nicely. One year, the Yeshiva University rowing team lost all of its races. To find out what they were doing wrong, they sent an observer to watch the Harvard University team in action. Three days later, he came back shell-shocked. 'You won't believe it,' he said. 'You know what we do. They do the exact opposite. They have *eight* people rowing and only *one* person shouting instructions!' British and American politics these days can sometimes seem like the Yeshiva University rowing crew.

Those are non-moral examples. The moral ones touch on more fundamental relationships. A marriage in which one or both partners acts selfishly is unlikely to last. A parent indifferent to the needs of his or her child will damage the child. A community where the members are not willing to bear their share of the burden of keeping it going – a group of free-riders – will cease to exist. A nation without a sense of collective identity and responsibility will split apart, as the United States and Britain have split apart since 2016. You cannot build a social world out of a multiplicity of I's.

Simultaneously with the rise of 'I' over 'We' since the mid-1960s, marriages, families and communities have all atrophied. Fewer people are marrying. They are marrying later. They are having fewer children. More marriages are ending in divorce. The result is that more people are living alone. In the United States, the proportion of single-person households has more than doubled in the past fifty years.[5] This is particularly so in large cities, where they represent 40 per cent of households. In Britain, in the twenty years between 1997 and 2017, there was a 16 per cent increase in the number of people living on their own.[6]

In the mid-1990s, the Secretary of State for the Environment invited the Archbishop of Canterbury, George Carey, the leader of the Catholics in England, Cardinal Hume, and myself as Chief Rabbi, to come and meet him. He told us that because of the breakdown of marriage, more people were living alone. The result was pressure on the supply of housing. Four hundred thousand new units needed to be built, he said, in south-east England alone. Could we not do something about it? Could we not make marriage attractive again? I thought this showed spectacular faith in the power of prayer, but even were a miracle to happen, it would take more than a generation to reverse the decline.

To be sure, there is a difference between living alone and feeling lonely. Not everyone who chooses the first feels the second. But there is a connection. Genetically we are social animals. Our ancestors, in the hunter-gatherer stage of humanity, could not survive alone, and they have left a trace of this deeply engrained in our emotional set-up. Separated from others, we experience stress. Many prisoners have testified that solitary confinement is as terrifying as physical torture. John McCain said of the five and a half years he was a prisoner-of-war in Vietnam that being kept solitary 'crushes your spirit and weakens your resistance more effectively than any other form of mistreatment'.[7] Obviously, social isolation is mild in comparison, but the body nonetheless responds by heightened awareness of potential threats in the environment, and the resultant stress eventually weakens the immune system.[8] That is one reason why most people seek company, the presence of others, the touch of another soul. The less there is of 'We', the more there is of loneliness.

*

A cartoon in the 4 November 2019 issue of *New Yorker* magazine showed Humphrey Bogart, wearing a white tuxedo and black bow-tie, sitting alone at a bar, a glass of bourbon in his hand. In front of him is an electronic device. He is turning to it and saying, 'Alexa, play "As Time Goes By".'[9] A poignant image for an age in which communication technology is smarter and faster than ever before, but in which human interaction, direct, face to face, other-focused, I–Thou, is all too rare. We are becoming a lonely crowd.

So serious has the problem become that in January 2018, Tracey Crouch was given the task of becoming what the press dubbed Britain's first ever 'Minister for Loneliness'. The appointment struck a chord. Loneliness is hardly new – it makes its first appearance in the second chapter of the Bible, when Adam finds himself without a partner and God says, 'It is not good for a person to be alone' (Gen. 2:18). But not until relatively recently has it been seen as a major health hazard. One of the factors prompting the appointment of a minister was a 2017 research report by the Jo Cox Commission on Loneliness that showed that more than nine million people in Britain feel lonely. Two hundred thousand older Britons had not had a conversation with a friend or relative in more than a month.[10]

A similar state of affairs exists in the United States. A 2018 Cigna survey showed that 46 per cent of Americans always or sometimes feel alone, and 47 per cent feel left out. One in four rarely or never feel that there are people who really understand them. Forty-three per cent feel that their relationships are not meaningful and that they are isolated from others. Fifty-four per cent feel that no one knows them well. The most distressed by loneliness were young people aged between eighteen and twenty-two.[11] The phenomenon is not confined to the West. In Ukraine, Russia, Hungary, Poland, Slovakia, Romania, Bulgaria and Latvia, 34 per cent of the population declared themselves lonely.[12] In Japan, meanwhile, there is an entire sub-population known as the *hikikomori*, numbering more than a million, of people who shut themselves up in their homes, seldom if ever venturing out and living in hermit-like seclusion.

As noted above, more people than ever in the West are living alone. Only half of American adults are married, down from 72 per cent in 1960.[13] More than half of those between the ages of eighteen and thirty-four do not have a steady partner.[14] More people are cohabiting rather than getting married, and the average length of a cohabitation is less than a third as long as the average marriage.[15] Fewer children are living as adults in close proximity to their parents. Corporations often call on individual workers to move to a different region or country, which further disrupts relationships. Isolation particularly affects the elderly. One-third of Britons and Americans over the age of sixty-five live alone, and more than half of those over eighty-five.

Then there is the phenomenon charted by Robert Putnam, the marked decline in membership of the kind of associations that used to bring people together on a regular basis – sports teams, local charities, religious congregations, and so on. Increasingly, people are using electronic means of communication rather than face-to-face contact, which itself is potentially dangerous, since the health benefits of relationships are quite often associated with actual physical presence.

Loneliness has serious health implications.[16] It has long been associated with psychiatric conditions such as anxiety, depression and schizophrenia. Recently, strong connections have also been established with physical conditions such as cardiovascular disease, stroke, cancer, dementia and Alzheimer's disease.[17]

There is a difference between loneliness and social isolation. The first is a subjective, self-reported state, while social isolation is an objective condition, usually defined as a lack of contact with family, friends, community and society. Social isolation is itself as harmful to health as smoking fifteen cigarettes a day and more harmful than obesity.[18] A 2015 study, tracking 3.4 million people over seven years, showed that individuals judged to be isolated had a 26 per cent greater risk of dying. If they lived alone, the risk was 32 per cent higher.[19]

Chronic loneliness is associated with raised levels of cortisol, a stress hormone, and high vascular resistance, which can raise blood pressure. It can also lead to a reduced capacity on the part of the body's immune system to fight infections. A 2012 study of patients over the age of sixty, in which 43 per cent reported feelings of loneliness, showed that they had higher rates of declining mobility and inability to perform routine daily activities.[20] The evidence by now is compelling that loneliness and isolation are significant health hazards, physically and psychologically.

Simply playing cards with friends once a week, or getting together over a cup of coffee, adds as many years to life expectancy as giving up a pack-a-day smoking habit.[21] People with active social lives recover faster after illness. A study done by the University of California in 2006 showed that of 3,000 women with breast cancer, those with a large network of friends were four times as likely to survive as women with few social connections.[22]

To be sure, not everyone likes company. There are people who find solace in solitude. They are alone without being lonely. But for the most part, life is about relationships. That is why loneliness can be depressing and dangerous.

*

One unexpected consequence of the loss of close connections has been described by the distinguished war correspondent Sebastian Junger in his poignant study of belonging, *Tribe*.[23] The question he sought to answer was why levels of post-traumatic stress disorder are so high among American servicemen today – the highest in history and possibly the highest in the world. His hypothesis is that when they return home, they are moving from the intense comradeship of the unit to the relative isolation of contemporary society. A soldier returning from combat today 'goes from the kind of close-knit group that humans evolved for, back into a society where most people work outside the home, children are educated by strangers, families are isolated from wider communities, and personal gain almost completely eclipses collective good'. The close bonds of belonging that would allow psychological wounds to heal are not there.

Loneliness, the sensed lack of human connection, touches on our essence as social animals. We are not the only such animals, but it is our ability to form extensive networks that differentiates us from other species. Our sociability is our humanity and this is deeply rooted in our evolutionary past. That is what morality represents: our commitment to others, our capacity to form bonds of belonging and care. Our sense of wellness depends on being part of one or several networks of relationship in which we are prepared to act for the benefit of others, knowing that they are prepared to do likewise for us.

So individualism comes at a high cost: the breakdown of marriage, the fragility of families, the strength of communities, the sense of identity that comes with both of these things, and the equally important sense that we are part of something that preceded us and will continue after we are no longer here. Edmund Burke said that a culture that broke the connection between past and future would have the result that 'the whole chain and continuity of the commonwealth would be broken. No one generation could link with the other. Men would become little better than the flies of summer.' The move from 'We' to 'I' has devastating consequences.

By contrast, strong family ties are life-giving in the most literal sense. Susan Pinker tells the story of a cluster of villages in Sardinia, where uniquely men lived to be as old as women – usually there is a difference of between five and seven years of life expectancy between the sexes – and where there are ten times as many centenarians as the average elsewhere. These villages, including the one she visited in Villagrande Strisaili in the Gennargentu mountains, are places where no one lives alone, where the elderly live with their children, where people are constantly popping in to see one another, social contact is high and people keep working in the fields as long as they can, not retiring until they reach their eighties or nineties.[24]

It turns out that one of the greatest aids to longevity is to live in a place where people honour old age. The people of these Sardinian villages, Susan Pinker writes, considered their centenarians communal property and were fiercely protective of their 'treasures' – the word one woman used to describe her 102-year-old uncle.

The elderly were respected, honoured, and constantly visited by members of their family, especially by the young. They were never left alone. Pinker calls this 'the village effect'. It's a striking example of the power of social connectedness. A close connection to friends and family is part of mental and physical health and a sense of a life that matters.

This sense of community is something religion has provided at important junctures in history. This was particularly so during the first half of the nineteenth century in Britain and America when there were great social dislocations as people moved from villages to cities during the Industrial Revolution. This was a traumatic experience for many. Sociologists describe it as the move from *Gemeinschaft* to *Gesellschaft*, from the face-to-face relationships that predominate in small communities to the anonymous encounters of strangers that make up much of city life. It took a sustained effort of outreach by the churches in both countries to recreate communities in urban environments, and this enabled them to combat some of the negative consequences of the social dislocation, from drunkenness to child abuse.

Judaism performed a similar role for immigrant Jewish families in America and Britain, who had known wrenching dislocation, fleeing from persecution and finding themselves strangers in a strange land. Almost immediately, they organised themselves into *landsmanshaft* organisations, mutual aid societies based on town or city of origin. These gave support to new arrivals, helping them to find places to live and work, assisting them through some of the cultural and bureaucratic challenges, and providing financial support when people were ill or out of work.

I saw this myself. My early years were spent among first-generation immigrant Jews who had come to Britain from Eastern or Central Europe before, or in some cases after, the war. They arrived with nothing, yet within one generation almost all of them had moved out of the inner-city ghettoes and had begun to make a life for themselves and their families. Working class in themselves, tailors, shopkeepers or street traders, their children mostly went to university and entered the professions.

Jews like my parents were poor, but they were rich in social capital. They had strong families and immensely supportive communities. They had an almost Calvinist ethic of hard work, together with a strong respect for scholarship and study. These values were embodied in the communities they made or joined. People helped one another.

Judaism tends to have a strong communal dimension. As one famous joke has it, Levy, the atheist, is asked why, when he does not believe, does he go regularly to synagogue? His reply: 'I go with Markowitz. Markowitz goes to talk to God, and I go to talk to Markowitz.' This may be true generally of minority faiths, and especially of immigrant communities. In a profound way, religion is the consecration of community, the place where our togetherness under God is given shape and strength.

In practical terms, our human connections shape us in ways of which we are not always consciously aware. Nicholas Christakis and James Fowler have documented the enormous impact social networks have.[25] If our friends are overweight, so probably will we be. If they don't smoke, the likelihood is that neither will we. We are affected not only by our close friends but also to a surprising extent by our friends' friends.[26] Indeed, most job opportunities come our way through these second-order networks, which are vastly more extensive than our close friends. Community plays an important role in the way our lives unfold, and is the living face of a shared moral order. All of which makes the breakdown of community deeply problematic at both a personal and societal level. Once we feel that we are really alone and cannot call

34

on neighbours for help, then we are part of a new social poverty, which can be demoralising and debilitating.

So our current individualism is liberating. We are free as never before to be as we wish and live as we choose. But there is a cost. The distinguished Canadian philosopher Charles Taylor put this well when he spoke of 'the spread of an outlook that makes self-fulfilment the major value in life and that seems to recognise few external moral demands or serious commitments to others'.[27] We can do things of which our ancestors could hardly dream, but what they found simple we find extremely hard. Getting married. Staying married. Being part of a community. Having a strong sense of identity. Feeling continuity with the past before we were born and the future after we are no longer here. More of us live alone, and loneliness means increased risk of chronic disease, dementia and mortality rates.

We are not made to live alone. Not only is the unprecedented atomisation of modern life bad for our health and happiness. It is also dangerous because it makes us vulnerable to the dangers that lie ahead: turbulence, change, unpredictability. When the environment changes, people who are members of strong and diverse groups are at a huge advantage. They contain people with different strengths, variegated knowledge, diverse skills, and by working together they can negotiate their situation with effectiveness and speed. They have collective resilience. A crowd of disconnected individuals does not have that strength. Loneliness is the single greatest fear of Millennials, according to a 2016 Viceland UK census. It ranks higher than the fear of losing a home or a job. Forty-two per cent of millennial women are more afraid of loneliness than a cancer diagnosis.[28]

Tip O'Neill used to say, 'All politics is local.' Morality is likewise. That, at any rate, is where it begins, among families and friends and neighbours. Morality places a limit on individualism. Those who seek the benefit of the group must pay the price. That is the meaning of the 'reciprocal' in reciprocal altruism. Those who try to take the benefit without paying the price are called free-riders, and they will sooner or later find themselves shunned by the group and left to survive on their own. This is a phenomenon that can be witnessed among all social animals, not just humans.

Morality, at its core, is about strengthening the bonds between us, helping others, engaging in reciprocal altruism, and understanding the demands of group loyalty, which are the price of group belonging. A sense of morality safeguards something deeply engraved within us, a legacy from the distant life's past, when we lived together in small groups. Then, as now, the ability to rely on the help of others when facing life's challenges is a powerful source of resilience. Sebastian Junger, whom we mentioned earlier, puts it starkly. Early humans were distinguished, he says, by two things that they did effectively: the systematic sharing of food and the altruistic defence of the group. These launched *Homo sapiens* on its evolutionary path, and they remain human needs:

> The earliest and most basic definition of community – of tribe – would be the group of people that you would both help feed and help defend. A society that doesn't offer its members the chance to work selflessly in these ways isn't a society in any tribal sense of the word; it's just a political entity that, lacking enemies, will probably fall apart on its own.[29]

One significant contribution of religion today is that it preserves what society as a whole has begun to lose: that strong sense of being there for one another, of being ready to exercise mutual aid, to help people in need, to comfort the distressed and bereaved, to welcome the lonely, to share in other people's sadnesses and celebrations. These moral responses have not disappeared: we see them whenever there is a communal tragedy, a shooting, a terrorist incident or a major accident. People come together to give help and support. Our wellsprings of altruism have not run dry. They are a large part of what makes us human. But we tend not to exercise them on a day-to-day basis. That is what we have lost in society at large, but what can still be found in religious congregations. These remain, as Robert Putnam went on to demonstrate in *American Grace*, our strongest living embodiments of social capital.[30]

That availability of collective strength that we find in strong communities held together by moral bonds is an important source of resilience that we will need as we face the kind of uncertainty that seems to be the mark of the twenty-first-century thus far. It is easier to face the future without fear when we know we do not do so alone.

We have lived through an extended period during which the 'I' has grown stronger at the expense of the 'We'. The result, as American sociologist Robert Bellah put it, is that our 'social ecology' has been damaged by 'the destruction of the subtle ties that bind human beings to one another, leaving them frightened and alone'.[31] In the long run, that is unsustainable. The human condition is overwhelmingly about relationships – about faithfulness, staying true, loyal and committed to one another despite all the tensions, setbacks, misunderstandings, backslidings, and all the multiple ways in which we fall short. It is about consecrating the bonds between us. It is about transcending our solitude.

The over-emphasis on 'I' and the loss of 'We' leaves us isolated and vulnerable. It is not good to be alone.

2

The Limits of Self-Help

It happened on our honeymoon. We had hitchhiked from the Swiss mountains to the Italian coast, finding ourselves at a little town called Paestum, an ancient place with fine Roman ruins. But it was the beach that drew us to it, and the sea. Rarely had the sea seemed more inviting than just then. There was just one problem. The Talmud tells us that one of the duties of a parent to a child is to teach it how to swim. Unfortunately, my parents never learned that page, and I never learned how to swim.

But as we sat on the beach and looked out across the water I realised that the shore must be sloping very gently indeed. People were far out into the sea and yet the water was only coming up to their knees. It looked safe just to walk out. And so it was. I walked out to where I had seen people standing just a few minutes before, and the water gently lapped against my knees. Then I started walking back to the shore. That's when it happened. Within a minute I found myself out of my depth.

How it happened, I'm not sure. There must have been a dip in the sand. I had missed it on my way out but on my way back I had walked straight into it. I tried to swim. I failed. I kept going under. I looked around for some possible source of rescue. The other people bathing were a long way away – too far to reach me, I thought; too far even to hear. Besides which, we were in Italy, I didn't speak the language and didn't know how to make myself understood. I was sure this was the end. As I went under for the fifth time, I remember thinking two thoughts. 'What a way to begin a honeymoon.' And, 'What is the Italian for "Help"?'

It's difficult to recapture the panic I felt. Clearly someone rescued me, or I wouldn't be writing now. But it did, at the time, seem like the end. As far as I can reconstruct that moment in my memory, I had already reconciled myself to drowning when someone, seeing me thrashing about, swam over, took hold of me, and brought me to the shore. He deposited me, almost unconscious, at the feet of my wife. I was too shocked to do or say anything. I never found out his name. Somewhere out there is a man to whom I owe my life.

That for me has always been what help is like. You put out a hand, and someone seizes it and lifts you to safety. Self-help would not have worked at all. I was the problem, not the solution. Help, for me, has always been other-help.

Nonetheless I am, I admit, a long-time devotee of self-help books. I have felt the fear and done it anyway. I have refrained from sweating the small stuff. I have experienced the life-changing magic of tidying. I know the power of now. I'm OK and you're OK. And I no longer sit worrying who moved my cheese. I have read more books on happiness than I can count, shelf-loads of them. And my commitment stretches way back to the classics of the genre. I have even read the very first: Samuel Smiles's *Self-Help* (1859), with its no-nonsense opening: 'Heaven helps those who help themselves.'

So I don't mean any criticism of such books, still less of those who read them, but one thing has always puzzled me from the outset. The obvious thing. Self, surely, is where it begins, not where it ends. It's the problem, not the solution. If I look back at my life I discover that it was always someone else who set me on a new trajectory. I suspect the same is true for most people. Someone who was there when we needed it, who listened as we poured out our problems, who gave us the encouraging word when we were about to give up, who believed in us more than we believed in ourselves. Or maybe it was actually someone who looked us in the eye and told us the honest truth: that we were self-obsessed, that we were wallowing in our emotions, that instead of thinking about how to develop the mindset to achieve great things, we should stop reading and start doing. Help, I have found time and time again, comes not from the self, but from others.

Two books have appeared recently, evaluating the entire self-help movement. One is Will Storr's *Selfie: How We Became So Self-obsessed and What It's Doing To Us*, the other Marianne Power's *Help Me*.[1] In the latter book the author describes how, at a bad point in her life, she made the decision to set aside a significant amount of time – in the end it turned out to be fifteen months – to live according to a whole series of self-help classics, a month at a time. She read them all and lived out what they told her to do. Some of it was amusing, while some was quite scary.

At the end, she tells us the result of fifteen months of self-help. Her debts had grown. Her productivity had plummeted. She was a stone heavier than when she began. 'I became irresponsible, selfish and deluded, watching inspirational videos on YouTube instead of doing actual work and spending money I didn't have on the basis that the universe would provide. Worst of all, I fell out with one of my best friends.' Marianne had become self-obsessed. In fact the books, by promising a happiness that was simply unattainable, made her more and more dissatisfied with the present situation.

The other recent book, Will Storr's *Selfie*, goes much deeper, being among other things a history of Western ideas about the self, going back to ancient Greece and medieval Christianity. Particularly powerful is his analysis of the movement that began in the 1960s and 1970s towards self-esteem. One of the sources of this idea was the psychologist Abraham Maslow, famous for his concept of the hierarchy of needs from the lowest – food and shelter – to the highest: actualisation and esteem.[2] The movement to promote self-esteem would, in the 1980s, eventually become an entire educational philosophy in Britain and America. Those who had self-esteem, it was believed, would fulfil their potential in a way that others would not.

What Storr reveals is that Maslow himself, in the months before his death in 1970, began to have profound doubts about the movement he had influenced. He had been carrying out tests on those with high scores of self-esteem. What he discovered was that they 'were more apt to come late to appointments with the experimenter, to be less respectful, more casual, more forward, more condescending', and various other antisocial behaviours. Carl Rogers, the American psychologist known for his practice of 'unconditional positive regard',[3] another strand of the self-esteem movement, also had second thoughts, seeing how it encouraged self-indulgence. Eventually he took to writing to those who wanted work at his Institute: 'Less self-esteem, please. More self-discipline.'

Storr shows how the self-esteem movement was based on shaky research – which comes first, the achievement or the esteem? – and led to an obsession with the self. Two contemporary researchers, Jean Twenge and W. Keith Campbell, have argued that the pursuit of self-esteem led eventually to an epidemic of narcissism, and that 'narcissism causes almost all of the things that Americans hoped high self-esteem would prevent, including aggression, materialism, lack of caring for others, and shallow values'.[4]

It is worth thinking about why self-help, in this peculiarly modern sense, has emerged – often as a substitute for what in previous centuries would have been a religious quest. The answer, I think, was given by the American scholar Philip Rieff in his book *The Triumph of the Therapeutic* (1966). One of his most insightful points was that in all previous generations, people helped those suffering depression or loss or bereavement by seeking to re-integrate them into the community.

That, for example, is the point of the ancient and still powerful Jewish custom of *shiva*: a bereaved family sit together for a week and are visited by members of the community and by friends. It is a period in which you are hardly ever alone. It is exhausting, but it achieves many things; above all, it prevents you from retreating into yourself. It softens the jagged edges of grief. What makes the therapeutic situation so different, said Rieff, a scholar of Freud, is that conventional Freudian psychoanalysis, at least, keeps you within yourself. It tends to see society and other people as the source of your distress.

There is a fascinating passage in the Talmud, describing an event in the third century, which tells of a certain rabbi who had the power of healing. When he laid his hand on someone who was ill, he was cured. Then, continues the Talmud, he fell ill himself and sent someone to fetch another rabbi to heal him. Why, asks the Talmud, did he not cure himself? It answers: *a prisoner cannot release himself from prison.*[5] It takes someone else to turn the key that unlocks the door.

Read any story of transformation and you will find a significant other. Stephen King, for example, in his book *On Writing* – written after he almost died, having been hit on a country road by a van – tells the story of how, in the early years of his marriage, he tried to write a novel, and found it intensely difficult. Eventually he completed a manuscript – a story about a schoolgirl with terrifying psychic powers. He read it through, and came to the conclusion that it simply did not work. He threw the manuscript into the waste-paper basket and went out for a walk, intensely depressed and on the point of giving up his ambition to be a writer altogether.

When he arrived back home many hours later, he found that his wife had rescued the manuscript from the waste-basket, and had read it. She told him that, yes, it would need to be edited and parts rewritten, but it had the makings of a fine work. When he told her that he simply could not convincingly write about the experience of a young girl, she said that she would help him on those parts, but she insisted that he stayed with the project. That is how *Carrie* was rescued. It became an immense bestseller, twice made into a film, in 1976 and 2013. Stephen King went on to become one of the most successful authors of our time, or any time.

Take a quite different sphere, that of leadership: any leader needs a mentor, a counsel, a wise voice that one trusts, who can look at a situation dispassionately and say, quietly and confidentially, 'Not a good idea.' It transpires that during much of her premiership, Margaret Thatcher relied on William Whitelaw in this capacity. He was Deputy Party Leader when she became

Prime Minister, and was later Leader of the House of Lords. He had the rare capacity to tell the woman known as the Iron Lady when she was wrong, in such a way that she was able to hear it. She respected his wisdom and knew he had her interests, as well as those of the country, at heart. As long as he was in good health, he moderated those of her policies that he thought were mistaken. After a stroke, in 1987, he was no longer well enough to fulfil this role, and in the view of many, this was the beginning of the end of her political career.[6] Though Margaret Thatcher remained as Prime Minister until 1990, her judgement became less sound and she began to lose touch with her party and the nation.

The same is true about the best leaders in many fields. There is usually someone empowered to whisper in their ear and say No. A leader cannot be *in* the fray and *above* it at the same time. Nor can any single figure embody all the requisite qualities: a young leader may lack experience; an experienced leader may lack youth and fail to see new opportunities. There must be at least one other voice – spouse, friend, advisor, trusted colleague – because the judgement of even the greatest will fail at times. These figures are often invisible to the public: they are helpful precisely because they are discreet. Yet they are often a leader's most important defence against disaster, and without them failure will eventually follow. A leader's strengths are his or her own, but it takes *someone else* to protect them from their weaknesses. Self-help is often no help at all.

The person who demonstrated most dramatically the transformative power of the voice-from-outside-the-self was the late Viktor Frankl. Frankl had been a psychotherapist in Vienna before the war. He was taken to Auschwitz. It was there that he realised that the most important thing he could do was to maintain the will to live and help others do so. The book he wrote about his experiences there, *Man's Search For Meaning*, is regularly cited as one of the most inspiring books of the twentieth century.

The first thing he had to do was to reframe his whole situation. The Nazis did everything they could to dehumanise their victims.

They took away all their possessions. They shaved their heads. They gave them numbers instead of names. Frankl's transform-ing insight was that, although the Nazis had taken away virtually every freedom and vestige of humanity from the camp inmates, there was one freedom they could not take away: the freedom to choose how to respond.

Frankl's first decision was to refuse to let the Nazis define his situation. He would not allow himself to see himself as a victim, as racially inferior, as a Jew. Instead he chose to see himself as a scientist, a psychotherapist, participating in an experiment to test what constitutes humanity. This kept his sense of freedom intact, and gave him his first victory over the murderers.

His next decision was to look out for others who seemed to be losing their will to live. He describes his method. He would listen carefully to their stories about themselves, and the people they had been before the war. He would then try, for each of them, to find a mission that was waiting for them, and that could only be fulfilled if they stayed alive. One of them had begun a series of travel guides, and Frankl persuaded him that he needed to live to complete the series. Another had a niece waiting for him in Canada, and he needed to survive in order to join her.

On the basis of his experience in the death camps, he devel-oped an entirely new method of psychotherapy that he called Logotherapy: psychological healing based on man's search for meaning. As he explained it later: the essence of this mission had to be a *call from outside the self*. This was as near he could come in secular terminology to the classic sense of mission as a call from God. As he later put it: we should not ask ourselves what we want from life. We should ask ourselves, what does life want from us.[7] There is a difference between the call from within and the call from outside: it is the difference between *ambition* and *vocation*. The former comes from the self, the latter from something outside and larger than the self. To give his fellow pris-oners the strength to survive, Frankl needed to take them outside themselves. As he explained it, 'being human is always directed, and pointing, to something or someone other than oneself: to a meaning to fulfil or another human being to encounter, a cause to serve or a person to love.' He called this self-transcendence and said that one achieves this 'not by concerning himself with his self's actualisation, but by forgetting himself and giving himself, overlooking himself and focusing outward.'[8]

Iris Murdoch, the philosopher and novelist, described something very similar that she called 'unselfing', and gave an example of how it may happen:

> I am looking out of my window in an anxious and resentful frame of mind, oblivious of my surroundings, brooding perhaps on some damage done to my prestige. Then suddenly I observe a hovering kestrel. In a moment, everything is altered. The brooding self with its hurt vanity has disappeared. There is nothing now but kestrel. And when I return to the thinking of the other matter it seems less important.[9]

The relentless first-person singular, the 'I', falls silent and we become aware that we are not the centre of the universe. There is a reality outside. That is a moment of transformation. She saw this as central to Plato's vision of morality: seeing the true, the good and the beautiful as something objectively there, not made up by us. In a similar if not identical way, Adam Smith defined the moral sense as the view of 'the impartial spectator'; that is, seeing a situation from outside the distortion-field of our own wants and desires.

That is what gives morality its unique power, central to the human condition. We are capable of two quite different experiences: call them the 'I' and the 'Me'. I am both subject and object. I feel my feelings as only I can feel them. That is the 'I' as subject. But I can also stand outside my feelings and pass critical judgement on them. That is the 'Me' as object. Standing outside, 'I' take into account other factors: the feelings of others, the likely consequences of my deeds, the duties and responsibilities I carry, and so on. This means that humans are capable of *second-order evaluations*. Like other animals, we have drives and desires. But unlike any other animal, we can ask: is this a desire I should seek to satisfy? Is this a feeling I should act on, or should I refrain from doing so? That ability to step back and see oneself from the outside is what makes us moral agents, capable of understanding that we have duties, obligations and responsibilities to others. Morality is the capacity to care for others. It is a journey beyond the self.

Sometimes someone from the outside can change the self-image of an entire group. One of the most moving films I have ever seen was produced by the BBC to accompany the opening of the Paralympic Games in London in 2012. Called *The Best of Men*, its subject was Dr Ludwig Guttmann, a Jew from a traditional Jewish family, who by 1933 was one of Germany's leading neurosurgeons. Then Hitler came to power and by 1935 all Jews were banned from the professions. Guttmann was able to continue working at a Jewish hospital until 1939, when he realised it was simply too dangerous for him to stay. So he came to England.

In late 1943 the British government, recognising what a remarkable doctor it had in its midst, asked Guttmann to head the first ever dedicated medical facility for the treatment of paraplegics. It was based at the hospital in Stoke Mandeville, Berkshire. When Guttmann arrived he was horrified by what he saw. The paraplegics, most of them soldiers injured in the war, were being kept horizontal in their hospital beds and heavily sedated. They were young men in their late teens and early twenties, yet the received medical opinion at the time was that, since they would never recover and never be able to walk, the most humane thing to do was to ease their pain until they died. At that time their life expectancy was between three and six months.

Guttmann realised that, though motivated by kindness, this was the worst possible way to treat the men. He was convinced they had a future, and his task was to find a way to help them make it. The first thing he did was to cut back their sedatives by half, because this was what was keeping them totally immobile. It hurt. Then he got them to sit up in their beds, and this too hurt. Then he starting throwing balls at them so that they were forced to play catch, and this hurt.

The other doctors and nurses, not understanding what Guttmann was trying to achieve, accused him of cruelty. The film showed Guttmann being summoned by a fellow doctor to a tribunal. 'These are moribund cripples,' the doctor said, looking at Guttmann. 'Who do you think they are?' Guttmann, looking him steadily in the eye, said, 'They are the best of men.' Hence the name of the film.

Eventually Guttmann got the paraplegics out of the ward in wheelchairs into the hospital garden and the fresh air. Then he started getting them to play games. He had the brilliant idea of placing some of the doctors into wheelchairs as well, and having them and the paraplegics compete. Not surprisingly, used as they were to the wheelchairs, the paraplegics won.

For the first time Guttmann saw real excitement on their faces, and he realised that sport was the way to give them back a passion for life. So he organised more games, and then a national competition, and finally in 1948 an international contest to accompany the Olympic Games. In 1968 Guttmann's efforts were rewarded when the International Olympic Committee recognised the parallel Olympics as an official part of the games. By the time the Paralympic Games came to London in 2012, they had grown to 4,302 participants from 164 different countries – the largest number ever – and their efforts were watched throughout the world. It was deeply moving to see how one man's determination had not only changed the way paraplegics were treated, but also the way they were seen.

Why did it take an outsider to see what none of his fellow doctors could see? I could not help thinking that at least part of it had to do with Guttman's experience as a Jew under the Nazis. They saw him as subhuman; he knew otherwise. Did this help him see the essential humanity in what others saw as 'moribund cripples'? One thing seems certain. There are times – not always, by any means, but sometimes – when help comes from the outside in, rather than from the inside out. The paraplegics found their own way back to life and hope and self-respect. But it took Guttman to open the door. A prisoner cannot release himself or herself from prison.

This is not to criticise self-help. But, in the end, we each have to take responsibility for our lives. The decisions, the willpower, the stamina and resilience are up to us. But for most of us, it is other people who make the necessary difference to our lives, guiding us, inspiring us, lifting us and giving us hope. It is the quality of our relationships that more than anything gives us a sense of meaning and fulfilment.[10] Most important of all, it is the ability to love that lifts us beyond the self and its confines. Love is the supreme redemption of solitude.

What makes morality so fundamental to our humanity is that it turns us outward. As Plato, Adam Smith and Iris Murdoch intimated in their different ways, the pursuit of the right and the good is not about self but about the process of unselfing, of seeing the world for what it is, not for what we feel or fear it to be, and responding to it appropriately. Morality is precisely un-self-help. It is about strengthening our relationships with others, responding to their needs, listening to them, not insisting that they listen to us, and about being open to others, sometimes experiencing the miracle that just as you are about to give up and go under for the last time, a hand reaches out and pulls you to safety and the rest of your life becomes a gift for which you thank God every day.

3

Unsocial Media

In the course of making a podcast together, a woman from Silicon Valley talked to me about her family. She had become concerned that her children were in danger of becoming addicted to social media. Their use of it was harming their social skills. They weren't fully attending to other people. They always had half a mind on their smartphones. The time they spent on Snapchat, Instagram and other social media was absorbing their energies and robbing them of sleep. Even when the family was sharing meals, they were still texting friends, their phones on their laps underneath the table.

After discussion, the family agreed that there was a problem and that they would deal with it together. The decision they took, she said to me, was that they would have one screen-free day a week – no phones, no tablets, no laptops, just face-to-face communication, being together. 'You will like the name we gave the day,' she said. 'We've decided to call it Shabbat.' She was right. I enjoyed the irony. Thirty-three centuries ago, Moses liberated the Israelites from slavery to Egypt. Now, the same institution is liberating young people from slavery to smartphones.

We need such liberation.

*

Social media emerged and spread with remarkable speed. Facebook, which claimed 2.41 billion monthly active users as of June 2019, was founded in 2004. YouTube followed in 2005, Twitter in 2006, Tumblr in 2007, WhatsApp in 2009, Instagram in 2010 and Snapchat in 2011. They were born out of an extraordinary convergence of innovations: the second phase of the Internet – Web 2.0, with its ease of posting user-generated content – smartphones and broadband connectivity. And they have been embraced worldwide. As of 2019, there were 5.1 billion owners of mobile phones, 4.3 billion users of the Internet, 3.4 billion users of social media.[1] In Britain, nine out of ten teenagers use social media.[2] In the United States, according to a 2018 Pew Research Center report, more than half of American thirteen- to seventeen-year-olds say they spend too much time on their smartphones, and 57 per cent have tried to cut back on their use of social media.[3] Never have more people been more widely, quickly and easily connected. This is a revolution that will prove at least as transformative as the (Western) invention of printing in the mid-fifteenth century.

In many respects it is benign. Given all the nay-saying about the negative impact of social media, some of which will appear in this chapter, it is important to note the positives. Social media connects families and friends across the world. Often nowadays, when I officiate at weddings, someone will be livestreaming the ceremony for the sake of relatives who, because of age, illness or distance, could not be present in person. That may seem a minor phenomenon but it can be a deeply moving one. Social media can enhance community. They have enormous educational potential. I use them heavily in my work as a way of teaching people across the globe. A 2018 Pew survey of attitudes towards social media on the part of American teenagers showed that 81 per cent feel more connected to friends, 69 per cent think social media helps them interact with a more diverse group of people and 68 per cent feel that they have people who will support them through tough times.[4] There is enormous power in these media for good.

But there are real problems also. In 2017 Jean Twenge, of the University of California, San Diego, published *iGen*, subtitled *Why Today's Super-Connected Kids Are Growing Up Less Rebellious, More Tolerant, Less Happy – and Completely Unprepared for Adulthood*,[5] a definitive account of the research evidence thus far of the impact of social media on children's physical and mental health. It makes a disturbing story.

Twenge documents the fact that recorded levels of life satisfaction among American teenagers stayed relatively stable until 2012, when they suddenly began to plummet. Likewise, numbers of teenage attempted and actual suicides stayed stable until they began to rocket in 2012. Why this particular year? Because, she argues, this was when 'iGen', or Generation Z – children born on or after 1995 – were in their teens. This was the first generation to grow up with both smartphones and social media as part of their taken-for-granted environment.

According to Twenge, the effects are substantial and disturbing. Teenagers in the United States are spending on average between seven and nine hours a day watching a screen: two hours a day on the Internet, two and a half hours texting on smartphones, one and a half hours a day on electronic gaming, half an hour on video chat, and two hours a day watching television (not all of this is necessarily sequential: they multitask).[6] This is robbing them of social time, time spent meeting and relating to people face to face.

In 2015, Sherry Terkel reported that the average American adult checks their phone every six and a half minutes. A quarter of American teenagers are connected to a device within five minutes of waking up. Most teenagers send a hundred texts a day. Eighty per cent sleep with their phones beside them. Forty-four per cent do not disconnect even in religious services or when exercising.[7]

There is accumulating evidence that smartphone exposure is robbing children of their sleep, not only because of the time they spend on them, but also because of the effect of the particular quality of light reflected from a screen – blue light – that has a negative effect on sleep. In one survey in 2015, 43 per cent of American teenagers reported that they had less than seven hours sleep a night, regarded as the minimum for good health. Children need sleep for their cognitive and emotional resilience.

The psychological effects are more disturbing still. Children compare themselves to the profile of their friends on the social media. They see those profiles and relate themselves negatively to them, forgetting that that profile itself has been carefully edited and curated. They are comparing their own reality with the highly selective version of other people on the screen. This leaves many of them feeling inadequate and depressed.

Meghan, the Duchess of Sussex, felt moved to warn of how young people's sense of self-worth was becoming skewed by pursuing 'likes' on social media and seeing Instagram photographs that have been edited to make people look more beautiful.[8] Shannon McLaughlin, aged eighteen, from Blackburn, told the *Guardian* in 2019, 'Since being diagnosed with depression and anxiety in my early teens, my mental health has definitely been affected by social media.' Partly this has to do with the fact that people share the positive things in their lives while editing out the negatives. 'Seeing that everyone was happy and enjoying life made me feel so much worse.' This had a physical as well as a mental dimension. 'I was constantly confronted by women with unattainably skinny bodies who were praised for the way they looked.'[9]

Comparing ourselves with others is one of the most deeply rooted of all human instincts, but the terms of the comparison change when we find ourselves measuring the reality of our own lives against the edited, sometimes artificially enhanced versions of other lives that we encounter on social media. One of the most striking new phenomena is FOMO (Fear of Missing Out), a term added to the *Oxford English Dictionary* in 2013. In the past, if your friends were invited to a party to which you were not, this may have given you some anxiety, but at least it wasn't public. Today, everything is public. Everything is shared. Everything is there for the presentation of self, and the selfie. Social media invite us into a world of 'advertisements for myself'[10] and a competition for attention that few can win.

Everything then becomes subordinate to the image, the post. A businessman whose job is arranging meetings between ordinary people and celebrities told me recently that in the past, people would pay for the privilege of meeting a star and would want to

spend ten minutes speaking to him or her. Today, the market for
what he offers is dominated by young people, and all they want,
he said, is a selfie of them together with the star to post on their
social media. Once the photo is taken, they leave. It is as if they
have begun to see the world not through their eyes but through a
lens. What exists is narrowed to what can be photographed.

The sheer cumulative impact of spending that amount of time
watching a screen, and responding to the rapid pace of social
profiles, is reconfiguring the brains of young people so exposed.
One study presented to the Radiological Society of North
America in 2018 reported that young people addicted to smartphone use showed chemical imbalances in the brain.[11] Another, in
the *Journal of the Association for Consumer Research*, showed
that the mere presence of a smartphone, even when switched
off, reduces cognitive capacity.[12] It is as if we have become so
attentive to our phones that we find it hard to concentrate fully
on anything else. The benefits of the smartphone as a hub for
information, entertainment and social stimulation, say the
researchers, may come at a cognitive cost.

It has long been suspected that the sheer pressure of information in the electronic and digital age has had the effect of
diminishing attention spans. To be sure, the evidence for this is
largely anecdotal. For the past few years parents have been telling me that they find it difficult to get their children to read a
book. If a story can't be told in five minutes, it can't be told at all.
One recently published study by researchers from the Technical
University of Denmark does, though, show that when it comes
to items in the news, global attention spans have indeed reduced
over time. So for example a 2013 Twitter global trend would last
for an average of 17.5 hours, while one in 2016 would last for
only 11.9 hours.[13]

Another research report, by researchers from the Boston
University School of Medicine, questions the use of smartphones
and tablets by parents to pacify very young children. When
parents use these devices to do this, they may be damaging their

social and emotional development.[14] Dr Jenny Radesky, one of the team that produced the report, said, 'If these devices become the predominant method to calm and distract young children, will they be able to develop their own internal mechanisms of self-regulation?'[15] These digital devices 'could be detrimental to later social-emotional outcomes when used as the principal way in which children are taught to calm themselves down'.

The end result of excessive use of social media is depression and stress-related symptoms such as eating disorders and drug and alcohol abuse. iGen'ers, says Twenge, are 'scared, maybe even terrified', as a result of their exposure to limitless screen time and the potency of the new media for cyber-bullying and other forms of intimidation. Recall her remark that they are 'both the physically safest generation and the most mentally fragile'.

This particularly affects teenage girls. A recent report by the Royal College of Paediatrics and Child Health in Britain revealed that 38 per cent of fourteen-year-old girls who spent more than five hours a day online felt miserable, tired, restless, worthless or tearful. A 2018 report by the Children's Society revealed that almost a quarter of fourteen-year-old girls in Britain had self-harmed in the course of a year.[16] Internet-induced depression is beginning to be recognised as a public health hazard in both Britain and the United States.[17] In April 2019, the British government announced plans to impose fines on Internet firms that permit potentially harmful content to be shared, including material promoting self-harm or suicide as well as terror and child abuse images.[18]

More and more, human interaction is no longer taking place face to face but electronically. Siblings text one another even when they are at home together. Teenagers say they prefer to communicate by text rather than in person because texting is less stressful. The end result is that they show a marked decline in empathy and social skills over previous generations.[19] They find it hard to maintain eye contact or undivided attention. Nowadays people even break up relationships by text message – surely a situation that absolutely demands personal presence to be even remotely humane. People apologise by text, but the recipient of the apology knows full well that the text is not the same as an actual physical expression of remorse. Sherry Terkel quotes a graduate student in economics describing what is missing when someone apologises to her by text:

> The texted "I'm sorry" means, on the one hand, "I no longer want to have tension with you; let's be okay," and at the same time says, "I'm not going to be next to you while you go through your feelings; just let me know when our troubles are over." When I have a fight with my boyfriend and the fight ends with an "I'm sorry" text, it is 100% certain that the specific fight will come back again. It hasn't been resolved.[20]

Some of the people who seem to have known best how damaging the new media can be are the very people who first made it possible. So, for instance, Steve Jobs, in a 2011 interview with the *New York Times*, disclosed that he forbade his children from using the iPad he had only recently launched, telling interviewer Nick Bilton, 'We limit how much technology our kids use at home.'[21] Tim Cook, who took over the leadership of Apple after Steve Jobs's death, has said that he does not want his nephew to be on social media.

In 2007 Bill Gates, creator of Microsoft, laid down a limit on the screen time his daughter was allowed when he saw that she had begun to spend extended time playing video games. His rule was that she was allowed no more than forty-five minutes of screen time on weekdays and an hour on weekends.

Evan Spiegel, the founder of Snapchat, has imposed a rule on his seven-year-old stepson, limiting him to ninety minutes of screen time per week. Spiegel himself revealed, in an interview with the *Financial Times*, that his parents did not allow him to watch any television at all until he was nearly a teenager. He says in retrospect that though this rule was difficult to live with at the time, it proved to be valuable because 'I spent a lot of time just building stuff and reading or whatever.'

Mark Zuckerberg, creator of Facebook, together with his wife Priscilla Chan, published an open letter to their newborn daughter, August, in 2017, explaining why they felt it was important for her 'to make time to go outside and play', because 'childhood is magical'.

That is the irony. These iconic figures in the development of computing, tablets, smartphones and social media understood early on the danger they posed to childhood and everything associated with it. They themselves did little to publicise the risks or actively seek to limit them. But what they sensed is now public knowledge. This great, empowering, democratising and connecting technology carries with it health hazards that are now documented and creating concern among politicians, medical experts, teachers and parents alike.

It is unhealthy to spend several hours a day in front of the screen. Not only does it damage physical and mental health; it is addictive and can cause depression. Not only does it inhibit the acquisition of social skills that any person needs in his or her transactions with the world; it results in shorter attention spans, damaging the capacity for sustained and focused thought. Most fundamentally, it leaves us morally underdeveloped, addicted to a search for popularity that has little to do with character, virtue or anything else, and that is the worst possible training for resilience or happiness in the real world of real people and real relationships.

*

Something is missing when human interaction is no longer face to face: the whole affective dimension that makes us living, breathing, feeling persons in relation with other persons. One of the prevailing assumptions in an age of science and technology is that communication is about the exchange of information – in which case it doesn't matter whether it is done face to face, or by letter, or email or text. Information I wanted to hand on to you has now been received by you.

But it isn't so. True communication involves personal presence. One of the first people to draw our attention to what is going on when two people meet and talk was the anthropologist Bronislaw Malinowski, who studied the inhabitants of the Trobriand Islanders in the 1920s. He noticed that a significant part of their day was spent talking to one another, but almost none of it took the form of information-exchange. Meaningless or trivial though it seemed, this chitchat was performing an important social function. It was creating relationship, 'bonding'. In the fugue of conversation we listen; we pay attention to another person. We reply, and the words we say are a response to the words we hear. Speech is the medium of relationship. He called this 'phatic communion', meaning speech as the touch of two selves, their presentness to one another, their mutual non-hostile exposure.[22]

Coming from a different direction, the Cambridge mathematician Alan Turing proposed a test for artificial intelligence. What would a machine have to be able to do for us to be convinced that it is a form of intelligent life? His answer was: we would have to be able to hold an extended conversation with it. The counterpoint of listening and speaking is at the heart of what it is to be a person – what it is to establish a moral, as opposed to a purely instrumental relationship.

Malinowski's idea was taken further by British anthropologist Robin Dunbar.[23] In the wake of important studies of primate behaviour, in which a great deal of alliance-building was done by animals grooming one another, Dunbar suggested that grooming was in fact the original function for which language was developed. It was about establishing ties of mutual responsibility, of building trust, of strengthening the group. The use of language rather than physical embrace meant that humans could extend their group to much larger numbers. Conversation-as-grooming means that talking together is about bonding together. It is about people coming to understand one another through all the subtleties of tone, eye contact, body language and the sharing of vulnerabilities that happen when we are bodily present for one another. Exchanging information electronically is not the same thing at all.

Something similar can be seen with friendship. A 2018 research exercise showed that the average person in Britain had 554 friends online, but only five true and close friends.[24] That is a measure of the difference between real and electronic friendship – between people you can turn to for help and who will make some sacrifice for you if you need it and people with whom you merely exchange information. Social media has an enormously positive role to play in allowing people to stay in touch with one another, share experiences and knowledge, and enhance interactions within a real community. But real interpersonal friendship needs an investment of time, intimacy and a degree of privacy.

Likewise trust in business. There are wonderful electronic modes of meeting: Skype, FaceTime, GoToMeeting and others. These are fine for the exchange of information or the expression of opinions. Yet for the most important interactions, business people still travel halfway across the globe so as to deal face to face with their opposite number. The establishment of trust is of the essence, and CEOs know that this can only be judged in a situation of physical interaction.

Or consider education. One of the most widely watched of all lecture series – it has been seen by 30 million Chinese – is Professor Michael Sandel's Justice 101 course at Harvard. There are a thousand people in the lecture hall, but the entire session is a conversation with individuals in the audience. It is as near as one can get nowadays to Socratic dialogue. This is, you feel instinctively, what it was like twenty-five centuries ago in Athens. Here the Internet is reminding us of what it itself cannot provide, the thrill of actually *being there* in direct conversation with one of the great teachers of the age – of acquiring a teacher and becoming a disciple.

Bonding, friendship, trust, discipleship: these emerge from face-to-face conversation and the subtle cues that accompany it and that shape the contours of human interaction, cues such as body language, posture, the speed and intensity of the words, the evenness or lack of it in the give-and-take of listening as well as speaking, and the powerful concomitant experiences of understanding and being understood. These are essential social skills. They are the choreography of interpersonal relationship. They emerge from the direct encounter between living, breathing, thinking, feeling human beings.

Social media have played a significant part in the move from 'We' to 'I'. In the world they create, I am on the stage, bidding for attention, while others form my audience. This is not how character is made, nor is it how we develop as moral agents. Morality is born when I focus on you, not me; when I discover that you, too, have emotions, desires, aspirations and fears. I learn this by being present to you and allowing you to be present to me. It is this deeply subtle interaction that we learn slowly and patiently through ongoing conversations with family, friends, peers, teachers, mentors and others. We develop empathy and sympathy. We learn what it is to receive acts of kindness and then to reciprocate them. Morality is about engaging with the raw human vulnerabilities of others that lie beneath the carefully burnished image, and about our ability to heal some of the pain. I learn to be moral when I develop the capacity to put myself into your place, and that is a skill I only learn by engaging with you, face to face or side by side.

These sensitivities and sensibilities live in the immediacy of the encounter and they are, for the most part, lost in electronic information-exchange. That, for instance, is why the Internet has a 'disinhibiting effect' – one of the factors in why people are ruder online than they would be in the physical presence of the person they are insulting. When the connection between us is not direct either in time or space, I am not forced to recognise you as a human being, and I can express whatever I feel without considering what you might feel at the receiving end. When that happens, I am unlearning morality.

The danger of Facebook, Twitter, Snapchat, Instagram and the rest is that they can seem at times to substitute for the real interactions essential to the human condition. Character is trivialised into personality, 'likes' take the place of genuine respect, and presentation of self takes the place of engagement with others. This can often seem more like narcissism than genuine personal growth.

*

Two famous Jewish thinkers of the twentieth century placed interpersonal relationships at the heart of their philosophies of the moral life. Martin Buber famously contrasted two modes of relationship: I–It and I–Thou. In an I–It relationship, we see the object of experience as something to be analysed, classified and quantified. My primary question is: to what use can I put this object in front of me? He called this, *experience*.

The other kind of relationship, I–Thou, he called *encounter*. Between us, there is relationship. We are part of the same world. We are capable of transforming one another. An enormous amount of communication in the modern world is done at the level of I–It. That is what makes us feel alienated, part of a primarily impersonal world. But what really matters to us ultimately is the encounter with another 'Thou'. The supreme example is the relationship we call love, and it is at the heart of moral and spiritual life. It is this that contains a signal of transcendence. Though Buber does not refer to him, it is something like this that William Blake was alluding to when he wrote:

> For Mercy has a human heart,
> Pity a human face,
> And Love the human form divine,
> And Peace, the human dress.[25]

Even more powerful is the account of morality given by the French philosopher Emanuel Levinas. Levinas believed that moral obligation is born at the moment when we encounter what he called 'the face of the other'. His view was that some basic act of recognition takes place when we make eye contact with another human being: here is a person to whom I have duties because he or she is a person, even if, in the biblical phrase, they are an orphan, a widow or a stranger. In this immediate, pre-reflective encounter, morality is born. 'The face speaks to me and thereby invites me to a relation', he wrote.[26] 'The face opens the primordial discourse whose first word is obligation.'[27] It is only when we encounter another human being that we begin to communicate and construct a shared world out of the act of communication: 'Meaning is the face of the Other, and all recourse to words takes place already within the primordial face-to-face of language.'[28]

To be fully human, we need direct encounters with other human beings. We have to be in their presence, open to their otherness, alert to their hopes and fears, engaged in the minuet of conversation, the delicate back-and-forth of speaking and listening. That is how relationships are made. That is how we become moral beings. That is how we learn to think as 'We'. This cannot be done electronically.

The immediacy of global connection offered by social media makes it, potentially, one of the wonders of our age. But it must not become a replacement for face-to-face relationships in real space and time, which is where the moral life is born, lives and has its being.

4

The Fragile Family

Traditionally, the supreme consecration of the 'We' within a culture has been marriage, two people coming together in a covenant of loyalty and love, to build a life, a home, and hopefully a family. That was the understanding with which I had grown up. So it was with a profound shock that, in 1967, I became conscious of the scope of the moral change that was taking place, when I found myself listening to a discourse about free love in the form of the BBC Reith Lectures! The Reith Lectures – six half-hour programmes of uninterrupted discourse from a single individual – are the BBC's intellectual event of the year, named after Lord Reith, first director of the BBC, and first given in 1948 by Bertrand Russell.

In 1967, under the title *A Runaway World*, they were given by Edmund Leach, Professor of Anthropology at Cambridge. Even as a teenager I used to listen devotedly to the Reith Lectures, not really understanding them but lulled into a gentle serenity by the sound of deep rumination. Little did I guess that twenty-three years later I would be delivering the lectures myself. In 1967, however, the thrust of Leach's argument was unmistakable. He was speaking to the mood of the moment – the new youth culture, pop music, psychedelic drugs, flower power, and the sexual revolution. This was, after all, the summer of the Beatles' *Sgt. Pepper's Lonely Hearts Club Band*.

It was what he said in the third lecture that made me sit up and take notice. He was talking about the new modes of sexual relationship that young people were developing, and the censorious views of an older generation. Leach sided unequivocally with the young. They should go ahead and develop new ways of living together. Then he said this: 'Far from being the basis of the good society, the family, with its narrow privacy and tawdry secrets, is the source of all our discontents.'

That was when I knew something extraordinary was happening. Leach was not a member of the counterculture of which he spoke. He was a distinguished representative of the academic establishment, one of the great and the good of the nation. And he was dismissing, with little less than disdain, the most significant institution of Western civilisation, the vehicle through which it transmitted, genetically and culturally, its past to the future, namely marriage and family life.

My first thought was: 'Speak for yourself, Professor Leach.' I knew that it was only because of the effort and sacrifices of my parents that I was able to go to university at all. I knew that in doing so, I was not just doing it for me. It was a way of making up for the opportunities my immigrant father never had. That, I guess, is true in general for second-generation immigrants. You will find it today among Hindus, Sikhs and others in Britain. You also find something similar among children of Chinese immigrants. Amy Chua's bestseller, *Battle Hymn of the Tiger Mother*, made many of us realise that Jewish mothers are signally outdone by their Chinese counterparts.

Almost all civilisations have developed ways of consecrating marriage and the family. What makes immigrant communities significant is the additional strain they face in adjusting to a new country and culture. Historically, the strength of Jewish families was the source of the resilience of Jewish communities that allowed them to survive the enforced exiles and expulsions, the ghettoes and pogroms, of a thousand years of European history. Family in Judaism is a supreme value. It's how we celebrate our festivals and sabbaths. A Jewish child always has a starring role at the Seder table on Passover night, where we are inducted into our people's history, and where our parents fulfil their first duty, namely to teach children to ask questions. Strong families create adaptive communities.

More generally, marriage is fundamental to the moral enterprise because it is the supreme example of the transformation of two

'I's' into a collective 'We'. It is the consecration of a commitment to care for an Other. It is the formalisation of love, not as a passing passion but as a moral bond. To see what is at stake we need to understand the difference between two things that look and sound alike but actually are not, namely *contracts* and *covenants*.

In a contract, two or more individuals, each pursuing their own interest, come together to make an exchange for mutual benefit. So there are commercial contracts that create the market, and the social contract that creates the state. A covenant is something different. In a covenant, two or more individuals, each respecting the dignity and integrity of the other, come together in a bond of love and trust, to share their interests, sometimes even to share their lives, by pledging their faithfulness to one another, to do together what neither can achieve alone.

A contract is a transaction. A covenant is a relationship. Or to put it slightly differently: a contract is about interests. A covenant is about identity. It is about you and me coming together to form an 'Us'. That is why contracts benefit, but covenants transform. Covenant is about the logic of cooperation. That is what differentiates marriage and the family from economics and politics, the market and the state, which are about the logic of competition.

To be sure, a marriage may have the external form of a contract, but its inner logic is that of covenant. That is how Israel in the biblical era understood its relationship with God, as a covenant. The Hebrew word *emunah*, often translated simply as 'faith', really means faithfulness, fidelity, loyalty, steadfastness, not walking away even when the going gets tough, trusting the other and honouring the other's trust in us. The prophets understood the relationship between humanity and God in terms of the relationship between bride and groom, wife and husband. Love thus became the basis not only of morality but also of theology. Faith is like marriage. This is what Hosea meant when he said in the name of God:

I will betroth you to me forever;
I will betroth you in righteousness and justice,

64

I in love and compassion.
I will betroth you in faithfulness,
and you will know the Lord (Hos. 2:21–22).

Marriage is fundamental to society because throughout history it has been the most fundamental way in which we recognise something beyond the 'I' of self-interest, namely the 'We' of the common good, cooperative relationships, shared identity and collective responsibility.

Alexis de Tocqueville understood this so well. There is, he said, 'no country in the world where the tie of marriage is more respected than in America or where conjugal happiness is more highly or worthily appreciated'.[1] In Europe, by contrast, 'almost all the disturbances of society arise from the irregularities of domestic life'.

Marriage, de Tocqueville believed, was the foundation of a free society: domestic peace equals social order. Lack of it equals social unrest. Yet this was the proposition being treated with disdain by Edmund Leach in the Reith Lectures. Leach, as an anthropologist, must surely have known the truth that, as James Q. Wilson would go on to put it, 'In virtually every society into which historians or anthropologists have enquired, one finds people living together on the basis of kinship ties and having responsibility for raising children.'[2] There are many types of family structure, just as there are many kinds of society, but almost none without some shared norms and forms.

In the 1960s, marriage and the family received the biggest blow they had ever encountered in Western civilisation. This was the result of many factors, among them the emergence for the first time in the West of a self-contained youth culture, the availability of birth control, and the passing of the shadow of war that had so strengthened the 'We' culture in Britain. The vehicles of cultural continuity had broken down and people felt on the brink of a new age radically different from the old.

It was Daniel Patrick Moynihan, writing in the United States in 1965, who first pointed out the enormous social risks that would attend the breakdown of the family unit. He was speaking at the time about African Americans. But what he said eventually proved true about American society as a whole.[3] Everything he predicted came true, but the spirit of the moment was unstoppable. For many, sex was no longer associated with marriage, or commitment, and became instead a leisure-time activity. Over the next generation, in Britain and America, fewer people got married, and those who did were marrying later. In 1968, 56 per cent of Americans between the ages of eighteen and thirty-one were married or heads of households; by 2012, this was true of only 23 per cent.[4] An unprecedented proportion of marriages – rising at times to 50 per cent, 42 per cent in Britain in 2017[5] – terminated in divorce, and almost one in two children were born outside marriage.

Marriage is often derided as a mere formality, a 'piece of paper', while cohabitation has come to be portrayed as an equivalent or substitute. Sadly, it is not so. In Britain, the average length of marriages that end in divorce is between eleven and twelve years,[6] and the average length of marriages as a whole is thirty years.[7] The average length of cohabitation in Britain and the United States is less than five years. The formal act of commitment that constitutes marriage makes a difference to the strength and durability of the relationship.

Despite the cultural shift of which Leach's Reith Lectures were a symptom, the majority of people do get married. And in recent years the divorce rate and that of teenage pregnancies have declined. But the consequences of those earlier changes are still with us. The collapse of marriage has created new forms of financial and moral poverty concentrated among single-parent families, and of these, the main burden is borne by women, who in 2011 headed 92 per cent of single-parent households. In Britain today more than a million children will grow up with no contact whatsoever with their fathers. A 1993 survey in Britain found that children living with cohabiting rather than married parents are twenty times more likely to become victims of child abuse.[8] It is hard to avoid the conclusion that family breakdown must be part of the explanation for the sharp increase among young people of eating disorders, drug and alcohol abuse, stress-related syndromes, depression, and actual and attempted suicides.

This is creating a divide within societies the like of which has not been seen since Disraeli spoke of 'two nations' a century and a half ago.[9] In the past few years, two of America's most distinguished social scientists published path-breaking works that came to the conclusion that the American dream – that everyone, given effort and enterprise, could succeed in life – had been broken for at least one-third of the population. The thinkers came from quite different starting points: Charles Murray of the American Enterprise Institute and the libertarian Right, and Robert Putnam of Harvard, and the communitarian Left. The libertarian Right tends to focus on individual choice, the communitarian Left on collective responsibility. Yet Charles Murray's *Coming Apart* (2012) and Robert Putnam's *Our Kids* (2015) were strikingly similar. Each gave dramatic force to their presentation by focusing on two communities, Belmont (in Boston) and Fishtown (in Philadelphia) for Murray, and two groups in Port Clinton, Ohio, one college-educated, the other not, for Putnam.

Their point is that segments of the population that used to live close to one another, interact, and generally belong to the same world, have diverged since the early 1960s. The well-off and well educated have prospered while the less successful and poorly educated have become progressively more deprived. They no longer inhabit the same social space at all. As their careers and remuneration have diverged, they live further apart physically and mentally, and their children have markedly different expectations.

To both Murray and Putnam, this is more than a minor fact. It calls into question the quintessential American proposition that everyone is equal in opportunity, if not in outcome. So great is the gap between the top third and the bottom third that equality of opportunity no longer genuinely exists. Social mobility is declining. The American narrative, which said that anyone with sufficient dedication could reach the heights, no longer rings true for a significant proportion of the population. A nation lives and is sustained by its ideals. But could one realistically say today, in the words of the Gettysburg Address, that the United States is 'dedicated to the proposition that all men are created equal'?

The difference begins in marriage patterns. All groups were affected by the sexual revolution in the 1960s, but the more successful group in each comparison recovered itself quite quickly and marriage was restored as a social norm. That was not the case with the poorer group, which saw a dramatic rise in cohabitation without marriage, non-marriage, divorce, and single parenthood. There is overwhelming social scientific evidence that children benefit from being brought up in a stable marriage by two parents, that divorce is harmful to the children, and single parenthood still more so: whether measured in terms of childhood aggression, delinquency, hyperactivity, criminality, illness and injury, early mortality, sexual decision making in adolescence, school problems, dropping out, emotional health, educational achievement, career success, and the ability to make strong and lasting relationships, marriage especially.[10]

In short, Murray (on the political Left) and Putnam (on the libertarian Right) told a similar story. The top third of society – in terms of financial security and education – had dabbled with the new freedoms of the 1960s and following, but had more or less returned to the old conventions and pieties. They married, they joined religious communities, they were intensely ambitious for their children. They made a point of living in the neighbourhoods with the best schools, or they sent their children to private schools, or gave them private tuition, and paid for them to enjoy extracurricular activities.

The bottom third was less able to swim against the current. Today, these people live almost on a different planet from their erstwhile fellow townspeople. There is an enormous burden on single mothers. There is a rise in child poverty, whether measured in terms of relative or absolute family income, or access to facilities. America now has one of the highest rates of child poverty in the developed world. There are whole communities without adult role models, where there is no one to discipline the teenage children. Inevitably, without adult role models, many of them are inducted into gangs, and from there into drug culture or petty crime, and find themselves in prison, all hope for a secure future utterly lost. These communities are places of educational under-achievement, high unemployment, high incarceration rates, and violence.

This entire lifestyle is not fully of their choosing. It follows directly from decisions made by their parents and grandparents. Some years ago, in the course of making a television documentary for the BBC on the state of the family in Britain, I spent a day with young offenders at a centre called Sherborne House. This place was their last chance of rehabilitation. If convicted of crime again they would be sent to prison. The young men there were mostly eighteen years old. They were all from broken, and many from abusive, families. When I tried to get them to talk about their childhoods, they refused to do so, out of loyalty to their families. So I changed the approach. I said, 'One day you will have children. What kind of father would you like to be?' That is when they started crying. They said things like, 'I'd be a tough father, but I'd make sure that there were rules, and whenever the children needed me, I would be there for them.' I found the experience deeply moving, and distressing.

These were young men with strong instincts for good, who if they had been born into a different kind of family environment might well be preparing to go to university themselves, instead of being given one last chance before being sent to prison. I believe that the injustice done to them by society is hard to forgive. A generation imbibed the idea of sex without responsibility and fatherhood without commitment, as if there were no victims of that choice. But there are victims, especially the children of dysfunctional and abusive families, who would never really have a chance to pursue their dreams and are mired instead in a culture of poverty, violence, prison and hopelessness. In both the United

States and Britain, one government after another has invested large sums in grants, initiatives and programmes, but none of these has significantly lowered rates of child poverty, and poverty is in any case only part of the problem. It is the emotional damage inflicted upon them from which they may well never recover. Having seen only a dysfunctional family in childhood, they have nothing on which to model their own behaviour in due time.

Yet establishment figures like Edmund Leach endorsed the 1960s sexual revolution that gave young people of the sixties the green light to go ahead and abandon the self-restraint that had made Britain and America the cultures they were. Nor was this pure accident. Many of them had been influenced by the work of anthropologist Margaret Mead, who in 1928 had published a famous book called *Coming of Age in Samoa*. She described it as a place of sexual *laissez-faire* without any kind of prescribed sexual morality, yet where people lived lives of idyllic happiness. In the 1980s a New Zealand anthropologist, Derek Freeman, contested many of her findings, though not all scholars agree with him. But no Western culture has allowed a sexual free-for-all, without codes or conventions governing marriage or parenthood, at least since the conversion of Constantine in the early fourth century.

Love as a moral bond in the form of monogamous marriage is one of the great achievements of the West, a remarkable combination of sociological realism and moral and spiritual beauty: marriage as the crucible of the love that brings new life into the world.

In the course of its evolution, a unique challenge was posed to *Homo sapiens* by two factors: we stood upright, which constricted the female pelvis, and we had bigger brains – a 300 per cent increase – which meant larger heads. So human babies had to be born more prematurely than any other species, and thus needed parental protection for much longer. This made parenting more demanding among humans than among other species, the work of two people rather than one.

Hence the relatively rare phenomenon among mammals, of pair bonding, unlike other species where the male contribution tends to end with the act of impregnation. Among most primates, fathers don't even recognise their children, let alone care for them. Elsewhere in the animal kingdom, the protective link between mother and baby is almost universal but one between father and baby is rare. So what emerged along with the human person was the union of the biological mother and father to care for their child. But then came culture and with it the third surprise.

Among hunter-gatherers, pair bonding was the norm. Then came agriculture, and economic surplus, and cities and civilisation, and, for the first time, sharp inequalities began to emerge between rich and poor, powerful and powerless. The great ziggurats of Mesopotamia and the pyramids of ancient Egypt, with their broad base and narrow top, were monumental statements in stone created by hierarchical societies in which the few had power over the many.

The most obvious expression of power among alpha males, whether human or primate, is to dominate access to fertile females, and thus maximise the spread of their genes in the next generation. Hence polygamy, which exists in around 95 per cent of mammal species and 75 per cent of human cultures known to anthropology. Polygamy is a powerful expression of inequality, because it means that many males never get the chance to have a wife and child, and women get only a part share in a husband they are unlikely to have had any part in choosing for themselves. And sexual envy has been, throughout history, among animals as well as humans, a – some say even the – prime driver of violence.

That is what makes the first chapter of Genesis revolutionary in its statement that every human being, regardless of class, colour, culture or creed, is in the image and likeness of God himself. In the ancient world it was rulers, kings, emperors and pharaohs who were held to be in the image of God. What Genesis was saying is that we are all royalty. We each have equal dignity in the kingdom of faith under the sovereignty of God.

From this it follows that we each have an equal right to form a marriage and have children, which is why, regardless of how we read the story of Adam and Eve – and there are differences between Jewish and Christian readings – the norm presupposed by that story is: one woman, one man. Or as the Bible itself says: 'That is why a man leaves his father and mother and is united to his wife, and they become one flesh' (Gen. 2:24). Monogamy did not immediately become the norm, even within the world of the Bible. But many of its most famous stories, about the tension between Sarah and Hagar, or Leah and Rachel and their children, or David and Bathsheba, or Solomon's many wives, are all critiques that point the way to monogamy.

What makes the emergence of monogamy surprising is that normally the values of a society are those imposed on it by the ruling class.[11] And the ruling class in a hierarchical society stands to gain from its own promiscuity and polygamy, both of which multiply the chances of their genes being handed on to the next generation. From monogamy the rich and powerful lose and the poor and powerless gain. So the establishment of monogamy goes against the normal grain of social change and was a triumph for the equal dignity of all.

This had huge implications for the moral life, especially in what has come to be known as the Judeo-Christian heritage. We've become familiar with the work of evolutionary biologists using computer simulations and the iterated prisoner's dilemma to explain why reciprocal altruism exists among all social animals. We behave to others as we would wish them to behave to us, and we respond to them as they respond to us. As C.S. Lewis pointed out in his book *The Abolition of Man*, reciprocity is the Golden Rule shared by all the great civilisations.

What was new and remarkable in the Hebrew Bible was the idea that *love*, not just reciprocity, is the driving principle of the moral life.[12] Three loves. 'Love the Lord your God with all your heart, all your soul and all your might.' 'Love your neighbour as yourself.' And, repeated no fewer than thirty-six times in the Mosaic books, 'Love the stranger because you know what it feels like to be a stranger.' Just as God created the natural world in love and forgiveness, so we are charged with creating the social world in love and forgiveness. That love is a flame lit in marriage and the family. Morality is the love between husband and wife, parent and child – uncommanded because it is assumed to be natural – extended outward to the world.

This led to the quite subtle idea that truth, beauty, goodness, and life itself, do not exist in any one person or entity but in the 'between', what Martin Buber called *Das Zwischenmenschliche*, the interpersonal, the counterpoint of speaking and listening, giving and receiving. That is why covenant – the moral bond that turns two or more 'I's' into a 'We' – is the central concept in the Hebrew Bible.

The Jews became an intensely family-oriented people, and it was this that saved us from tragedy. After the destruction of the Second Temple in the year 70, Jews were scattered throughout the world, everywhere a minority, everywhere without rights, suffering some of the worst persecutions ever known by a people, and yet Jews survived because they never lost three things: their sense of family, their sense of community, and their faith.

And these values were renewed every week on Shabbat, the day of rest when we give our marriages and families what they most need and are most starved of in the contemporary world: namely time. While making the television documentary for the BBC, referred to earlier, on the state of family life in Britain, I took the person who was then Britain's leading expert on child care, Penelope Leach, to a Jewish primary school on a Friday morning.

There she saw the children enacting in advance what they would see that evening around the family table. There were the five-year-old mother and father blessing the five-year-old children with the five-year-old grandparents looking on. She was fascinated by this whole institution, and she asked the children what they most enjoyed about the Sabbath. One five-year-old boy turned to her and said, 'It's the only night of the week when Daddy doesn't have to rush off.' As we walked away from the school when the filming was over, she turned to me and said, 'Chief Rabbi, that Sabbath of yours is saving their parents' marriages.'

What makes the traditional family remarkable, a work of high religious art, is what it brought together: sexual drive, physical desire, friendship, companionship, emotional kinship and love, the begetting of children and their protection and care, their early education and induction into an identity and a history. Seldom has any institution woven together so many different drives and desires, roles and responsibilities. It made sense of the world and gave it a human face, the face of love.

For a whole variety of reasons – some to do with medical developments like birth control, in vitro fertilisation and other genetic interventions; some to do with moral change, like the idea that we are free to do whatever we like so long as it does not harm others; some to do with a transfer of responsibilities from the individual to the state, and other and more profound changes in the culture of the West – almost everything that marriage once brought together has now been split apart. Sex has been divorced from love, love from commitment, marriage from having children, and having children from responsibility for their care.

No one surely wants to go back to the narrow prejudices of the past – loveless marriages, authoritarian families, harsh parenthood and the rest. But our compassion for those who choose to live differently should not inhibit us from being advocates for the single most humanising institution in history. The family – man, woman and child – is not one lifestyle choice among many. It is the best means we have yet discovered for nurturing future generations and enabling children to grow in a matrix of stability and love. It is where we learn the delicate choreography of relationship and how to handle the inevitable conflicts within any human group. It is where we first take the risk of giving and receiving love. It is where one generation passes on its values to the next, ensuring the continuity of a civilisation. For any society, the family is the crucible of its future, and for the sake of our children's future, we must be its defenders.

PART TWO

Consequences:

The Market and the State

5

From 'We' to 'I'

How did it happen, this move from 'We' to 'I', from society to self, from 'out there' to 'in here'? We've seen some of the symptoms, from loneliness to self-help to social media's focus on self-presentation. But these are part of a larger story, one deeply embedded in the history of the West, and it is this larger story I want to sketch out in this chapter.

When and why did people in the West start seeing themselves as individuals? Some date it to the Hebrew Bible, with its statement that every human being is in the image and likeness of God. Others trace it to the great Greek philosophers like Socrates, or to the Stoics. Larry Siedentop has made a compelling case for Christianity as having liberated the individual from the sometimes-suffocating embrace of the family.[1] A strong argument could be mounted for the Italian Renaissance, especially the document that has come to be seen as its manifesto, Pico della Mirandola's *Oration on the Dignity of Man*. There is some truth in all these suggestions, but there can be little doubt that something decisive happened between the fifteenth and seventeenth centuries, in the interval between the end of feudalism and 'the birth of the modern'.[2]

People begin writing autobiographies. Artists start painting self-portraits. Rembrandt (1606–69) did so repeatedly: over forty paintings, thirty-one etchings and seven drawings of himself. People lived, increasingly, in private rooms. The French psychologist Jacques Lacan argued that the sense of an 'I' closely corresponded to the mass manufacture of glass mirrors.[3] All roads in the late seventeenth century, writes historian Christopher Hill, led to individualism: 'More rooms in better-off houses, use of glass in windows . . . replacement of benches by chairs – all this made possible greater comfort and privacy for at least part of the population.' Privacy, he argues, 'contributed to the introspection and soul-searching of radical Puritanism, to the keeping of diaries and spiritual journals'.[4]

One of the key turning points was the Reformation, Luther purportedly nailing his ninety-five theses to the door of the church in Wittenberg, and his epoch-making assertion of individual conscience: 'Here I stand, I can do no other.' Luther was hardly a revolutionary: he sought not something new but something old that he believed the Catholic Church had forgotten, namely the primacy of the individual's direct encounter with God, the 'I' of faith unmediated by the 'We' of the Church. His concept of the 'priesthood of all believers' – he derived it from the New Testament, though the verses he quotes are adapted from the verse in Exodus where God says to the Israelites, 'You shall be to Me a kingdom of priests and a holy nation'[5] – was intended to relocate authority from an external institution to the individual believer and his or her direct encounter with God through their reading of sacred texts and personal openness to divine grace.

Luther's significance in the history of moral thought, argues moral philosopher Alasdair MacIntyre, is that for the first time we encounter the absolute individual, the person-as-such over and above any social roles into which they have been cast. When we die, says Luther, we do so irreducibly as ourselves. No one else can do this for us. 'It is as such, stripped of all social attributes, abstracted, as a dying man is abstracted, from all his social relations, that the individual is continually before God.'[6] No one else can make our decisions for us. Nothing in the culture or social structure can relieve us of our ultimate responsibility to decide how to live and what to believe. All depends on the individual. That was one turning point.

A century later, there were two other turning points, equally fateful. The first came from Descartes (1596–1650), father of modern philosophy, in his attempt to build an account of human knowledge on the foundation of radical scepticism, the systematic questioning of everything. Famously he concluded that there was one thing he could not doubt: 'I think; therefore I am.' What made this a turning point was that the religious heritage of the West had, as one of its foundations, the moment that Moses at the burning bush asked God for his name, to which God replied, 'I am that I am.'[7] The revolutionary nature of the Cartesian method lay in the move from the divine 'I am' to the human 'I am' – from a theocentric to an anthropocentric view of reality, whose full implications would later be articulated with shattering force by Friedrich Nietzsche.

The other came from intellectual radical Thomas Hobbes (1588–1679). *The Leviathan* is the first great work of modern political philosophy, and what is striking about it is that it dispenses entirely with metaphysical or theological doctrines, such as the divine right of kings, and takes as its starting point the self-interested individual. Any situation in which individuals are free to pursue their own desires without constraints will rapidly descend into what he called a state of nature, a 'war of every man against every man', in which there is constant fear of death.

What we have and others desire will be taken from us, by force if necessary. Therefore it is in the interests of each to forgo some of their rights and powers, handing them over to some central agency, a Leviathan, who will use that power to ensure the rule of law within and the defence of the realm without. The hero of Hobbes's narrative is the atomic individual, the 'I' considered without regard to culture or class, or constitutive attachments to family and faith. Thus the modern concept of the social contract was born, and the 'I' moved to the centre of the intellectual world of the post-Reformation West.

A key figure in helping it further on its path to ascendancy was Immanuel Kant. Kant placed supreme emphasis on the human power of reason, and on the capacity of the mind to construct the world, not as it is in itself, but as it is perceived by us. He interiorised reality. The best way of understanding his writings on morality is to think of them as a translation of Lutheranism into the language of secularity.

The biblical idea that we are each in the image and likeness of God became, in Kant's translation, the principle: treat other human beings as ends, not means. Luther's Pauline insistence on faith, not works, became Kant's assertion that nothing is unconditionally good except a good will. Morality for Kant, like faith for Luther, lives within the mind or soul. It is not what we do but what we intend and why that matters. Finally, and crucially, for Kant as for Luther, authority lies not in external institutions but in the inner life of the individual. Doing good because someone else – God or society – so commanded constitutes *heteronomy*, a law made by someone other than me, and does not constitute moral behaviour. Morality requires *autonomy*, meaning that I have legislated it for myself.

Viewed one way, Kant and Luther are opposites. Kant believed in reason, Luther in revelation. The Reformation evoked human self-abasement: only God can make us good. The Enlightenment exuded human self-assertion: we alone can achieve true knowledge through reason and observation. But both placed the human individual at the heart of the moral life. Kant's concept of autonomy, in particular, proved fateful.

Kant did not believe that this was a recipe for Hobbesian chaos: what the Bible in Judges describes as a situation in which 'Everyone did what was right in his own eyes.' To the contrary, he believed his system meant that everyone would arrive at the same moral law. He laid down three conditions. First, a moral law had to treat others as ends, not means. Second, it had to be a categorical, not hypothetical imperative, meaning that it had to be absolute and unconditional. Third, it had to be universal. As he put it, 'Act only on that maxim which you can at the same time will that it should become a universal law.' In retrospect, though, it seems almost incomprehensible that all humanity would, even if they used reason alone, unswayed by emotion, converge on the same moral principles. It is an occupational hazard of philosophy, at least in the Western mode, to mistake what seems compelling now for what is true, if anything, in all cultures and ages. Kant's benign vision of a world of self-legislating saints and sages could not last long, and it did not.

Two lonely nineteenth-century geniuses, one deeply religious, the other profoundly anti-religious, yet both highly critical of society and its conventions, both fascinated by masks, role-distances and multiple identities, made the leap from Kant's dream of reason to a profoundly non-rational world of radical personal choice. The first was the Danish theologian Søren Kierkegaard (1813–45).

In a dazzling and wholly original work, *Either/Or*, Kierkegaard sets out, in the form of two personae, two radically different modes of existence: the aesthetic, with its life of the senses, and the ethical, with its commitment to righteousness and duty. These constitute two different worlds of feeling and thinking; they amount to two different lives. Each is coherent and consistent in itself but radically incompatible with the other. Which then to choose? There are no criteria by which you could make a rational choice. All you could do was decide, non-rationally. You had to make a leap of faith. For the first time a thinker had set out what Isaiah Berlin was to call the incommensurable. Not all values can be realised in a single life. The Platonic idea of the harmony of the true, the good and the beautiful had been exploded beyond repair. In placing at the centre of the moral life this essentially non-rational choice, not of what to do but of who to be, Kierkegaard should be seen in retrospect as the first existentialist.

The other figure was Friedrich Nietzsche, the thinker rightly regarded as the most important progenitor of the postmodern world. His writings lend themselves to an almost infinite range of interpretations, but central to his work was his view that the whole conception of morality as it had been understood throughout the history of Christianity was to be overthrown in what he called a 'transvaluation of values'.[8]

Nietzsche was the first to proclaim that God is dead and we have killed him. So radical was the assertion that he put it in the mouth of an imagined madman in *The Gay Science*. But he was far more than merely an atheist. His view was that the entire Judeo-Christian moral heritage was nothing less than the revenge of the powerless against the powerful; the retribution exacted by slaves against their former masters. It was a sustained exercise in *ressentiment*. Everything we had come to think of as virtue, compassion, kindness, was in fact a way of caging, neutering the reality of human nature, which was, he believed, shaped and dominated by the will to power.

In the competition for power, most people fail, but some succeed and impose their will on others. Such a person Nietzsche called an *Ubermensch*. Christianity opposed this way of life in the name of justice and equality. But Nietzsche believed that the Christian era was at an end, and rightly so, because in returning to nature, we would find ourselves returning to the world of the epic heroes of the pre-Socratic world of the Greeks. This was, in fact, the conclusion to which Bernard Williams was drawn, as he says in perhaps his finest book, *Shame and Necessity*. Nietzsche did not say what would happen to the rest of us in a world ruled by pre-Socratic heroes, but the short answer must be that that was not his concern. For Nietzsche, winners count; losers do not. A world ruled by the will to power is not a moral world as we recognise it.

Nietzsche's influence on the contemporary world is almost incalculably immense. He was one of the first to believe that language and ideas were merely a mask hiding an underlying battle of wills, a struggle for power. He thus became the originator, later followed by Marx and Freud, of the hermeneutics of suspicion. There are no truths, he said, only interpretations. Nietzsche thus became one of the sources of late twentieth-century postmodernism.

Kierkegaard and Nietzsche between them effectively destroyed the foundations of morality as they had been known in the West for many centuries, and each proposed in its place a profoundly personal, subjective vision of the moral life, in which choice was of the essence: not choice as it had always been known, between good and evil as defined by the prevailing culture, but rather to define good and evil themselves in an act involving the totality of one's being. The 'I' had become not just the principal character in the moral drama, but its author, the writer of its rules.

This was understood in quite different ways in different cultures. In France it became existentialism, as expounded by Sartre and Camus. Our existence precedes our essence, as Sartre famously put it. Any mere acceptance of society and its roles – Sartre has a lovely word-portrait of the waiter who consummately plays the role of being a waiter – constitutes *mauvais foi*, bad faith. We are here to be ourselves, he thought, not act out a role dictated by society. Later, as we will see in the chapter on post-truth, this became the mood and movement known as postmodernism, led by Foucault, Derrida and others.

In the Anglo-American world its most significant expression was the theory known as emotivism, the view that moral judgements do not reflect any objective reality. They are no more than a disguised way of expressing our feelings and subjective valuations, a way of saying, 'I like this; like it too.' Morality thus ceased to be what it had usually been understood as being, a shared code by whose rules the members of a group agreed to abide, even if only tacitly, and became a mere matter of personal taste.

The end result was an ethic without agreed principles or object-ive truths. It was a world of relativism, subjectivism, and a new and dominant idea, namely *authenticity*, or as it is sometimes called, *expressive individualism*. The moral imperative, different in substance for each of us, is to become ourselves.

While Kierkegaard and Nietzsche were constructing their philosophies, two other figures, one a political commentator, the other a sociologist, made important observations. The political commentator was the French aristocrat Alexis de Tocqueville in his dazzlingly perceptive account, published in the 1830s: *Democracy in America*. What he discovered in America was a phenomenon he had never encountered before, and it was so new and strange that he had to devise a new word to describe it. The word he coined was *individualism*.

He emphasised that by this, he did not mean egoism. He was not referring to people being selfish and riding roughshod over the needs and feelings of others. 'Our fathers knew of egoism', he writes, which he defines as 'a passionate and exaggerated love of self'. Individualism is different. It is less a failing of character than an environment, 'a feeling which disposes each citizen to isolate himself from the mass of his fellows so that, having created a small company for its use, he willingly leaves society at large to itself.'[9]

De Tocqueville saw this as the single greatest danger to democratic freedom in the long run. People would simply cease to interest themselves in the welfare of others, and they would leave that responsibility to the state, which would grow ever larger until it became a kind of benign tyranny.

> Each of them, living apart, is as a stranger to the fate of all the rest; his children and his private friends constitute to him the whole of mankind. As for the rest of his fellow citizens, he is close to, but does not see them; he touches them, but he does not feel them; he exists only in himself and for himself alone; and if his kindred still remain to him, he may be said at any rate, to have lost his country.[10]

De Tocqueville foresaw the risks of what I described in the first chapter as outsourcing. People would leave everything that did not concern them personally to the state, and this would eventually lead to the end of democratic freedom. The only thing that protected America from this outcome was the strength of its families, communities, churches and charitable organisations, in other words, its moral environments where people actively cared for one another. De Tocqueville's warning still echoes today. Lose those environments of face-to-face encounter, where the moral sense is exercised, and eventually you will lose liberty.

The sociologist, one of the pioneers of the discipline, was Émile Durkheim. In his work *Suicide* (1893), Durkheim argued

84

that in any society in a state of anomie – that is, lacking a shared moral code – there would be a rise in suicide. He did not see how a society could survive the loss of what he called *la conscience collective*, the unifying body of ideas, beliefs and attitudes that give shape and coherence to our shared social world. Not only would society fragment; so too would individuals, and many of them would be unable to cope. That, I believe, is what is happening in our time.

In the United States, for example, there was a 30 per cent increase in suicides between 2000 and 2016. It rose by 1 per cent a year until 2006 and by 2 per cent a year for the next decade. There was a 50 per cent increase in suicides among girls and women during the same period,[11] and among people aged between ten and thirty-four it has become the second most common cause of death.[12] In Britain in 2017, suicide rates among fifteen- to nineteen-year-old males were the second highest since records began in 1981, and the rate among girls and women of that age was the highest since records began. This is not in itself proof that Durkheim was right. Every tragedy of this kind has its own unique set of causes. But the figures are suggestive. A world without shared meanings is one in which it is easy to feel lost.

Anomie, it seems to me, aptly describes the state we inhabit today: a world of relativism, non-judgementalism, subjectivity, autonomy, individual rights, and self-esteem. The gains of this long process have been many, but the loss, too, has been profound. The revolutionary shift from 'We' to 'I' means that everything that once consecrated the moral bonds binding us to one another – faith, creed, culture, custom and convention – no longer does so. The energy now localised in the 'I' has been diverted from family, congregation and community, all of which have now grown weak, leaving us vulnerable and alone.

An individualistic universe may be free but it is fraught with loneliness, isolation, vulnerability and nihilism, a prevailing sense of the ultimate meaninglessness of life. We are, in the title of Sherry Turkle's book, *Alone Together*. That is the price of radical individualism, massively accelerated by smartphones, social media and the loss of contexts in which we form enduring moral commitments. Everything has become immediate, transactional and presentational. We hide behind our profile and become the masks we wear.

Hence the contemporary paradox: we can communicate instantly across the globe but often find it difficult to chat with our next-door neighbour. Yet, as Robert Hall puts it in his book *This Land of Strangers*, 'the truth is, relationships are the most valuable and value-creating resource of any society. They are our lifelines to survive, grow and thrive.'[13] As the editors of a recent collection of studies, *The Crisis of Connection*, put it: 'In place of the "we," we have been left with the "me," the solitary individual, whose needs, wants, and desires take precedence over the collective. Human society has evolved to a stage where the rights of the individual, particularly those with wealth, power, and status, supersede all other rights and responsibilities.'[14]

What do porcupines do in winter? asked Schopenhauer. If they come too close together, they injure one another with their spines. But if they stay too far apart, they freeze in the cold. It is not easy to get the balance right, and in human society there is no homeostasis, no mechanism that adjusts to the temperature outside. As long as the market economy and the liberal democratic state last, we will never be forced close to one another as people were in the premodern age, nor would we want to be. But we cannot stay as we are, for the human world is growing colder and the winds more biting and ferocious. We need a little more 'We' and a little less 'I' if we are to negotiate some of the challenges the present century still has in store for us.

6

Markets Without Morals

In September 2018, a parliamentary report was published into the collapse of one of Britain's largest construction companies, Carillion. The company had gone into liquidation in January 2018 with debts of some £7 billion pounds. Many people suffered as a result. More than two thousand lost their jobs. Carillion's 30,000 suppliers faced massive financial losses. So did the company's 28,500 pensioners. Taxpayers faced costs of £150 million. New hospital facilities in Liverpool and Birmingham, intended to relieve pressure on the National Health Service, have been put on indefinite hold. Yet while the firm was heading towards catastrophe, its board of directors continued to award themselves large bonuses.

The parliamentary report was scathing:

Carillion's rise and spectacular fall was a story of recklessness, hubris and greed. Its business model was a relentless dash for cash, driven by acquisitions, rising debt, expansion into new markets and exploitation of suppliers. It presented accounts that misrepresented the reality of the business, and increased its dividend every year, come what may. Long term obligations, such as adequately funding its pension schemes, were treated with contempt. Even as the company very publicly began to unravel, the board was concerned with increasing and protecting generous executive bonuses.[1]

Sadly, in our time, this is an instance of behaviour that has become all too common. One of the early examples was the collapse of Enron in 2001. As Bethany McLean and Peter Elkind document in their book *The Smartest Guys in the Room*,[2] Enron, an American

energy, commodities and services company, had been named by
Fortune magazine as America's 'most innovative company' for
six years in succession. It employed 29,000 people. Each year its
profits increased and its stock price rose. It was held up as a role
model for other businesses to follow.

At the height of its success, a young journalist Bethany
McLean wrote an article asking how Enron was able to record
such extraordinary profits, especially at a time of economic turn-
down. Essentially, she was working to a simple dictum that could
have spared many people much grief and loss, namely: *if it looks
too good to be true, it probably is.* By the end of 2001 Enron
and its hitherto respected accounting firm Arthur Andersen
were revealed to have engaged in prolonged systematic fraud
and insider trading. Enron filed for bankruptcy. The accounting
firm was dissolved. The entire culture of corporate governance
in the modern economy came under a shadow from which it has
not emerged. In 2018, the British Academy published a report,
Reforming Business for the 21st Century, in which it argued
that 'corporations were originally established with clear public
purposes', but only in the past fifty years has that purpose been
confined to profit. This, it said, has damaged 'corporations' role
in society, trust in business and the impact that business has had
on the environment, inequality, and social cohesion'.[3]

The Enron scandal took place in the United States, but the
corrosion of morals – the failures of honesty, integrity, responsibility, transparency and accountability – was clearly beginning
to affect the entire corporate culture of the West. Shortly after
the Enron collapse, I had one of the most poignant conversations of my life, with (Lord) Arnold Weinstock, widely regarded
as the leading British industrialist of his generation. He was a
role model; his methods had been written about and studied in
business schools throughout the world. He had led his company
to sustained growth for decades and did so while exercising firm
and principled financial caution. He regarded this as an essential
responsibility of business leadership. Business, he had told me

some years earlier, is not about short-term profit, but about long-term benefit to the public, shareholders and employees alike.

Now, though, in his late seventies and approaching death, he was a pale shadow of his former self. He looked like a broken man. He was not religious, but he had called me to say that he wanted to tell me something before he died. What he told me was this: 'I gave my life to building the business. I paid myself a reasonable salary, but a modest one. My successor pays himself ten times as much, and he has driven everything I have built to ruin.' As I later discovered, this was true, and everyone in the business world knew it: his successor had made a series of irresponsible acquisitions, completely ignoring the principles that had led the organisation to greatness for four consecutive decades, and leading it instead to catastrophic losses and ruin.

One of the underlying factors of this change in corporate culture in Britain and America was doubtless the financial deregulation in the 1980s that came to be known respectively as Thatcherism and Reaganomics. I have no criticism of that policy. It was right for its time. The 1970s was a period of deep depression in both countries, economic, social and psychological. Deregulation kick-started four successive booms that led to sustained economic growth from which most of us have benefited, directly or indirectly.

But not equally. Since 1980, the average pre-tax income of the top 10 per cent of Americans has doubled. That of the top 1 per cent has risen threefold. That of the top 0.001 per cent has risen more than sevenfold. During this same period, the average pre-tax income of the bottom 60 per cent of American workers has remained static or has declined in real terms.[4] In Britain, the ratio of rewards of CEOs to average employees moved from 45 to 1 in 1998, to 120 to 1 in 2010.

In the year of the 2008 crash, the stock market fell by 30 per cent, while salaries of top executives rose by 10 per cent.[5] J.P. Morgan, founder of the bank that bears his name, once said that no one at the top of a company should earn more than twenty times that of those at the bottom. Today top salaries at major corporations go far beyond this. The reality is even worse than it appears at first sight: in many corporations, much of the lowest-paid work is now outsourced to contractors, so that the poorest paid do not figure on the company's payroll at all. There has been a major realignment of the economy in Britain and America, from a relatively egalitarian era in the 1950s, in the wake of the Great Depression and the Second World War, to a highly inegalitarian one now. This is not an accident. It has taken place during the period when the age of 'We' mutated into the age of 'Me'. If the corporation's purpose is no more than the pursuit of profit, why should that not apply to individuals in positions of power? Why should they not translate their sense of self-worth into financial reward? When only profit counts, what then happens to service, loyalty and duty to others?

The most dramatic, indeed scandalous, element of the 2008 crash was the result of the development of financial derivatives using credit default swaps, essentially allowing banks to leverage their deposits on an unprecedented scale by outsourcing the risk, somewhat in the way that we do as individuals when we take out an insurance policy. The risk was diminished by the strategy of slicing and dicing the risks into packaged products, each containing tiny portions of a large number of loans. This minimised the effect of any individual debt failure, but in fact it exposed the entire chain of financial instruments and institutions to systemic collapse. So inter-connected were they that the entire global banking system turned out to be at risk once any part of it collapsed. The main impact of these new derivatives was to the benefit of the housing market in the form of enabling subprime mortgages, that is, mortgages that would not normally be granted for lack of security.

At the time, this seemed a positive way of extending home ownership throughout the United States. Interest rates were at a record low and the flood of new buyers seemed set to be a non-stop boom for the housing market. Everyone would benefit. Many, many people would own homes for the first time. They would have a capital asset that would increase in value over time. Meanwhile the banks were able to leverage their capital to a degree unheard of before. Everyone stood to gain. No one stood to lose.

It was at this time, early on in the process, that more people should have applied the same simple dictum that Bethany McLean did in the case of Enron. If it looks too good to be true, it probably is. In fact, someone did: none other than Warren Buffett, consistently the most successful investor of the past fifty years. In 2002 he was already calling subprime mortgages 'financial weapons of mass destruction'.[6] In 2007 former options trader Nassim Nicholas Taleb published a book entitled *The Black Swan: The Impact of the Highly Improbable*, an argument for, among other things, the unreliability of economic predictions. As Donald Rumsfeld said in a different context, we know about the known knowns and the known unknowns, but not the 'unknown unknowns', factors that we never thought of but that nonetheless have a decisive effect on markets.

Booms turn into busts, profits into losses, and people suffer. Recall the Jeff Goldblum character in the film *Jurassic Park* who reminds Richard Attenborough that all his contingency planning is based on rational predictions, ignoring such significant ideas as chaos theory, non-linear equations and strange attractors. 'If there is one thing the history of evolution has taught us it's that life will not be contained.' Then he adds: 'But your scientists were so preoccupied with whether or not they could that they didn't stop to think if they should.' That seems to be the truth about those complex derivatives.

The crash, beginning with Lehman Brothers in the United States and Northern Rock in Britain, was horrific. So global and interconnected has the world's banking system become that one of the first and major casualties was Iceland, population 300,000, not hitherto recognised as one of the world's leading financial centres. The easy availability of cheap credit had tempted many smaller players to overcommit, and they were among the first and worst sufferers when the tide turned.

Luckily at least one of the lessons of the Great Crash in 1929 had been learned. Governments stepped in by way of central banks and bailed the banks out, at the most massive cost. In the end it was not the 'smartest guys in the room' who saved the day, and certainly not the mathematicians who had created securitised risk in the first place, nor the bankers themselves, who turned out only to have the vaguest knowledge of what subprime mortgages actually were. It was, of all things, government, whose role in the financial sector had been drastically curtailed by the deregulatory process in the 1980s and whose role in the global economy had increasingly been downplayed as irrelevant in the intervening years. It was their sense of moral responsibility to their populations as a whole that rescued the economy from collapse. In the end, the market needed to be saved by something that was not the market and did not work by the market's principle of self-interest.

It was what happened next that left a bad taste in the mouth that has not gone away in the meantime. Having been rescued by the government as being 'too big to fail', the banks continued to award bonus payments to their senior staff. In one notorious case, a senior banker who had awarded himself £30 million in salary and bonuses drove the bank he presided over almost to oblivion. Only because it was deemed 'too big to fail' was it saved by the government.

The public as a whole suffered deeply. In Britain and America over a million houses were repossessed. The people promised a home of their own for the first time found themselves homeless again. To restore some kind of balance to government finances, programmes of austerity were introduced in one country after another. People as a whole, especially those dependent on government services, suffered as a result, while to all appearances the senior bankers who might rightly have been held responsible for their suffering received bonuses for their pains. Stalin is believed to have said: 'The death of one man is a tragedy, the death of millions is a statistic.' The crash of 2007/8 showed us that something similar is true in the world of finance.

Nor has the inequity and iniquity ceased since then. Bankers' salaries and bonuses continue to rise, while the income of those in the bottom of the population continues to stay static or fall. As noted in the first chapter, in 1965 the ratio of chief executive to worker pay in the United States was 20:1. Today it is 312:1.[7] This has significantly damaged public perceptions of businesses and their leaders. In Britain, Noreena Hertz recorded a massive fall in young people's trust in large corporations to do the right thing. Two generations ago, 60 per cent of people trusted them to do so. Today that figure is only 6 per cent.[8] In America a 2018 Deloitte Millennial Survey produced figures tending in the same direction. In a single year, between 2017 and 2018, the percentage of young people who believed that businesses behave ethically fell from 65 per cent to 48 per cent, and the percentage of those who believe business leaders are committed to helping improve society fell from 62 per cent to 47 per cent. It was reported that 75 per cent believe business leaders focus on their own agendas rather than considering the wider society, and 62 per cent think that the leaders of said companies have no ambition beyond wanting to make money.[9] None of these attitudes is necessarily true, but collectively they are indicative of a profound loss of trust in business, and the capacity of the market to regulate itself in the interests of the common good.

Seemingly, today's young people concur with the judgement of the first great philosopher of the market economy Adam Smith, who wrote in *The Wealth of Nations*: 'People of the same trade seldom meet together, even for merriment and diversion, but the conversation ends in a conspiracy against the public, or in some contrivance to raise prices' – we might include mention of salaries and bonuses. What has happened to drive CEO pay out of all proportion to that of the rest of the workforce – not just as salary but also in the form of bonuses, share options and other benefits – is what looks uncommonly like collusion between senior executives and board members, without thought of what is best for employees, communities and nations involved.

This itself is only one example of the larger problem, however, which is that the market is better at creating wealth than distributing it, and equitable distribution requires something other than self-interest. It needs a sense of the common good, of the 'We' not just the 'I'. Markets need morals.

If these comments are critical it is not because I claim any expertise in the field (though I initially went to university to study economics). Rather it is because in 1992, early in my tenure as Chief Rabbi, I and a brilliant young rabbi, Pinchas Rosenstein, created the Jewish Association of Business Ethics (JABE), which functioned with great distinction for some twenty years. We feared that financial deregulation might create perverse incentives and moral hazard – what George Bernard Shaw in a different context called 'the maximum of temptation combined with the maximum of opportunity' – and we sensed that the time was right to enlist the advice of leading business people within our community. They agreed: the group consisted of CEOs of some of Britain's leading public companies, top professionals – lawyers, accountants and economists – and a representative group of Britain's top financial journalists. What this showed was that CEOs themselves appreciated the need for a moral dimension in business and financial decision making.

JABE did not just sit and deliberate, like a kind of localised World Economic Forum. We went out to schools, to engage high school students in reflection on some of the moral choices they would have to make. The journalists wrote scenarios. A team of professional actors played them out. The pupils then gave their own reflections: what they would do in the circumstances and why. Only then did the business people and professionals explain to the students what they would have done, and at the very end a rabbi explained the position of Jewish law on the matter. Stripped of denominational content, the material was made available to all secondary schools in Britain under the heading of Money and Morals.

It was some of the same business leaders who told me in 2008 how appalling they felt had been the behaviour of the bankers and financial institutions in the wake of the crash. They were shocked that the banks had taken such risks with other people's money. They were outraged that the bankers had not only rewarded themselves so generously in the first place, but also provided themselves with a golden parachute so that they stood to gain substantially not only if they succeeded but even if they failed: the classic case of moral hazard.

Moral hazard occurs when one party is involved in risk-taking, but knows that, should the decision turn out to be a bad one, someone else will pay the price. When this happens, there is a distortion in the decision-making process. Because the potential gain is high and the cost of potential loss will be borne by others, there is an incentive to take high-risk decisions that would not otherwise be justified. The assumption behind the derivatives involved in subprime mortgages was that they effectively outsourced the risk. Besides which, if anyone considered the risk of massive defaults, they surely believed – rightly as it happens – that the major banks were too big to fail: if governments allowed them to do so, whole nations would suffer. So the bankers did not have skin in the game in the way that their customers did. They were not going to lose, whatever the outcome. While the global economy was on the brink, I did not encounter a single report of a banker expressing remorse, guilt or shame that others were suffering while they walked free and without loss. They seemingly could not understand the moral enormity of the irresponsibility they had perpetrated against trusting customers.

A basic sense of justice as fairness is deeply embedded in human instinct, observable even in young children.[10] 'It's not fair' is one of the first moral propositions we articulate. Such a sense of innate justice is not even exclusive to humans. All social animals feel something like this. There is a famous TED Talk given by the great primatologist Frans de Waal – the video is available online.[11] In part of it there are two capuchin monkeys in adjacent cages, performing an exercise for their keeper. Their task is to hand the keeper a stone through the mesh of the cage. The keeper then rewards them each time by giving them a slice of cucumber.

Then the keeper does something different. He rewards the first monkey with a grape. Monkeys like cucumber but they like grapes more. The second monkey observes this closely. The keeper then turns to it. It hands the keeper a stone, and he then gives it a slice of cucumber. The expression on the face of the monkey is a study in moral indignation. It looks at the cucumber and at the keeper, then in disgust flings it as far as it can throw it. It does this a second time when the keeper offers it another slice of cucumber.

Nothing could illustrate more dramatically how fundamental is a sense of justice as fairness, the very thing that is threatened in circumstances of moral hazard. Contemplating the success of Bill Gates of Microsoft, the late Steve Jobs of Apple, or Jeff Bezos of Amazon.com, people might question specific policies of their companies, but they would nonetheless see them as genuine risk takers who had put their entire future on the line. They had much to lose as well as much to gain. Moral hazard offers the upside of risk with no downside, and that offends our sense of justice as fairness. To most people, the self-exculpating, self-rewarding behaviour of bankers in our time has shown the market at its amoral worst.

Too often, from the collapse of Enron until today, we have seen people at the top of major corporations and financial institutions pursuing short-term policies, taking unsustainable risks, awarding themselves absurdly large salaries and bonuses, and leaving employees, pensioners and the public to pay the costs when the house of cards collapsed.

The moral case for free market economics is, in my view, overwhelming. It has proved to be the best antidote to general poverty ever invented. In the space of a single generation it has lifted over a hundred million people from poverty in India, and almost a billion in China, a transformation unprecedented in history. It produces massive incentives for creativity, our most miraculous gift as members of *Homo sapiens*. Would Microsoft or Apple or

Google – and all the technological innovation they have brought us – have existed outside a market economy? Would artificial intelligence have arisen, with its extraordinary promise of, for example, medical innovation and improved diagnostics? The free market has liberated people in a way that Marxism never could.

What is more, as A. O. Hirschman, the Harvard economic historian, showed in his classic study, *The Passions and the Interests*, the market was seen by Enlightenment thinkers Adam Smith, David Hume and Montesquieu as a powerful solution to one of humanity's greatest traditional weaknesses: violence. When two nations meet, said Montesquieu, they can do one of two things: they can wage war or they can trade. If they wage war, both are likely to lose in the long run. If they trade, both will gain. That, of course, was the logic behind the establishment of the European Union: to so lock together the destinies of its nations, especially France and Germany, that they would have an overwhelming interest not to wage war again as they had done to such devastating cost in the first half of the twentieth century.

Bernard Mandeville, the renegade thinker who in 1714 published *The Fable of the Bees*, otherwise known as *Private Vices, Public Benefits* – a work that in many ways anticipated that of Adam Smith – scandalised the British public by suggesting that avarice, a private vice, could be turned, through economic activity, into public benefit. Note, though, that this is not what Adam Smith advocated. Smith spoke not of passions but of interests. His most famous line was: 'It is not from the benevolence of the butcher, the brewer, or the baker that we expect our dinner, but from their regard to their own interest.' Smith did for economics what Hobbes had done for politics. He showed that self-interest led logically to the creation of a system of commercial contracts, as it did *vis-à-vis* the state in the form of a social contract.

The Enlightenment thinkers, Smith, Hume and Montesquieu, knew that religion was loosening its hold on people; that the authority of the Church had been compromised by the violence and warfare it had led to between Catholic and Protestant. They searched therefore for a more neutral, secular basis for the key institutions of society, namely what Bishop Butler called 'cool self-love', and what Alexis de Tocqueville called 'Self-interest rightly understood'. However, none of them ever assumed that a market could function without morals.

As mentioned earlier, Adam Smith himself wrote a major work of moral philosophy, *The Theory of Moral Sentiments*, before he wrote *The Wealth of Nations*. Its opening sentence tells us immediately the context within which he conceived the working of the market: 'How selfish soever man may be supposed, there are evidently some principles in his nature, which interest him in the fortune of others, and render their happiness necessary to him, though he derives nothing from it except the pleasure of seeing it.' He took it for granted that to be human is to have a moral sense – this was the shared assumption of the figures of the Scottish Enlightenment, including David Hume and Adam Fergusson. That interpersonal relations should be governed by morality was fundamental to his understanding of what it is to be human.

Yet David Hume, even in the eighteenth century, can be found warning against the perils of consumerism: 'This avidity alone, of acquiring goods and possessions for ourselves and our nearest friends, is insatiable, perpetual, universal, and directly destructive of society.'[12] So there remains the risk of tension between self-interest and the common good. How, in practice, is this resolved? In recent years, people have turned from purely theoretical accounts of human behaviour to social science experimentation. Significant studies have been conducted to consider the decision-making process, when it is a question of balancing considerations between selfishness on the one hand and fairness on the other.

One classic example is the so-called Ultimatum Game.[13] There are two players, a proposer and a recipient. The proposer is given $10 and has the option of giving any portion of this to the recipient. The only proviso is that if the recipient refuses the offer, then the proposer loses the entire $10. On a strictly rational basis, the proposer should offer one dollar. The recipient should accept it, because it is better than nothing. In actuality, however, in most cases the proposer gives half or close to half, either out of their sense of innate fairness or in fear that the recipient will refuse to accept a smaller amount because of their same sense of what would be fair.

More striking still is the Public Goods Game. Here there are four players, unknown to one another, each of whom is given $20. The game is a series of rounds in which the players put money in the middle, the total is doubled, and then given back equally to all the players. Each player receives a report detailing how much money he or she now has and what the other players did. So, for example, if everyone puts $20 in the middle, this is doubled, and given back to the players, who now each have $40. If, on the other hand, three players put their full $20 in the middle, while one does not, the $60 in the pot is doubled to $120, and each is given $30, so that three of the players have $30 while the one who did not put any money in the common pot now has $50. It pays to let other people contribute to the common good while you hold back.

This condition, however, does not last. The players quickly notice that one of their number is not contributing, and one by one they all cease to do so. There is now no common good, only individual private goods. People give up their potential gains because their sense of justice is outraged. More interestingly, when given the option, the overwhelming majority of players are willing to pay money to a third party to take money away from non-contributors.[14] On the face of it this is odd. Why sacrifice something of your own to punish someone else? Yet the logic is strong. The temptation to be a free-rider – to benefit from public goods without contributing your share, to care for the 'I' not the 'We' – is powerful, so the disincentive has to be even more so. Even though this costs us something, we see it as the necessary price for public goods.

There is no question that the behaviour of banks, other financial institutions and CEOs of major corporations has generated much anger at the most visceral level. After all, gut instinct is what drives our feelings of justice as fairness. But that behaviour is the logical consequence of the individualism that has been our substitute for morality since the 1960s: the 'I' that takes precedence over the 'We'. How could we reject the claims of traditional morality in every other sphere of life and yet expect them to prevail in the heat of the marketplace? Was that not the point of the famous speech delivered by the actor Michael Douglas in the film *Wall Street* that 'Greed – for lack of a better word – is good'? Greed 'captures the essence of the evolutionary spirit', he said: it marks 'the upward surge of mankind'.

In a world where the market rules and its operation is driven by greed, people come to believe that their worth is measured by what you earn or can afford and not by qualities of character like honesty, integrity and service to others. Politics itself, because it can assume no shared morality among its citizens, ceases to be about vision, aspiration and the common good and becomes instead transactional, managerial, a kind of consumer product: vote for the party that gives you more of what you want for a lower price in taxes. You discover that politicians are claiming unwarranted expenses or getting paid for access: in short that politics has come to be seen as a business like any other, and not an entirely reputable one. That is when young people no longer get involved in politics. Why should they? If all that matters is money, they can make more of it elsewhere.

Any position of leadership, however, makes you responsible to the people who have entrusted some part of their destiny to you. That applies to businesses, financial institutions and global corporations. Without morals, markets cannot function. The very words we use imply as much. The word 'credit' comes from the same root as *credo*, 'I believe'. 'Confidence', the presence or lack of which shapes markets, comes from the Latin root 'fides', meaning to have faith in someone or something. 'Fiduciary' has the same origin. Trust, the lack of which produced the banking crisis of 2008, is predicated on trustworthiness. These are, or were, fundamentally moral terms. When there is a breakdown of trust, something significant is going wrong.

The market economy has generated more real wealth, eliminated more poverty and liberated more human creativity than any other economic system. The fault is not with the market itself, but with the idea that the market alone is all we need. Markets do not guarantee equity, responsibility or integrity. They can maximise short-term gain at the cost of long-term sustainability. They cannot be relied upon to distribute rewards fairly. They cannot guarantee honesty. When confronted with flagrant self-interest, they combine the maximum of temptation with the maximum of opportunity. Markets need morals, and morals are not made by markets.

They are made by schools, the media, custom, tradition, religious leaders, moral role models and the influence of people. But when religion loses its voice and the media worship success, when right and wrong become relativised and all talk of morality is condemned as 'judgemental', when people lose all sense of honour and shame and there is nothing they will not do if they can get away with it, no regulation will save us. People will continually outwit the regulators, as they did by the so-called 'securitisation' of risk that meant no one knew who owed what to whom.

Markets were made to serve us; we were not made to serve markets. Economics needs ethics. Markets do not survive by market forces alone. They depend on respect for the people affected by our decisions. Lose that and we will lose not just money and jobs but something more significant still: freedom, trust and decency, the things that have a value, not a price.

7

Consuming Happiness

When the 'I' predominates over the 'We', the market mindset spreads to other aspects of life where it does not belong. The most striking example is the pursuit of happiness. It begins to lose its connection with morality and starts to be associated with the products, services and experiences that we can buy. In both the Greek and Judeo-Christian traditions, happiness was intrinsically related to virtue. It was seen as the result of a life lived in accord with ethical ideals. Since the 1960s, however, it has increasingly reshaped itself to fit the contours of a consumer society driven by self-gratification. The result is that we have become less happy, or at least not more so. As Richard Layard argues in *Happiness: Lessons from a New Science*, incomes have doubled in the past century in Britain and America, but people are no more happy now than they were then.[1] We are, I suggest, searching for happiness in the wrong places. We may even be searching for the wrong thing entirely.

It was Aristotle who gave the West its most influential analysis of happiness. He believed that its pursuit was at the heart of all human endeavour.[2] We undertake all activities for the sake of some good, but there is only one good that we seek as an end in itself and for no other reason, namely *eudaemonia*, his term for happiness. This central idea was for him inextricably connected with the moral life. Happiness is, he said, an activity of the soul in accordance with virtue. It is a matter of living well and faring well. Yes, there are material prerequisites of a happy life. You cannot achieve it if you are desperately poor or seriously ill. Faring well is therefore not entirely under our control. Everyone pursues happiness, but not everyone achieves it. Some fail through no fault of their own. But for the most part *eudaemonia* is a matter of living nobly, courageously, temperately and wisely. It is not about having wealth or popularity or power. It is about what kind of human being you become.

Something similar to Aristotle's account is to be found in another great source of Western values, the Hebrew Bible. The book of Psalms begins with the sentence: 'Happy is the one who does not walk in step with the wicked or stand in the way that sinners take or sit in the company of mockers' (Ps. 1:1). Elsewhere we read, 'Happy are those who uphold justice, who practise righteousness at all times' (Ps. 106:3) and 'Happy are those whose way is blameless, who live according to the Lord's instruction' (Ps. 119:1). Again the assumption is clear. Happiness, or blessedness – the terms are almost interchangeable – means living in accord with the word and will of God, which is how the Bible construes the moral life. It means doing well, living in harmony with the fundamental values embedded in the universe by its Creator.

It was only in the late seventeenth century that happiness began to be thought of in terms of feelings, of private experience. John Locke spoke about it as sensible pleasure. Its most rudimentary form, he said, was 'so much ease from all pain, and so much present pleasure, as without which anyone cannot be content'. Its highest form is simply 'the utmost pleasure we are capable of'.[3] This was an important shift, from *eudaemonia*, happiness as a state of being-and-doing, to *hedonia*, a state of feeling, the pursuit of pleasure. Yet Locke and those who followed him still believed that human nature would lead people to feel happiness in doing virtuous actions, and pain or unease at acting otherwise. Thomas Jefferson, who included 'the pursuit of happiness' as one of the inalienable rights set out in the American Declaration of Independence, took it for granted that happiness is inseparable from the moral sense, and that the essence of virtue is doing good to others.[4]

According to all these views, and throughout an overwhelming majority of the history of the West, happiness has had an inextricably moral dimension. It is about doing good, not just doing well oneself, and about virtue, not just about pleasure as an end in itself. There is an enormous gulf between these positions and today's understanding of happiness in terms of private experience and self-reported life satisfaction. To be sure, there were exceptions. Epicurus (Greece, 341–270 BCE) was a hedonist who believed that the good life consisted of the pursuit of pleasure and the avoidance of pain, though he would not have agreed at all with the values of consumerism. He believed it was important to limit desire, not inflame it; he would have argued for simplicity of living, peace of mind and contentment. But for most other classic thinkers it would have made no sense at all to say that you could find happiness by focusing solely on your own pleasure. For Aristotle, and for the Bible, that would have been a contradiction in terms. What then happens to happiness when it is decoupled from the moral sense and instead linked to the mindset of the market?

Ours is the most affluent age in history. Standards of living have risen consistently over the past fifty years. We can travel around the world, be in touch with friends, buy almost anything we like, see our favourite films, read our favourite books, find out the answer to almost any question, instantly and without friction. Even a generation ago, the access to information and freedom of communication we enjoy today, courtesy of smartphones, apps and the Internet, would have been absolutely inconceivable. Life expectancy in the UK in 1900 was forty-seven years for men, fifty for women, and in 2017, seventy-nine years for men and eighty-three for women, an increase of between two and three extra years in every decade. We are, quite simply, better off, better-informed, healthier and freer than any previous generation.

Yet, to take one symptom of contemporary dysphoria, in the course of the past decade, the life satisfaction of teenagers has plummeted. Drug taking, from marijuana to opioids to heroin and crystal meth, has rocketed. We noted in the chapter on social media that rates of depression, stress-related illness, and attempted and actual suicide have risen sharply among today's teenagers. More people than ever say that they are lonely. Some of the most affluent societies in the world are way down the list of happiest populations, Britain at fifteenth, the United States at eighteenth.[5] To quote Richard Wilkinson and Kate Pickett in *The Spirit Level*, their book on market economics, 'It is a remarkable paradox that, at the pinnacle of human material and technical achievement, we find ourselves anxiety-ridden, prone to depression, worried about how others see us, unsure of our friendships, driven to consume and with little or no community life.'[6] How could this have happened?

One reason is that a consumer society focuses attention on what we do not (yet) have, rather than on what we do. It depends on inducing a widespread mood of envy and avarice. It distorts our system of values in absurd ways. Can it really be a sane conclusion that happiness means the must-have designer handbag, or the wildly expensive handmade Swiss watch that you 'never really own', merely 'look after for the next generation', but which tells the time no better than the one you can buy for almost nothing? The flaunting of the lifestyles of the rich and famous is calculated to induce envy and misdirect attention from what people are to what they have.

The absurdity of consumerism has reached a height in the form of fashions and lifestyles adopted by the rich to seem like the exceptionally poor. Hence the fashion for extreme thinness. Throughout history, being thin has been a sign of poverty, and the opposite for wealth. The very words for *honour* and *weight* are, in most languages, the same or closely similar. Now these values are reversed. Or take the fashion for wildly expensive ripped jeans designed with great skill to look as if one had nothing else to wear, and they had been worn for years, their colour faded and their fabric torn. You can spend a fortune to look as if you were down and out and needed clothes from a charity shop.

The latter could be dismissed as a superficial example perhaps, but the deeper point is that by constantly inflaming our discontents, an advertising-driven, consumer society that ostensibly aims at happiness becomes in the end a system for the production and distribution of unhappiness. As a former director of General Motors Research Lab once put it, advertising is the 'organised creation of dissatisfaction'.[7] Happiness is good for us, but it is bad for business. Hence we have to be induced to see it as always lying just around the corner, immediately after the next product we buy.

A consumer society, in short, encourages us to spend money we don't have, on products we don't need, for a happiness that won't last. The reason such happiness does not last lies in the fundamental difference between *hedonic* happiness, a momentary feeling of pleasurable sensation, and *eudaemonic* happiness, which is the lasting feeling brought by having lived a good, mean-ingful and worthy life. Hedonic happiness requires constant stim-ulation. Hence the idea of the 'hedonic treadmill': getting what we want only temporarily satisfies desire.[8] We almost immediately find new things to desire, so that though we may find ourselves better off materially, we do not become happier psychologically.

The lure of the market becomes ever more seductive. In the past, advertising appeared in newspapers or between television programmes, directed at all of us in general and none of us in particular. Targeted advertising based on our Internet search history has changed all that. As Yuval Harari has pointed out in his important book *Homo Deus*, we can now be manipulated, not in groups, but specifically as individuals.[9] We have reached the point at which, according to Harari, Amazon, Google and the social media know us better than we know ourselves. This, as he says, makes us highly vulnerable, because groups can gather together and fight back. Individuals cannot.

An all-out battle is currently taking place for human atten-tion. When asked who his main competitor was, Reed Hastings, co-founder and CEO of Netflix, replied: sleep. Many of the new media depend on capturing and monopolising people's atten-tion. By releasing all the episodes in a new series at the same time, Netflix intensified the phenomenon of 'binge watching' – non-stop viewing of all the episodes of a series in one or two sittings – earlier initiated by DVD box sets. In recent times YouTube, which used to show the video you wanted and then suggest some more, now automatically displays another video unless you do something to stop it. Facebook, Instagram and other social media invite extended engagement by constant updates, new hashtags and the like. Their aim is to become, in the title of Adam Alter's book from which these examples are taken, *Irresistible.*[10] Media like these are intentionally aiming at becoming addictive. As one member in a debate in the House of Lords put it, they have become 'crack cocaine for kids'.

Living in a consumer society inflames our discontent. It feeds our sense of inadequacy. It encourages us to make comparisons with other people. Social media in particular has created entirely new sources of unhappiness. We have already seen the negative impact on teenagers of comparing themselves with the carefully curated images of their Facebook friends. More generally, in a consumer society we act to be envied rather than admired. That is a problematic basis on which to construct a life. Back in the seventeenth century, Spinoza explained it thus:

> Everyone's true happiness and blessedness consist solely in the enjoyment of what is good, not in the pride that he alone is enjoying it, to the exclusion of others. One who thinks himself the more blessed because he is enjoying benefits which others are not, or because he is more blessed or more fortunate than his fellows, is ignorant of true happiness and blessedness, and the joy which he feels is either childish or envious and malicious. For instance, a person's true happiness consists only in wisdom, and the knowledge of the truth, not at all in the fact that he is wiser than others, or that others lack such knowledge: such considerations do not increase his wisdom or true happiness.[11]

The trouble with this analysis is that although it is undoubtedly correct, to live by it we need to use our thinking-slow, rational, prefrontal cortex part of the brain. We also carry within us, however, the limbic system, sometimes described as the chimpanzee brain (in the language of Jewish mysticism, *nefesh ha-behamit*), which is intensely focused on status within the group. It is this part of the brain that generates feelings and moves us to action, and it is here that we do feel passionately about whether we have more or less than our neighbour.

This means that the potential for endless dissatisfaction is easily activated. Instead of feeling happier because we have more than we had last year, we can find ourselves focusing on the fact that others in our reference group also have more, so we continue to strive, comparing ourselves against them. Edward and Robert Skidelsky argue that this is why one of John Maynard Keynes's most famous predictions failed to come true. In 1930, on the basis of calculations of increasing productivity, Keynes came to the conclusion that, in the future, people would only work three hours a day, or fifteen hours a week. For the rest they would enjoy leisure and all that it made possible. This is how he envisaged that future:

> I see us free to return to some of the most sure and certain principles of religion and traditional virtue – that avarice is a vice, that the exaction of usury is a misdemeanour, and the love of money is detestable, that those walk most truly in the paths of virtue and sane wisdom who take the least thought for the morrow. We shall once more value ends above means and prefer the good to the useful.[12]

Keynes was not often wrong, but he was on this. In actual fact, working hours have hardly diminished, and in some occupations have increased over time despite all the impact of automation and technology. A 2014 Gallup report, for example, estimated that the average full-time worker in the United States works forty-seven hours a week, not significantly fewer than in 1930 when Keynes delivered his prediction, when the average was forty-eight hours a week.[13] Besides which, half a century ago only 20 per cent of mothers worked. Today, 70 per cent of American children live in households where all adults are employed.[14] The Skidelskys argue that the reason is precisely that we are competitive, that we constantly compare ourselves with others. 'At no level of material wealth will I feel satisfied with what I have, because someone will always have more than I do.'[15]

The market is not just companies and corporations, buying and selling, profits and losses. It is also a mindset, a mentality, a way of looking at things. Some people have even suggested that it has become a religion – retail therapy, salvation by shopping, remission of sins by credit card – whose cathedrals are shopping centres and whose most heinous sin is the failure to upgrade to this year's model of car or phone. It becomes a way of understanding and enacting the human condition, telling us that anything can be bought or sold, that everything has a price. This is a flawed way of seeing the human condition.

There are many values that the market undermines. Take loyalty. Loyalty means sustaining our commitment to a person or a cause through the bad times as well as the good ones. Loyalty means *not* making constant comparisons in search of a new brand, the smarter product, the better deal. Yet it is precisely those comparisons that the market encourages us to make. It devalues loyalty; in fact it makes it look ridiculous. Yet lasting relationships, marriage in particular, depend on loyalty. We are not freely floating atoms on an ocean of possibilities. We have attachments, to our family, our friends, our colleagues, our neighbours. Social capital, at all levels, is built out of loyalties. Without them, our whole personal world loses its richness and texture.

The market mindset can encourage companies to think in ways that marginalise loyalty. Until relatively recently, the big companies did their own manufacturing. This meant they had significant numbers of employees, to whom, to a greater or lesser extent, the company had obligations of loyalty, specifically in relation to their own workforce. The global economy has changed this completely. The big brands no longer do their own manufacturing. They outsource this, usually to low-wage economies. This means that they can often simply abdicate responsibility for low pay and poor working conditions. The entire constellation of values has been outsourced to other companies, countries and cultures far away.

Or consider the effect of market values on sport. Over several decades now, sport has become big business. The richest clubs buy the best players, managers and coaches and win the big competitions. Even the exceptions find themselves forced to game the same system. In the film *Moneyball*, for example, based on the book of that name by Michael Lewis, Aaron Sorkin tells the true story of how a mathematician, a 'quant', devised an algorithm by means of which, using computer analysis, a team could buy players of a higher quality at a lower cost than others using more traditional means of selection. That was the entire drama. To be sure, it had an edge. It showed how with sufficient ingenuity a team with limited financial resources could outperform others that were much richer. It was a challenge to the hegemony of cash: that richest is best. But it was still, in the end, a film about money rather than sport.

There are many films about baseball as a metaphor for the human spirit – *The Natural*, *Field of Dreams* and others. What makes sport so gripping is that it is about loyalty and courage, hard work and practice, team spirit and the power of inspiration to lift a group of people to greatness. *Legacy*, James Kerr's book about the New Zealand All Blacks rugby team, is about character, humility, responsibility, sacrifice and ritual.[16] These are not market values. Turning any sport into a set of algorithms, in which individual effort and collective endeavour are marginalised and return on investment prioritised, is essentially removing sportsmanship from the game and turning it into something smaller and less human. What happens when human beings are deemed to be inefficient, and are replaced by robots? What then becomes of sport? What becomes of us?

One vivid example of how a market mindset can transform and undermine an institution is given by Dan Ariely in his book *Predictably Irrational*. He tells the story of a day-care centre in Israel that decided to fine parents who arrived late to pick up their children, in the hope that this would discourage them from doing so.[17] In fact, the exact opposite happened. Before the imposition of fines, parents felt guilty about arriving late, and guilt was effective in ensuring that only a few did so. Once a fine was introduced, it seems that in the minds of the parents the entire scenario was changed from a social contract to a market one. Essentially, they were paying for the centre to look after their children after hours. Some parents thought it worth the price, and the rate of late arrivals increased. Significantly, once the centre abandoned the fines and went back to the previous arrangement, late arrivals remained at the high level they had reached during the period of the fines. It seemed that once the market mindset had been introduced, it was very hard to go back to the previous situation of social contract mediated by a sense of guilt.

Given the discontent that we have seen to be inherent in a market-led, sensation-driven, pleasure-seeking approach to happiness, what is there to be said for a recovery of the older philosophical and religious tradition that sees happiness in terms of a life well led?

A powerful piece of evidence is to be found in one of the most famous medical research exercises of recent times, known as the Nun Study. Directed by David Snowdon of the University of Kentucky Medical Center, it studied the health pattern of some seven hundred nuns of the School Sisters of Notre Dame, with particular reference to Alzheimer's disease. The nuns were aged between 75 and 107, and what gave the study its fascination and depth was the access the researchers had to their autobiographies, written when they were in their early twenties, more than half a century earlier.

This particular order required novitiates to write a brief account of their lives on entering the order, and the researchers used linguistic analysis to draw a picture of their personalities at that early age. One of their findings was that the more the early autobiographies expressed positive emotions like gratitude, happiness, hope and love, the more likely the nuns were still to be alive sixty years later. The correlations they discovered were so specific that they were able to predict with 85 per cent accuracy which of the nuns would develop Alzheimer's and which would not. The difference in life expectancy between the thankful and (relatively) thankless was, on average, seven years. Being grateful adds years to your life.[18]

More research has been done on this connection between happiness and long life in recent years. Sonja Lyubomirsky, of the University of California, Riverside, reports that a group of participants who were asked to write down five things for which they were thankful once a week for ten weeks tended to feel more optimistic and more satisfied with their lives than control groups.[19] Other studies have shown that on days when individuals focus on and express thankfulness, they experience more positive emotions. Gratitude encourages the savouring of positive experiences. It bolsters feelings of self-worth. It helps people cope with stress. It inhibits invidious comparisons with others. It encourages moral behaviour – grateful people are more likely to help others. It tends to dissipate negative emotions such as anger. And it counteracts the hedonic treadmill.[20] Gratitude is the opposite of the mindset of a market-led, consumer society. It is about satisfaction with what we have, not hunger for what we do not have.

Other examples have been assembled by Stephen Post, Professor of Bioethics and Family Medicine at Case Western Reserve University in the United States, that show the positive impact of giving and altruism on health. He calls this the science of love. In his book, *Why Good Things Happen to Good People*, he documents a study by Paul Wink of Wellesley College that showed how giving in high school predicted strong physical and mental health into late adulthood.[21]

Another study, undertaken by Doug Oman from the University of California, Berkeley, showed that the mortality rates of those who volunteered for two or more organisations reduced by 44 per cent.[22] A series of studies among American teenagers showed that those who are giving, hopeful and socially effective are also happier, more active, involved and excited than their less engaged contemporaries.

Neal Krause of the University of Michigan found that adults who gave social support to others experienced reduced anxiety over their own situation when under economic stress. In another study, he found that offering emotional support to others helped people forgive themselves for their own mistakes.[23] Psychologist Stephanie Brown of the University of Michigan discovered, after a five-year study of elderly couples, that those who did not provide support to others had higher rates of mortality.[24]

Allan Luks, author of *The Healing Power of Doing Good*, and one of the pioneers in this field, has spoken about 'the helper's high', the feeling of exultation or uplift that 50 per cent of people feel when they help others. Forty-three per cent report feeling stronger and more energetic. Thirteen per cent say they experience fewer aches and pains.[25]

The connection between altruism, health and happiness is complex, and it would be wrong to oversimplify it, but there is enough in this research to suggest that the classic conception of happiness still has validity. We do feel better for helping others, for being concerned with the common good, for what Aristotle called 'exercising the soul in accordance with virtue'.

Yet another dimension of happiness has to do with the strength or otherwise of our social connections, our relationships with family and friends. This too has been documented by Sonja Lyubomirsky, who quotes in support the famous statement of the Jewish sage Hillel (first century BCE), 'If I am not for myself, who will be? But if I am only for myself, what am I?' Put simply, she says, 'happy people have better relationships than their less happy peers'.[26] They tend to be good at their friendships and family connections. They are likely to have a wide circle of friends and companions, a loving relationship and social support. The causality runs both ways. Friends make people happy, but happy people find it easier to make friends. And it is that complex set of human ties that creates the environment of support, good feeling, resilience, trust that make up the matrix of a happy life.

This finding is backed up by one of the longest of all longitudinal research exercises, the Grant Study, begun in 1938, which has tracked the lives of 268 Harvard students – at that time, Harvard was a male-only college – for more than eighty years, seeking to understand what characteristics – from personality type to intelligence to health, habits and relationships – contribute to human flourishing. For over thirty years, the project was directed by George Vaillant, whose books *Aging Well* and *Triumphs of Experience* have explored this fascinating territory.[27] In an interview published in the March 2008 newsletter to the Grant Study subjects, Vaillant was asked, 'What have you learned from the Grant Study men?' Vaillant's response was, 'That the only thing that really matters in life is your relationships to other people.'[28] A 2017 summary of the study concluded: 'Close relationships, more than money or fame, are what keep people happy throughout their lives . . . Those ties protect people from life's discontents, help to delay mental and physical decline, and are better predictors of long and happy lives than social class, IQ, or even genes.'[29]

If this is so, then happiness really is more about the 'We' than about the 'I'. The findings of the Grant Study help explain the discontents of the consumerist logic of the marketplace. Far more than what we buy or earn or own, happiness is a matter of what we do, what we are and how we relate to others.

There is a superb commentary on this in a very ancient text, the biblical book of Ecclesiastes. Its author is the man who had everything, yet nothing of what he owns makes him happy:

> I enlarged my works: I built houses for myself, I planted vineyards for myself; I made gardens and parks for myself and I planted in them all kinds of fruit trees . . . I collected for myself silver and

gold and the treasure of kings and provinces . . . Thus I considered all my activities which my hands had done and the labour
which I had exerted, and behold all was vanity and striving after
wind and there was no profit under the sun (Eccl. 2:4–8, 11).

Note the repeated use of the first-person singular. Nowhere else
in the Bible is it used so relentlessly and repetitively: 'I built for
myself, I made for myself, I bought for myself.' This is the supreme
expression of the 'I', and all it yields is 'vanity and striving after
wind'. Many people read the book and conclude that its theme is
disillusionment. However, this is not so. The author does discover
something that relieves his world-weariness, namely *joy*, a word
that appears seventeen times in the course of this short book.
What redeems life and etches it with grace is joy in your work
('Sweet is the sleep of the labouring man'), joy in your marriage
('See life with the woman you love'), and joy in the simple pleasures of life. Take joy in each day.

Joy in the Hebrew Bible is essentially shared. It is a phenomenon of 'We'. A husband must make his wife rejoice (Deut.
24:5). Festivals are to be occasions of collective rejoicing, 'you,
your sons and daughters, your male and female servants, the
Levites in your towns, and the strangers, the fatherless and the
widows living among you' (Deut. 16:11). Bringing first-fruits to
the Temple involved collective celebration: 'you and the Levites
and the strangers in your midst shall rejoice in all the good things
the Lord your God has given to you and your household' (Deut.
26:11). Joy is happiness shared. Something of this biblical insight
has been restated by David Brooks in his recent book *The Second
Mountain*, subtitled *The Quest for a Moral Life*. He argues that
happiness 'involves a victory for the self' while joy 'tends to
involve some transcendence of self'.[30]

One intriguing finding in recent happiness research has to do
with time and focus. Sonja Lyubomirsky divided participants in a
test of the impact of gratitude into two groups. One was instructed
to count their blessings three times a week (every Tuesday, Thursday

and Sunday), the other to do so just once a week (every Sunday night). The second group recorded higher levels of happiness at the end of the test, but not the first. Lyubomirsky speculates that the three-times-a-week group may have become bored, coming to see the task as a chore, whereas the once-a-week group continued to find it fresh and meaningful.[31] She found something similar when it came to altruistic behaviour. Two groups were asked to perform five acts of kindness a week for six weeks. The first group was instructed to do them at any time during the week, but the second group had to do all five acts on one specified day each week. Only the second group became happier.[32]

This is a powerful scientific finding that explains why the Sabbath, which I mentioned in connection to smartphones and social media, has had such a powerful effect on cultures that have adopted it. The Sabbath is a focused one-day-a-week antidote to the market mindset. It is dedicated to the things that have a value but not a price. It is the supremely non-market day. We can't sell or buy. We can't work or pay others to work for us. It's a day when we celebrate relationships. Husbands sing a song of praise to their wives. Parents bless their children. We take time to have a meal together with family and friends. In the synagogue we renew our sense of community. People share their joys – a new child, a bar or bat mitzvah, an engagement, a forthcoming wedding – with others. The bereaved find comfort for their grief. We study the Bible together, reminding ourselves of the story of which we are a part. We pray together, thanking God for our blessings.

The Sabbath is in fact one way of living out John Maynard Keynes's vision of an age of limited work in which leisure becomes a way of celebrating the human spirit. What makes the Sabbath so transformative an institution even today is that it does not involve waiting for the Keynesian moment of the fifteen-hour week to arrive, if indeed it ever does. It takes the utopian future and translates it into now, making it still the most effective form of work–life balance ever devised. It is a day of gratitude, when the restlessness of the week subsides and we find refuge in an oasis of rest.

The Czech economist Tomáš Sedláček, in his book *The Economics of Good and Evil*,[33] argues persuasively that what we need is a 'Sabbath economics', to create a pause in the endless pursuit of more, so that we may celebrate what we have, rather than fixate exclusively on what we do not yet have. It is paradoxical, Sedláček notes, that there had to be a command to rest on the seventh day. One would have thought that the desire for such rest would be natural. However, there seems to be something in our nature that seeks to maximise, to continue relentlessly and indefinitely to seek more and yet more. The end result is exhaustion, physical, emotional, psychological. Far better, he argues, to create the kind of balance envisaged by the Bible: six days of striving followed by one of relaxing, enjoying, pausing and resting.[34]

The Sabbath is one way of setting limits to the market and its mindset, focusing on the dimension of time. There are other ways, too: values such as loyalty that are not sacrificed to the pursuit of profit; aspects of happiness that derive not from what we earn or own or buy but from what we contribute to the lives of others; and gratitude for what we have rather than yearning for what we do not have. Market values are not the only ones that count. There are others necessary for personal happiness and the collective beatitude that constitutes a good society. Marriage is not a transaction. Parenthood is not a form of ownership. Universities are not intellectual vending machines. Healthcare is distinct from wealth care. Neighbourhoods should not be gilded ghettoes. Politics should not be a form of power for sale.

The market has its uses and they can be great and good, but there are spaces in our lives that should and must be protected from it. Our humanity matters more than our profitability.

8

Democracy in Danger

The sociologist Peter Berger once speculated about the appearance among *Homo sapiens* of the first intellectual: 'After centuries during which people did nothing but rhythmically bang away with stone implements and keep the fires from going out,' he said, 'there was someone who interrupted these wholesome activities just long enough to have an idea, which he or she then proceeded to announce to the other members of the tribe. We can make a pretty good guess as to what the idea was: "The tribe is in a state of crisis." '[1]

Today's intellectuals have left us in no doubt as to where they feel the West is today. Consider the titles of some major recent books about the state of Western liberal democracy: *How Democracy Ends. Why Liberalism Failed. The Strange Death of Europe. The Suicide of the West. How Democracies Die. Can Democracy Survive Global Capitalism? The Retreat of Western Liberalism.* And so on. In the wake of the 2016 presidential election, Yale Politics Professor Timothy Snyder wrote a book entitled *On Tyranny* – it became a bestseller. Madeleine Albright, the first woman to become US Secretary of State, published a book in 2018 entitled *Fascism: A Warning.* It too became a bestseller. These are not the usual jeremiads in what has hitherto been a resilient, optimistic, can-do American culture. The intellectuals are telling us that the tribe is in a state of crisis.

Two key votes in 2016, the presidential election in the United States and the Brexit vote in Britain, were uncommonly bitter and divisive. The rifts they opened up in the body politic have not healed in the intervening time. Rather they have grown deeper and more rancorous. In one European country after another, the feeling has been palpable that the established parties are out of touch with the electorate and unresponsive to their concerns. The far right and the far left have been gaining, sometimes at the expense of other parties, sometimes by internal takeover of an established party. The electorate has searched for new faces from outside the normal run of politics. Populism is at its highest level in the West since the 1930s.

There have been riots throughout Europe. In 2018 alone riots occurred in Belgium, Holland, Germany, Austria, Sweden, Hungary and Albania. Meanwhile, in the United States, on 11–12 August 2017, the small and graceful town of Charlottesville, home of the University of Virginia, which was founded and designed by Thomas Jefferson, became the venue of a white supremacist rally, a threatening alliance of white nationalists, members of the new alt-right, neo-Confederates, neo-fascists and neo-Nazis. The marchers carried rifles, Nazi symbols and swastikas, and banners with antisemitic and anti-Muslim slogans. There has been nothing like this in American politics in a very long time.

Throughout the West, trust in politicians and governments has fallen to new lows. In Britain at the beginning of 2016 only 36 per cent of the British public expressed trust in the government. By the start of 2017 this had fallen further to 26 per cent. Only 18 per cent trusted political parties to do what is right, and only 19 per cent trust the party leaders to do so. As for the United States, in 1958 three-quarters of the electorate said that they trusted the government to do the right thing all or most of the time. By 2017 the figure was a mere 18 per cent. According to the Pew Research Center, this loss of trust was evident across age groups and racial and ethnic divides.[2]

A research project undertaken by Yascha Mounk of Harvard and Roberto Foa of the University of Melbourne suggests that Millennials (those born in or after 1980) are losing faith in democracy. Only a third of them regard civil rights as 'absolutely essential' in a democracy, compared to 41 per cent of the previous generation. More than a quarter dismiss the importance of free elections, and only a minority declare themselves interested in politics, as compared to their elders, of whom a majority did so. In 1995, only 16 per cent of young Americans thought democracy was a 'bad system' for their nation, but in 2011, nearly a quarter did so.[3]

There are obvious reasons why this might be so. The world, under the vortex of forces unleashed by the Internet, instantaneous global communication, smartphones and social media, is undergoing the kind of change that occurs only rarely in history. The most obvious comparison is with the invention of printing in the mid-fifteenth century. Political systems can collapse under such disruptive innovation. The very nature of power is changing, becoming less centralised and more diffused.[4] The democratic institutions we have inherited from the past were made for a different age and a slower pace of change. Technology moves fast, while the democratic process is slow. The problems we face today, economic, social and environmental, are global, while our most effective political structures are at best national. It would be astonishing if our democratic structures were *not* strained under such circumstances.

Nonetheless, my concern here is to chart the deeper forces at work in our world, and in particular the moral underpinnings of a free society. To understand them, we have to go back to two founding moments that shaped the political cultures of the West: the American Declaration of Independence (1776) and the *Déclaration des droits de l'homme et du citoyen*, 'The Declaration of the Rights of Man and of the Citizen', issued by the French Revolutionary Assembly in 1789. Both were turning points in political history, and they each created a secular nation-state. They were both couched in terms of rights, and they were both heavily influenced by earlier philosophical theories: in the case of America, those of Thomas Hobbes and John Locke, and in France those of Jean-Jacques Rousseau. But they represented very different understandings of politics, even though they appear at first sight to be saying roughly the same thing.

The American Declaration states: 'We hold these truths to be self-evident, that all men are created equal, that they are endowed by their Creator with certain unalienable Rights, that among these are Life, Liberty and the pursuit of Happiness . . .' The French Declaration begins: 'Men are born and remain free and equal in rights.'

There are two obvious differences between these formulations. One is that the American Declaration is explicitly religious. It refers to the 'Creator'. The French Declaration is explicitly secular. This reflected a profound difference between the role of religion in the two countries. As de Tocqueville noted: 'In France I had almost always seen the spirit of religion and the spirit of freedom marching in opposite directions. But in America I found they were intimately united and that they reigned in common over the same country.' That is an important point, but not for here.

I want instead to focus on the second difference, the word *unalienable* that appears in the American but not the French version. What does it signify? We will not understand the contemporary loss of trust in politics without it. The American Declaration is based on one kind of social contract, that of Hobbes and Locke. The French, by contrast, is based on the social contract as conceived by Rousseau. They generated two quite different political cultures.

Thomas Hobbes asked: why do people establish governments? What is the basis of the authority of the state? He answered that without a government, people would be competing for the same limited supply of goods. If I obtain more than you, you will try to take it from me, by force if necessary, and if you can't defeat me on your own you will gather enough people to do so together. Life will be lawless, and each of us will live in constant fear of death. There are failed states in the world today in which lawlessness remains sadly prevalent and many people do live in fear.

Each of us, therefore, has an interest in giving up some of our powers – our rights – to some central body which then uses that power to establish the rule of law internally and the defence of the realm from warring nations externally. To create this contract, we *alienate* certain of our rights, meaning, we hand them over to the central law-enforcing body. But there are certain rights we *cannot* hand over without defeating the whole purpose of the contract. That is the meaning of *unalienable*. For Hobbes, this was the right to life. Since, for him, the entire social contract was to protect us from the fear of death, the right to life is non-negotiable. Locke added two more, liberty and property, which the American Declaration finessed into 'liberty and the pursuit of happiness'.

On this view of the social contract, the authority on which the state rests is 'the consent of the governed', meaning all its citizens, as individuals, pursuing their own interest. They want certain things – their lives, liberty and property – protected by the government, and that is all. This is a theory of limited government, in which rights represent the things we refuse to hand over to the state. Rights are the protected private spaces of our lives, which the state may not enter. That is what *unalienable* means here. It represents the lines that the state may not cross.

Rousseau's view of the social contract was quite different. He agreed with Hobbes and Locke that without a state people would always be in conflict with one another, given the existence of private property. We each have interests: we want what other people have. Therefore the state cannot be about satisfying our interests *as individuals*, because there is no way of satisfying them all. The state is about addressing our interest as a *collective* body seeking the common good. Rousseau called this the *volonté générale*, the 'general will'. The French Declaration explicitly invokes this idea in its Article 6: 'The law is the expression of the general will.'

The general will is not the sum total of the wills of individuals, which Rousseau called the 'will of all'. It is something else entirely. It is what we are deemed to want as a collective entity. Any individual who says, 'I don't want the common good; I want my own private and personal good', is deemed by Rousseau to be mistaken, because deep down, since he wants to live in society, he wants the common good. That is why Rousseau notoriously said that, in such a case, we – that is, the state – may have to 'force him to be free'. We understand the individual's deep desires better than he does.

Rousseau's social contract is *not* based on the consent of the governed as private individuals. It is based on a politics of all-of-us-together, meaning us as a collective personality. Seeking the common good, we hand over to the state the right to act on our behalf as a corporate body. It is easy to see how the pursuit of the liberty of all-of-us-together might involve sacrificing all our freedom as private individuals. J.L. Talmon called this kind of politics 'totalitarian democracy'.[5]

To be fair to Rousseau, he anticipated that this kind of politics could only work in small city states like the Athens of antiquity or Calvin's Geneva, the city in which he lived. The best example in recent times is the Israeli kibbutz. Everyone takes part in decision making, all property belongs to the group, not to individuals, and everyone has his or her task to do for the sake of all. Even on this small scale, the freedom of all-of-us-together is exceptionally restrictive of the freedom of each-of-us-as-individuals. Applied to a whole society, it can quickly become terrifying. Utopian politics, whether in its Rousseau-inspired French revolutionary form or its later Marxist version, eventually becomes a dystopian nightmare, and sooner rather than later. During the Reign of Terror (1793–4) that followed the French Revolution, 16,594 people were sentenced to death. That is what can happen when we pursue the 'common good' at the cost of individual liberty.

Rousseau, who died in 1778, would have been horrified at the use to which his philosophy was put. But his version of the social contract is a theory of maximal, not minimal, government, and his version of 'rights' was the opposite of that of Locke, Jefferson and the Anglo-American tradition. Rights on this view do not define an area into which the state may not intrude. To the contrary, they represent claims upon the state that only political action on the part of the state can bring about.

So, despite the fact that their founding documents begin with very similar declarations, the Anglo-American and French approaches to politics, the state and human rights are very different indeed. What tends to hide this from us is the fact that the two declarations use the same words: liberty and rights. But in using these words they mean very different things and create different kinds of political culture.

The greatest difference is that in the Anglo-American version, it is not the state that produces the highest social goods. It is the people who do so by coming together as families, communities and voluntary associations. The task of the state is to protect this space from the intrusion of politics. On the French revolutionary model, meanwhile, rights were delivered by the state, while families, communities and voluntary associations were, in the eyes of the philosophers of the Revolution, a distraction and a danger, because they were arenas in which people came together to promote their own interests as they saw them, instead of leaving it to the state to create the common good.

To put it another way, on the Anglo-American model there are three key social arenas: the state, individuals, and civil society. It is the third sector, civil society, that is seen as most vital to the health of democracy, because that is where we come together at a local level, forming moral communities where people help one another in face-to-face and side-by-side relationships, to do together what we cannot do alone. It is this area, smaller than the state but bigger than the individual, that creates and sustains what Tocqueville called the 'art of association', and that he held to be the necessary 'apprenticeship of liberty'.

On the French revolutionary model there are only two arenas: the state and the individual. The state works for the common good, leaving individuals free to do whatever they like so long as they do not harm others. To put it in the terms in which we have been speaking throughout, on the French model there is the market where we produce and consume as individuals, and there is the state where we function as a collective. *Everything collective is political, a matter of power.* On the Anglo-American model, there is something over and above the state and the market, namely the multiplicity of places where we come together not because we are paid to (the market), nor because law forces us to (the state), but because we are moral beings who care about the neighbour and the stranger. *Not everything collective is political. Some of it is moral, a matter not of power but of conscience, duty and virtue.* This is where the moral life is at its strongest, where we are constantly exercising our altruistic muscles, and where we form the friendships and loves that redeem us from our solitude.

Having travelled this far, we can begin to see where the argument is heading. Somehow, almost without noticing it, in the past half-century, the French model has come to dominate both Britain and America. Rights have ceased to be restrictions on the scope of the state, and have become instead entitlements, demands for action by the state. How did this happen? According to Harvard law professor Mary Ann Glendon, in her now-classic book *Rights Talk*, 'To a great extent, urbanisation, industrialisation, bureaucracy, geographic mobility, mass culture, and centralisation of political power have accomplished the project of the French revolutionaries, bringing citizens everywhere into ever more unmediated relationships with government.'[6] As communities atrophy and voluntary associations lose their power, people turn to the state to meet their needs. Society withers, the scope of government continually increases, and the old Anglo-American vision of limited state intervention ceases to compel the imagination of citizens. That is why the term 'rights' is today understood more and more in both Britain and America in the French sense as demands upon the state, rather than in the Locke–Jefferson sense as the non-political civil space in which we exercise our responsibilities to others so that they too can experience civic dignity.

As the moral sense has mutated from the 'We' to the 'I', almost all the institutions of civil society – marriage, the family, communities, congregations, houses of worship and the rest – have atrophied. They may still be strong in certain localised areas, but not in the nation as a whole, especially not in urban areas, suffering from poverty, unemployment and evincing the symptoms of despair, from graffiti on the walls to drug dealers on the streets.

What happens when civil society grows weak and all that is left are the market and the state? That is when people begin to make demands of the state that the state cannot satisfy. The state cannot create strong families or supportive communities. It cannot provide children with stable and responsible parents. It can finance schools, but it cannot create inspiring teachers. It cannot generate the work ethic, self-control and resilience that are vital if individuals are to escape the vicious circle of poverty and unemployment and lead lives of happiness and hope.

The state is about power. Families and communities are about people. They are about personal relationships and lifting one another from depression and despair. When these are lost from civil society, they cannot be outsourced to the state. The state is and must be impersonal. Therefore it cannot help when the damage is deeply personal. The strength of the Anglo-American model as it evolved in the nineteenth and early twentieth century was that it did not rely exclusively on the state. Whether in churches, friendly societies, trade unions or ethnic enclaves, people helped one another at a local level, in often life-changing ways.

The 'We' made the 'I' stronger, because it showed people what they could achieve by working together without relying wholly on the state. When there is only the state, people's expectations are not and cannot be fully met. Rights are increasingly thought of as entitlements at the very time that the 'We', the feeling of collective responsibility, has grown weaker. The result is the secession of the successful: the rich who separate themselves off and do not recognise any special responsibility to the poor.

One of the most significant moments in the triumph of the French model was the United Nations Universal Declaration of

Human Rights (1948), whose style and wording is much closer to the French Revolutionary version than to the American Declaration of Independence. This is fine as a statement of ideals, but a French-style rights-based culture, translated into the global economy of the twenty-first century, generates conflicts it cannot resolve and expectations that cannot be met. In Mary Ann Glendon's words, 'the new rhetoric of rights is less about human dignity and freedom than about insistent, unending desires'. Rights talk, she says, 'easily accommodates the economic, the immediate, and the personal dimensions of the problem, while it regularly neglects the moral, the long-term, and the social implications'.[7]

Unmet expectations generate a mood of betrayal and resentment. People lose faith in politics and politicians, perhaps rightly so. That is when potentially dangerous phenomena begin to appear: riots, anger, violence, and widespread cynicism about the value of democratic freedom. People begin to turn to 'strong' leaders who mobilise public anger to attack elites in the name of the people. That is how populist politics is born.

Such populism is born out of real grievances, genuine distress, and a widespread sense of injustice and humiliation. The suffering is real, as key texts such as J.D. Vance's *Hillbilly Elegy* and Arlie Russell Hochschild's *Strangers in their Own Land* have made clear about the America of the 2016 presidential election, and as David Goodhart showed for Brexit Britain in his *The Road to Somewhere* (2017). People *have* been betrayed. The institutions in which they put their trust did not honour the responsibility they had taken on. Too often the interest that concerned the elites has seemed to be overwhelmingly their own. Leadership in many fields has been cavalier, corrupt or simply incompetent.

Populist politics is (to adapt the words of Marx) 'the sigh of the oppressed creature, the heart of a heartless world, and the soul of soulless conditions'. But populism is unlikely to deliver redemption.

Populist politics involves magical thinking. The belief that a strong leader, with contempt for the democratic process, divisive rhetoric, relaxed about the truth or otherwise of his or her utterances, ignoring the conventions of normal politics, appealing directly to the people, blaming the state of the nation on some subgroup of the nation, or perhaps on neighbouring nations and peoples, and speaking not to the better angels of our nature but to the worst, can restore a nation's former greatness – that is magical thinking.

Populist politics often does deliver genuine gains, in the short term. But as the realisation begins to dawn that the problems are deeper and more intractable than people thought, populist leaders have to produce scapegoats to blame for their failure – elites, the media, immigrants, Muslims, Jews – and then the vortex of authoritarianism begins, sweeping aside rights, justice and liberty itself. One of the first people to warn us of this was Plato, who said that democracy would always degenerate into tyranny. He knew this from his own experience. Athens was where democracy was born, introduced by Solon in 594 BCE, and it was Athens, two centuries later, that sentenced Plato's teacher, Socrates, to death for corrupting the young by teaching them to question.

It is genuinely sad to see how, almost without people noticing, Britain and the United States have abandoned their own unique tradition, that of Locke and Jefferson, and instead embraced the Rousseau-esque French revolutionary model of rights as claims against the state, instead of rights as the protection of individuals *from* the state, so that they could achieve by their own local, cooperative, altruistic efforts what politics and power cannot achieve, namely a devolved sense of responsibility for the welfare of others.

If we continue to adopt the French model of rights and stop believing in the existence of a significant arena of individual responsibility, we will lose the sense of common morality that finds its natural home in families and communities. We will be left only with the market and the state. The market cannot deliver distributive justice. The state cannot deliver dignity and resilience, civility and responsibility, for and in its citizens. The state can deliver much: health, welfare, education, defence and the rule of law. But it cannot deliver the active citizenship that creates, daily, in myriad local contexts, the face-to-face care and compassion that constitute the good society.

Remove the moral matrix of civil society and eventually you get populist politics and the death of freedom in the name of freedom. It is the wrong road to take.

9

Identity Politics

Try the following thought experiment: imagine taking your prodi-giously bright, artificially intelligent robot, Robbie, who has become your valet, personal assistant, advisor, coach, motivator and unfailingly upbeat friend, to a (British) football match. Never having been exposed to such an experience before, Robbie duly prepares itself by ingesting everything on the Internet about foot-ball, learning enough of the laws and facts of the game in a few hours to be able to defeat even the most fanatical human football fan on any quiz about the game. Whatever there is to know, it knows.

During the match it processes all the information presented by its various sensors. When the game is over you ask Robbie whether it enjoyed the experience. 'Absolutely,' it replies, but then it asks, 'Am I right in thinking that football is a game?' 'Correct,' you reply. 'So whatever the result, the universe continues on its regular way?' 'Just so,' you reply. 'So why does everyone get so excited? Why did there used to be so much violence? Why did Bill Shankly, the Liverpool manager in the 1960s and early 1970s, say, "Some people believe football is a matter of life and death, I am very disappointed with that attitude. I can assure you it is much, much more important than that"? *Why do people get so excited about a game?*'

That is a not-unimportant question. The Turing test of artificial intelligence asks whether a computer can carry on a conversation with a human being without the individual being able to tell they are speaking to a computer. I suggest a differ-ent test: could a computer understand the passions aroused by a sports contest? This is human behaviour at its most irrational and most powerful. It has to do with identity, with our need to identify with a group whose existence is maximally affirmed when it clashes with another group. This idea makes very little sense at the level of the rational brain, the prefrontal cortex, the 'thinking slow' bit of the human mind. How could AI make sense of it? Yet the point is anything but theoretical, because time and time again the West has overestimated human rationality – most notably in the eighteenth century in the form of the Enlightenment – and underestimated the power of our tribal passions, whether focused on nation, religion, ethnicity, political party or the myriad other ways we define who and what we are.

We are social animals. For hundreds of thousands of years our hunter-gatherer ancestors lived in small groups, and that has left an indelible mark on our psychology. From this derives much of the best, as well as much of the worst, of human nature. We are, by and large, altruistic towards the members of our own group, and at least potentially aggressive towards members of other groups, especially when we see them as threatening to our own.

This inherent 'groupishness' lies at the heart of identity: I am who I am because of the group or groups to which I belong. I am because we are. Who the 'We' is taken to be depends to some extent on personal choice – the group with which I choose to identify. To some extent it depends on the wider culture – are its primary fault lines in terms of class, or income, or education, or ethnicity, or religion, or nationality, or some other factor? Different cultures are stratified on different lines. And to some extent it has to do with fate rather than choice: I did not choose who my parents were, or what their genes predisposed me to become. But identity, in the sense in which it has come to dominate politics today, is not something private and personal. It is something I share with the members of my group that I have come to see as the most important dimension of my life.

Identity was not a key word in the public conversation until the 1950s, when the work of psychologist Erik Erikson brought it into prominence. The phrase 'identity politics' is more recent still, dating back no earlier than the 1980s. Yet it has come to be seen as one of the key dimensions of contemporary politics in the West, seized by both the Right and the Left for their own purposes. The Left has focused on groups that have come to see themselves, not wrongly, as marginalised, oppressed and victimised: African Americans, women, minority religions, the gay and lesbian communities, and most recently, transgender individuals. The right, particularly in its populist versions, has increasingly addressed itself to another group, poor white males, often outside the main urban centres, who have reached the conclusion that their voices have not been heard by the governing elites, who have been busy attending to, and placating, the other minorities. It was this so-called 'white backlash' that is thought to have played a part in both the Brexit vote and the American presidential election of 2016.

In the wake of those elections, three significant thinkers have brought out books on the subject: Mark Lilla (*The Once and Future Liberal*), Anthony Appiah (*The Lies that Bind*), and Francis Fukuyama (*Identity: Contemporary Identity Politics and the Struggle for Recognition*). All three argue that identity politics is a clear and present danger to liberal democracy. It fragments the body politic and balkanises society. It discourages talk about the common good. It can quickly turn into the politics of grievance and competitive victimhood. This creates a vicious circle of social divisions leading to divisive politics that deepen and harden social divisions. It is one of the causes of the Us-versus-Them mentality that leads to populism, which itself, as we have seen, is a warning signal of democracy in danger.

However, as my football-based thought experiment shows, identity politics is not new. It is the latest iteration of a story that goes back before the birth of civilisation. For most of history it has played itself out in the form of war. One of the great achievements of civilisation has been to domesticate it in the form of team games. The extraordinary passion that fans bring to the support of their team owes its origin to the primal, irrepressible need to belong: to identify with something larger than Me.

We need to keep this history in mind because we will not under-stand identity politics until we realise that it is the latest chapter in a sequence of events that, like so much else, goes back to the seventeenth century.

Recall that of all forms of identity, historically the deepest and most tenacious has been that of religion. When a single faith was dominant throughout the nation, it bound the members of the society to one another. Hence the traumatic nature of the internal battle within Western Christianity following the Reformation. As long as wars are fought *between* nations or empires, as happened during the Crusades, identity tends to be strengthened, not weakened. We are never as altruistic as when we go to war on behalf of our group: the nation, the empire, the faith. During the battle there is selflessness and sacrifice. Thereafter, for the victors, there is pride; for the defeated, a time of collective heal-ing. But throughout the conflict, the boundaries are clear. It is 'Us' versus 'Them'. Trauma, though, occurs when the war turns inward, when a section of what was previously 'Us' becomes a new 'Them'. That is what happened within Western Christendom after the Reformation, dividing Catholic from Protestant in one nation after another. That is when, to heal the trauma, a deter-mined effort was made by the thinkers of the Enlightenment to *abolish identity in the name of the universal*.

This was the utopian vision of the eighteenth century, the 'dream of reason'. Once Descartes had shown that you can philosophise without dogmatic assumptions, and Newton had demonstrated that you can explain the universe without theological or teleo-logical ideas, why could not the same be said about the human condition? One of the pioneers here was the great humanist, Michel de Montaigne. He had witnessed France descend into inter-nal warfare over religion no fewer than three times between 1562 and 1570. Then in 1572, the St Bartholomew's Day Massacre of Huguenots began with the slaughter of 3,000 in Paris and saw as many as 70,000 killed elsewhere in France. Disturbed by the violence he saw about him, Montaigne retreated to his study to reflect on the nature of humanity. On one of the beams of his study he had engraved the words of Terence (c. 195–159 BCE): 'I am human and I think nothing human alien to me.' That was to be the guiding light for Montaigne and those who followed him for the next two hundred years.

What eventually emerged under the influence of Montaigne was a belief in the power of reason to help us rise above the tribal instincts and warlike habits that had allowed even sincere Christians to murder one another in the name of the God of love and forgiveness. We had to think beyond the divisions of colour, class, culture and creed: from men to Man, from human beings to humanity-as-a-whole. That was central to the philosophy of Immanuel Kant, who in the eighteenth century laid down as one of the criteria of morality the principle of universalisability: 'Act only on that maxim which you can at the same time will that it should become a universal law.' This was the beatific vision, of the world before Babel.

It was given immortal expression in Beethoven's musical setting, in the ninth symphony (1822–4), of Schiller's 'Ode to Joy': *Alle Menschen werden Brüder / Wo dein sanfter Flügel weilt* ('All people become brothers / Where your gentle wing abides'). Another classic expression was given by the poet Shelley in his 1818 poem *Prometheus Unbound*, with its idyllic vision of humanity:

> Sceptreless, free, uncircumscribed, but man
> Equal, unclassed, tribeless, and nationless,
> Exempt from awe, worship, degree, the king
> Over himself; just, gentle, wise; but man
> Passionless? no, yet free from guilt or pain . . .[1]

This was one of the noblest visions in the history of the West. But it was hopelessly utopian, and ultimately unsustainable. It ignored our need for identity, our inescapable desire to belong to a group. So, in a classic case of the return of the repressed, the old focus on identity came roaring back in the nineteenth century, in the form of the Counter-Enlightenment, Romanticism, and the celebration of the more irrational forces that shape who we are.

Post-Enlightenment European thinkers no longer based identity on religion. That would have constituted a return to the divisions that had prompted the Enlightenment in the first place. Instead, they focused on three secular substitutes for religion: nation, race and class. Nor did they think, as eighteenth-century philosophers had done, in terms of timeless truths. Instead the nineteenth century was gripped by the idea of history: of time as the vehicle of evolution, progress, and the journey from primitive to ever more sophisticated cultures. That is what Hegel brought to philosophy, Darwin to biology, and anthropology to the West's understanding of itself in relation to the now burgeoning study of other cultures.

Throughout the entire history of civilisations, there have been nations. But nationalism – not the mere fact, but the ideology of nationhood – was a product of the nineteenth century. Scholars have differed in their explanations for its genesis. One obvious cause was the Industrial Revolution and the dislocations it created in the move of populations from the country to the city and from the field to the factory, William Blake's 'dark satanic mills'. Ernest Gellner attributed nationalism to the new need, in an industrialised economy, for widespread education and an increasingly standardised curriculum.[2] Benedict Anderson traced it to the new information technology of national newspapers, echoing Hegel's remark that modern man had substituted reading the news for morning prayer.[3]

New social structures were emerging. Henry Sumner Maine (1822–88) said that modernity involved the move from *status* to *contract*. Society no longer mirrored the hierarchical structure that was thought to be embedded in nature, so that your status was determined by the class into which you were born. Instead it was based on a humanly created social contract. Others described it as the shift from *fate* to *choice*. The German sociologist Ferdinand Tönnies (1855–1936) spoke about the difference between *Gemeinschaft* and *Gesellschaft*: the warm, closely knit local communities of earlier ages as against the new, emerging, rule-driven, urban, impersonal society of strangers.

Whatever the precipitating factors, in the wake of the French Revolution and the birth of the secular nation-state thinkers began asking what constituted a nation. There were powerful political movements at work reshaping the boundaries of Europe, led first by Napoleon in France, and later by Bismarck in Germany and Garibaldi in Italy. One of the influences on which they drew was the German thinker Johann Gottfried von Herder (1744–1803), who had emphasised the role of language and culture. Nations, he argued, have distinctive sensibilities, shaped over the centuries and transmitted from generation to generation by the language they speak and the cast of mind that language creates. Herder was not himself a nationalist, but he was a key figure in the reaction against Enlightenment universalism. 'The savage', he wrote, 'who loves himself, his wife and child with quiet joy and glows with limited activity of his tribe as for his own life is in my opinion a more real being than that cultivated shadow who is enraptured with the shadow of the whole species'.[4]

Other intellectual currents were at work in the nineteenth century. There was a fascination with natural history, with the discovery of extinct species and the realisation that the universe was much older than had been thought. No less a figure than Newton (1643–1727) had devoted a significant amount of time to establishing the precise chronology of creation, believing on the basis of the Bible that the universe was less than six thousand years old. There was a new interest in anthropology and the study of 'primitive' cultures. And there was the idea of the evolutionary origin of species. Even before Darwin, Jean-Baptiste Lamarck had already put forward a theory of evolution, later rejected in favour of the path-breaking work of Charles Darwin and Alfred Russell Wallace, first publicised in 1858.

The almost inevitable outcome of these three theories, once they were connected with one another, was the so-called 'scientific

Identity Politics

study of race', initiated by the French naturalist Georges Cuvier (1769–1832) and carried forward by figures like Arthur de Gobineau (1816–82) in France and Ernst Haeckel (1834–1919) in Germany. On this view the various human races were as different as biological species, and this could be measured by physique, phrenology and other physical factors, such as the shape of the foot. Racial purity, a doctrine first developed in Spain in the fifteenth century, thus reappeared in Europe in the nineteenth century. To it was added an even more toxic pseudo-science, social Darwinism, propounded by the English philosopher Herbert Spencer (1820–1903) and adopted by Ernst Haeckel in Germany. Not only did this justify imperialism, colonialism and slavery, it also gave pseudo-scientific legitimacy to the idea that the same law applies in history as in biology: that the strong survive by eliminating the weak. It also provided a new basis for nationalism, namely race itself. The nation became not just a political entity or a cultural one but a biological phenomenon. This was extraordinarily dangerous because it could be used to claim, as it was by the Nazis, that anyone not ethnically Aryan was not a real part of the German nation and constituted a real and present danger to its racial purity. Race, then, was the second substitute for religion.

The third was Marxism, the idea that the real dynamic of history had little to do with nation or race and everything to do with class and the ownership of the means of production. Marx himself famously spoke of communism as a substitute for religion. He called religious suffering 'at one and the same time, the expression of real suffering and a protest against real suffering'. It is, he said, 'the sigh of the oppressed creature, the heart of a heartless world, and the soul of soulless conditions'. It is 'the opium of the people', meaning that it helped dull the pain of the suffering of working people everywhere, but though it relieved the affliction, it did not cure it. In place of religion would come a new economic order that would end the exploitation of the poor by the rich. Marx, not unlike the *philosophes* of the French Revolution, promised a secular messianism, achieved by overturning existing structures of power.

All three movements offered a strong sense of belonging in place of the abstract, identity-less, human-being-as-such that was the human person as understood by eighteenth-century rationalism. This was one of the great transformations in the history of the West, from the Age of Reason to that of Romanticism and Revolution. In place of the universal came a new sense of the particular, whether defined by nation, race or class. Instead of focusing on what united humanity, thinkers started to focus on what makes us different. These ideas, born in the nineteenth century, bore bitter fruit in the twentieth. Nationalism gave rise to two world wars. Racism led directly to the Holocaust. Marxism led to Stalin, the Gulag and the KGB. If we add Chinese Communism to the mix, collectively these movements led to the loss of some 100 million human lives.

In the wake of these traumas, a new flight from identity – be it nation, race or class – began in the 1960s. This time, refuge was sought not in the *universal*, as it was in the eighteenth century, but rather in the name of the *individual*. The inspirations for this movement we have already mentioned in an earlier chapter: Kierkegaard and Nietzsche. In addition, there was at this time considerable reflection on the part of intellectuals as to how it was that the Holocaust could have happened in the midst of post-Enlightenment Europe. Some, like Theodor Adorno and Max Horkheimer, spoke about the authoritarian personality and the danger of a culture that valued absolute obedience to someone else's authority. Figures like Herbert Marcuse, an icon of the New Left, dedicated to sexual rather than economic and political revolution, spoke of the psychological costs of repression and the moralisation of *eros*. Postmodernists like Jacques Derrida and Michel Foucault undermined all the certainties of modernity itself – the objectivity of science, the authority of tradition, the meta-narratives that the West had told itself for two thousand years, even basic concepts like 'truth' and 'text' – radically subjectivising and relativising the foundations on which the Enlightenment was based, substituting everywhere the individual for the universal.

Thus was born the counterculture of the 1960s, gathering to itself the energies of post-war affluence, the contraceptive pill, the new youth culture, protests against the Vietnam War, the 1968 riots in the United States following the assassination of Martin Luther King Jr, and in Paris against capitalism, consumerism and traditional values, and the beatific gathering at Woodstock in 1969.

The poet laureate of the new movement was Bob Dylan, whose lyrics to 'The Times They Are a-Changin'' (1963) announced the coming of the counterculture, inviting mothers and fathers throughout the land not to 'criticize what you can't understand'. Their sons and their daughters were now beyond their command. Eight years later, John Lennon, in 'Imagine' (1971), wrote the baby boomers' equivalent of Shelley's *Prometheus Unbound*, a vision of a world without countries, religions, heaven or hell; a world with nothing to kill or die for.

This was Europe's second great flight from divisive concepts of identity (Lennon's 'countries' and 'religion'), and like the first it was profoundly utopian. The liberalism of the 1960s was built on the premise of the individual as the bearer of rights, and of autonomy as the supreme value of the social order. Its key theoreticians were two Harvard philosophers, John Rawls on the social justice Left and Robert Nozick on the libertarian Right. Essentially, you could do anything you liked so long as it was legal, fair and involved no harm to others.

Within less than a decade, however, a number of outstanding thinkers, among them Alasdair MacIntyre, Michael Sandel, Michael Walzer, Charles Taylor and Robert Bellah, were pointing out that this abstract individual with no attachments to any group, this 'unsituated self' as Sandel put it, was not true to life. We are not mere individuals. We are social animals, embedded in a network of relationships – families, friends, colleagues, neighbours, co-workers and co-worshippers – and some of these are constitutive of our sense of self. The 'I', in and of itself, has no identity. We are who we are because of the groups to which we belong. To be sure, liberalism allows us to enter or leave such groups as we choose: that is what makes it liberal. It turns potentially coercive groups into voluntary associations. But community is essential to identity, so these thinkers argued, and they became known collectively as 'communitarians'.

While this was happening at an intellectual level, another development was taking place at a political level in Europe and the United States: multiculturalism. This was a response on the part of governments to the demographic changes in Europe and America brought about by a rise in levels of immigration. I have written elsewhere about why I believe that multiculturalism, embarked on for the highest of motives, was a disastrous policy, misconceived and profoundly damaging to the social fabric of every society into which it was introduced.[5] Intended to promote the integration of minority ethnic and religious groups into the wider society, instead it led to segregation. Meant to promote tolerance, it has given rise to new and dire forms of intolerance. It turned society from a home into a hotel, in which each group has its room but where there is little if any sense of collective belonging.

The first country to introduce multiculturalism, and the first to regret it, was the Netherlands. When asked why they were against it, the Dutch people interviewed said, because they were in favour of tolerance. When asked for their explanation of the difference between the two, they tended to reply that tolerance means ignoring differences; multiculturalism means making an issue of them at every stage.[6] In the words of Paul Sniderman and Louk Hagendoorn, two scholars who made a study of the negative impact of multiculturalism on Dutch society, 'The benefits of tolerance are large and the costs negligible. By contrast, the material benefits of multiculturalism appear negligible and the costs high.' Explaining this, they say, 'Sharing a common identity builds support for inclusion; bringing differences of ethnic and religious identity to the fore evokes the very exclusionary reactions it is meant to avoid.'[7]

Identity politics deepens the fragmentation caused by multiculturalism, adding to it not just culture and ethnicity but also other forms of identity based on gender and sexual orientation. There is a real danger here of the splitting of society into self-segregating, non-communicating ghettoes. One of its axioms is that 'Only a member of my group can understand my pain.' This is the very opposite of Terence's dictum 'I think nothing human alien to me.' Over three hundred years the West has, with some success, developed an ethic of tolerance and respect for difference, and in a liberal society the prejudice and discrimination that undoubtedly still exist are to be fought wherever they occur. But that is precisely incompatible with an identity politics that builds walls around minorities, allowing no one else to enter, and at the same time insists on recognition from the wider society. As Mark Lilla told students at Rutgers University in 2016, 'You cannot tell people simultaneously, "You must understand me" and "You cannot understand me." '[8]

This reaction against liberal individualism, like the nineteenth-century reactions against Enlightenment universalism, will end in tragedy. It turns difference into exclusion and suspicion. It builds walls, not bridges. It abdicates the hard work of understanding, respecting and working with and for the people not like us. It encourages a mindset of victimhood and oppression. It abandons ideas of the common ground and the common good. The identity politics of the contemporary Left – itemised in the 2016 American election campaign into women, Hispanics, 'ethnic Americans', the LGBT community, Native Americans, African Americans, Pacific islanders and ten other groups[9] – generates its own equal and opposite reaction on the part of the newly resurgent far right – white supremacists in the United States, the National Front in France, the Party for Freedom in Holland, the Alternative for Germany, and the Freedom Party in Austria, alongside authoritarian governments in Hungary and Poland.

One symptom of political malaise has been the return of anti-semitism to every country in Europe, to the point at which 40 per cent of Europe's Jews have considered leaving their home country according to a 2018 poll by the European Agency for Fundamental Human Rights.[10] That this should have happened within living memory of the Holocaust is almost unbelievable. Its significance is that historically the emergence of antisem-itism into the political mainstream has invariably been an early warning sign of societal breakdown. When people search for a scapegoat like the Jews to blame for their ills, they are displaying the first signs of societal dysfunction and democratic collapse. What was heralded as a growth in tolerance has led to new intol-erances, grievances, resentment and rage.

So identity politics is the latest chapter in the long story of the West from the Reformation to today. It began with the eighteenth-century Enlightenment escape from particular identities to a universal humanism. This led to the nineteenth-century Counter-Enlightenment in the form of nationalism, racism and Marxism. In the 1960s an escape began from group identities into individu-alism, and since the 1980s there has been a counter-reaction in the form, first of multiculturalism, then of identity politics.

There is, or there should be, an alternative to these extremes. It involves focusing on society rather than the state. Society is about the moral values we share. The state is about the pursuit and application of power. The battle for recognition and the right to be different belong to a just and compassionate soci-ety, not the liberal democratic state. For the more than two decades I was Chief Rabbi, we worked together, the Church of England, Catholics, the Free Churches, Hindus, Sikhs, Muslims, Buddhists, Jains, Zoroastrians and Bahai, together with the Jewish community, to promote good community relations, mutual respect, and personal friendship. We were able to do this precisely because we were not politicised; because we were acting together as British citizens under the sheltering canopy of a liberal democratic state; because we were driven by the ethical and spiritual values of our respective faiths; and because we were not competing for power.

Nations are enriched by diversity, and integrated diversity coexists with a shared national identity. The best way I have found of putting it is: *By being what we uniquely are, we contribute to society what only we can give.* That is a way of being Christian or Hindu or Muslim or Jewish while being proud to be English. And precisely because of the rise of the far right to meet the newly resurgent far left, it becomes very urgent indeed that we recall George Orwell's fundamental distinction between patriotism and nationalism. Nationalism, which he opposed, is 'inseparable from the will to power'. Its abiding purpose is to secure ever more prestige for the nation: 'Nationalism is power hunger tempered by self-deception.' Patriotism, by contrast, he defined as 'devotion to a particular place and a particular way of life, which one believes to be the best in the world but has no wish to force upon other people'.[11]

Without patriotism, a cohesive sense of belonging and identity is impossible. But patriotism belongs to civil society, that is, to the moral community whose shared values we live by as citizens. If there is no such thing as a national moral community, if civil society atrophies and dies while all that is left are the competitive arenas of the market and the state, then liberal democracy is in danger. Identity politics is a symptom of the breakdown of national identities and the institutions of civil society. Lose the moral basis of society and you will then have what Hobbes described as 'the general inclination of all mankind, a perpetual and restless desire of power after power, that ceaseth only in death'. That is no recipe for the collective grace of a free society.

10

Time and Consequence

I like jokes because sometimes they express philosophical ideas that are hard to formulate in other ways. There is one very old Jewish joke that has a bearing on the argument of this book:

> An old Jewish man and a young Jewish man are travelling on the train. The young man asks: 'Excuse me, what time is it?'
> The old man says nothing.
> 'Excuse me, sir, what time is it?'
> Again, the old man stays silent.
> 'Sir, I'm asking you what time is it. Why don't you answer?'
> The old man says: 'Young man, the next stop is the last on this route. I don't know you, so you must be a stranger. If I answer you now, there will be a relationship between us. I will have to invite you to my home. You are handsome, and I have a beautiful daughter. You will both fall in love and you will want to get married. So tell me, why would I want a son-in-law who can't even afford a watch?'

In other words: small actions can have large consequences.

My argument has been that the dysfunctions of the market and the state that we see today, together with some of the isolation and loneliness discussed in Part 1, are the result of a fateful experiment in the 1960s throughout the West, based on the adoption of the idea that you can have a society without a shared moral code. That would have been regarded in most eras as an impossibility. Society was always the dimension of the 'We' within existence. It is where people were mindful of and acted for the common good. Moralities might change and evolve over time, but they were the text and texture of our common life.

For much of history, societies were held together by religion. In the mid-nineteenth century, when figures like Matthew Arnold and George Eliot began to have doubts about religious faith, morality seemed to be a substitute, and the result was an intensely moralistic age. How did we get from there to here? How did we come to believe that you could have a society that was no more than a collection of individuals, engaged in the pursuit of self-interest, who merely happened to live in roughly the same place at the same time?

My argument will be that Western thought has all too often been insensitive to the dimension of time. Any decision has consequences. Those we can foresee are for the most part short term. Those that are long term are below the horizon. This simple idea has huge implications that are often forgotten. Hence the resonance of the joke: in the long term, small actions have large consequences.

The argument over the liberalisation of morality and law that brought about so many of the changes we have seen in the past fifty years was led in Britain by two outstanding intellects: the distinguished judge, Lord Devlin, and the equally distinguished Oxford Professor of Jurisprudence, H.L.A. Hart. The question each tackled was: should society legislate for morality, or should that be left to individual conscience?

In a powerful 1959 lecture, Lord Devlin argued that a shared morality is essential to society.[1] A society is not simply a collection of individuals doing what they like so long as they do not harm others. It has, essentially and inescapably, a foundation in shared beliefs about the right and the good. 'Without shared ideas on politics, morals, and ethics no society can exist.' He continued: 'If men and women try to create a society in which there is no fundamental agreement about good and evil they will fail; if, having based it on common agreement, the agreement goes, the society will disintegrate.'[2]

He held that any society is entitled, through its laws, to protect itself from internal as well as external dangers, and that 'an established morality is as necessary as good government to the welfare of society'. He continued:

> Societies disintegrate from within more frequently than they are broken up by external pressures. There is disintegration when no common morality is observed, and history shows that the loosening of moral bonds is often the first stage of disintegration, so that society is justified in taking the same steps to preserve its moral code as it does to preserve its government and other essential institutions.[3]

In a series of lectures in 1962, H.L.A. Hart disagreed.[4] He did not challenge the idea that society needs shared moral principles, but not all of these needed to be enforced by the civil law. Indeed they should not be, because there are other conflicting values, among them liberty, privacy and respect for individual conscience. There is no general decision procedure, valid at all times and under all circumstances, to distinguish those areas where behaviour should be legislated and those where it should be left to personal conviction and choice. In general, therefore, he advocated the view set out, a century earlier, by John Stuart Mill in his 1859 essay, *On Liberty*, where he stated that 'the only purpose for which our power can be rightfully exercised over any member of the civilised community, against his will, is to prevent harm to others. His good, either physical or moral, is not a sufficient warrant.'

Hart won the day and John Stuart Mill's principle became the unquestioned and unquestionable understanding of liberty – as Isaiah Berlin put it, 'liberty from' rather than 'liberty to' – and the basic principle of Western liberal democracies today. What was considered almost unspeakably radical in 1859 had become taken-for-granted common sense in 1962.

There is, though, one problem with most theories of morality and society, namely the factor of time. The debate between Lord Devlin and H.L.A. Hart in the late 1950s and early 1960s seemed relatively simple. Hart argued that society would not fall apart if one legalised things hitherto forbidden, whereas Devlin thought it would. The natural assumption is that in a disagreement like this, one view will prove right, the other wrong. There is, though, a third possibility: that Hart and Devlin were both right, but they were thinking in different time spans.

Hart was an academic at Oxford, while Devlin was a senior British judge. Hart knew ideas. Devlin saw people. He knew from personal experience that ideas that sounded right in one generation could nonetheless result in the young offenders of the next. Hart *thought* of the consequences. Devlin *saw* the consequences. I suspect that Devlin, who had a strong historical sense, was simply thinking more long term than was Hart.

Illumination on this idea came, a decade later, from a seemingly completely unconnected field. At the 139th meeting of the American Association for the Advancement of Science in 1972, a paradigm-shifting scientific idea was first formulated: chaos theory, the principle that the flapping of a butterfly's wings in Brazil could cause a tornado in Texas.

The basic premise of chaos theory is that complex systems (like weather, in this example, but all the more so for human society) are in principle unpredictable. This might sound trivial, but it is not. It refutes one of the most famous theories of the scientific Enlightenment: Laplace's principle, published in 1814, of causal or scientific determinism. This is what Laplace said then:

> We may regard the present state of the universe as the effect of its past and the cause of its future. An intellect which at a certain moment would know all forces that set nature in motion, and all positions of all items of which nature is composed, if this intellect were also vast enough to submit these data to analysis, it would embrace in a single formula the movements of the greatest bodies of the universe and those of the tiniest atom; for such an intellect nothing would be uncertain and the future just like the past would be present before its eyes.

147

In brief: tell us everything about now, and I will tell you with absolute certainty what is going to happen a hundred or a thousand years from now. A few months later, Laplace went to Napoleon to tell him his theory. Napoleon asked him, 'Tell me, where is God in your theory?' Laplace replied in words scientists and atheists have recited ever since as a proof of their victory over something as irrational as religion: '*Je n'ais pas besoin de cette hypothese*', I have no need of such a hypothesis. In other words: we have moved beyond such superstitions as religion. Science will tell us all we need to know. Given sufficient data, we can predict the future with absolute precision and certainty. Chaos theory tells us that this is not so. Complex systems are unpredictable. Laplace's theory turns out to have been rationalistic hubris: confident, and wrong.

This has moral consequences too. Perhaps the best-known and most often cited ethical principle in modern times has been Jeremy Bentham's utilitarianism: act to produce the best possible consequences, the greatest happiness for the greatest number. This is controversial, however, and many questions have been raised about it. Are all forms of happiness to be reckoned the same? Can happiness be quantified? How do you weigh the happiness of the majority against the rights of a minority? Are there some things we should not do whatever the consequences? And so on. But one of the most fundamental questions is the one raised by the joke: the question of time. *For how long* are you responsible for the consequences of your actions? For immediate consequences only, or for distant ones also? For those I intend, or for unintended ones also? For those that are foreseeable or for all?

How, in any case, in a complex system like a human society, do you identify clearly the consequences of an earlier phenomenon? How do you know what would have happened otherwise?

How long term should our thinking be?

Why would I want a son-in-law who can't even afford a watch?

How do you factor in the dimension of time, when thinking about moral issues? Chaos theory tells us that any complex system is unpredictable, and humanity is certainly a complex system. Karl Popper taught us that 'the human factor is the ultimately uncertain and wayward element in social life'.[5] We can never know how people will respond to a given event, or how others will respond to their response. So we have a problem at the very heart of utilitarianism: we have no way of knowing what the long-term consequences of any decision will be, especially when many people will be affected.

The libertarian thinker, Friedrich Hayek, suggested that the only way of planning for the future was to learn from the past. In his last book, *The Fatal Conceit*, he made a very important case: for the free market and its 'extended order' to emerge, so too must a certain kind of morality.[6] For many thousands of years, human beings had lived in small bands of hunter-gatherers, and it was during that long pre-history of *Homo sapiens* that our instincts were formed. Those instincts – of solidarity and altruism – allowed our ancestors to live together in close face-to-face groups, and without the group no isolated individual could have survived for very long.

However, a significant change had to take place in the way people related to one another in order for mankind to be able to make the transition from the small group or tribe to the larger and more open associations needed for complex societies and economies. Instincts were no longer sufficient. Instead their role had to be undertaken by rules relating to private property, standards of honesty, contract, exchange and so on. How these rules first developed is irrelevant. What matters is that they emerged and spread. The groups who adhered to them found themselves able to grow and spread more successfully than others. Don't look at what people intended to happen, argued Hayek; look at what actually happened.

Often our societal rules involve people acting against their instincts, so they had to be taught through habit rather than simply by appeal to inclination. Moral education became a matter of imitation, learning by doing, the handing on of tradition by habituation. Morality itself consisted largely of 'Thou shalt not's' – prohibitions that served as boundaries, within which free human action could be directed and contained, much as the banks of a river contain and direct the flow of water. It was this kind of morality that made possible humanity's transition from tribal societies to civilisations, in which ever larger associations of individuals and groups could develop their specialisations and yet meet their needs through the relatively peaceful process of trade and exchange.

So it was in the past. But Hayek could never take the free society for granted. It was, he believed, vulnerable on two counts. On the one hand there was the perennial danger of a retreat into primitive group solidarity, with its hatred of the outsider. On the other there was the seductive voice of reason's 'fatal conceit' that by conscious intent and deliberate planning we can improve on the morality of the past and re-design our basic human institutions. This, he felt, was the essential error, not only of socialism, but also of liberals like John Stuart Mill, who regarded traditional moral constraints as mostly dispensable, the unwanted baggage of a more superstitious age.

This led Hayek to reflect on the role of religion in preserving moral traditions, despite the fact that he himself was a self-confessed agnostic. We owe it to religions, he said, 'that beneficial traditions have been preserved and transmitted at least long enough to enable those groups following them to grow, and to have the opportunity to spread by natural or cultural selection'.[7]

The striking feature of religion, for Hayek, is its humility, even reverence, towards the great moral institutions without which our 'extended order' could not have developed. It guards against what he calls 'the rationalist delusion that man, by exercising his intelligence, invented morals that gave him the power to achieve more than he could ever foresee'. Religion sees morality as given by God. Hayek saw it as the result of evolutionary forces. What these two views held in common, though, was a strong and principled opposition to the idea that individually or collectively we can devise a better system by rational thought alone, so as to maximise happiness or some other good. The law of unintended consequences will always defeat our best intentions.

In the light of Hayek's argument, whether or not he would have put it this way, there is a case for listening, when on the brink of great social change, to the voice that says: think long. Learn from history. See what worked, and what failed, in the past. Don't fool yourself that you can predict and control the future. You may be setting into motion processes that will do great harm, but this will not be immediately apparent. You will hear people arguing with absolute certainty that they are sure that a development is safe, and it may be years, decades before the danger ensues. That is what Hayek meant by 'the fatal conceit'. That is how good people make bad decisions.

The discontents of the twenty-first century that we see today did not occur immediately after the 1960s. It took two generations for them to emerge. But we see one graphic example in the case of drugs.

*

It is 25 January 2019. A film opens in London. *Beautiful Boy* is a searing account of a father whose son has become a drug addict, and his attempt to rescue him from psychiatric illness, crime, violence and premature death. It is a powerful film, made memorable by the surely Oscar-worthy performances of its two lead actors, Steve Carell and Timothée Chalamet. It is all the more compelling because it is based on a true story, set out in two autobiographies, one by the father, the other by the son: David and Nic Sheff.

Nic is twelve when his father discovers that he has been taking marijuana. Nic promises his father that he will give it up, but he doesn't. Little by little, he graduates to more serious drugs – cocaine, crystal meth and heroin. He becomes an addict. Repeatedly his father wrestles with him and takes him into rehabilitation. For a while Nic breaks the habit, but each time, tempted by opportunity, he relapses. He degenerates into an almost feral figure. He steals from everyone, including his own young brother. He sleeps in the open, overdoses and almost dies. His father, though, refuses to give up on him, and it is this that saves him. A note at the end of the film tells us that Nic has been clean now for eight years. There is no softening of the message, no upbeat moral. It is a wrenching story, and one repeated in more lives than we know.

It begins with marijuana, often thought to be harmless, no more damaging than alcohol or cigarettes. This turns out to be wrong. Though debate on the subject continues, there is significant evidence that marijuana is a gateway drug. One study found that those addicted to it are three times more likely to become heroin addicts.[8] Another found that cannabis users were three to five times more likely to experience opioid problems three years later.[9]

In February 2019, Alex Berenson, an award-winning novelist and former journalist on the *New York Times*, published a book called *Tell Your Children: The Truth About Marijuana, Mental Illness, and Violence*. His warning was stark. As marijuana's use has become more socially acceptable – indeed, even as it has been legalised in several American states – so the evidence has become ever more compelling that marijuana use is linked to mental illness and violent crime.

In the United States, psychosis rates among young people doubled between 2008 and 2017. And over a similar period the number of Americans who use cannabis daily has been rising rapidly, from three million in 2006 to eight million in 2017. The medical evidence is not conclusive, but it is suggestive. The type of cannabis in use today is much more potent than that of the 1970s. Then, the percentage of the chemical responsible for its psychological effects, THC, was around 2 per cent. Today it is more than ten times as much. Research in Finland and Denmark has recorded a significant rise in psychosis corresponding to a rise in marijuana use. A 2019 report in the UK estimated that people who use high-strength cannabis daily are five times more likely to have a first episode of psychosis.[10] In 2012, a study of more than nine thousand American men found that marijuana use was associated with a doubling of domestic violence.[11]

Berenson decided to write the book, he says, when his wife, a psychiatrist who works with mentally ill criminals, told him that the one thing they had in common was that they *all* used marijuana. Yet, as Alice Thomson noted in *The Times*, New York State has announced plans to legalise cannabis for recreational use, 'admitting that it would make $300 million in the first three years from tax revenue'.[12] If this is their motivation then it is the mindset of the market gone mad.

This is only part of a yet more serious tragedy. As David Brooks reported in the *New York Times* in 2017, two and a half million Americans are currently addicted to opioids. The rate of death from this cause rose from 8,200 annually in 1999 to 33,000 in 2015. As Brooks notes, this means that more Americans died from opioid addiction in the two years of 2014 and 2015 than in the entire Vietnam War. The Centers for Disease Control and Prevention in Atlanta reported in 2015 that people addicted to prescription opioid painkillers are forty times more likely to be addicted to heroin.[13]

In Britain, cocaine use has more than doubled in the past five years according to 2019 research findings by forensic scientists at King's College London.[14] According to the National Crime Agency, seizures of cocaine trebled from 42.8 tonnes in 2013/14 to 122.9 tonnes in 2017/18. Senior police and government figures have argued that this massive increase reflects the increased distribution of drugs and hence the number of drug dealers and gangs operating in Britain, with a parallel rise in drug-related violence. In February and March 2018 the murder rate in London was higher than in New York for the first time in recorded history. There has been an epidemic of often fatal knife crime. David Gauke, Justice Secretary, said that 'those who take cocaine at dinner parties are responsible for fuelling the violence on London streets'.[15] His words were echoed by Metropolitan Police Commissioner Cressida Dick: 'There's a whole group of middle-class people who will sit around happily thinking about global warming, fair trade, environmental protection and organic food, but think there's no harm in taking a bit of cocaine. But there is. It causes misery.'[16]

Now travel back in time to 1967. On 26 May the Beatles released their new album, *Sgt. Pepper's Lonely Hearts Club Band*. It was heavy with drug-related associations. Those who knew about such things might already have detected the influence of marijuana on *Rubber Soul* (December 1965) or of psychedelic drugs on *Revolver* (August 1966). But *Sergeant Pepper* had an LSD feel about it. There was John Lennon's 'Lucy in the Sky with Diamonds', with its 'cellophane flowers' and 'kaleidoscope eyes'. Ringo was getting high with a little help from his friends, and the last song, 'A Day in the Life', had as its refrain, 'I'd love to turn you on.' I remember that spring differently, because it was then that I started studying philosophy and reading about the Hart–Devlin debate.

Lennon did not shy away from the dangers of psychedelic drugs: 'He blew his mind out in a car.' He even hinted at the involvement in drug taking of the upper classes of London society: 'They'd seen his face before; nobody was really sure if he was from the House of Lords.' The Beatles had been taking amphetamines since 1960 to help them stay awake during the marathon sessions in German nightclubs, then Bob Dylan introduced them to marijuana in 1964. But it was a London dentist in 1965 who gave Lennon and George Harrison sugar cubes laced with LSD, only informing them after they had ingested it. Lennon was angry and found the experience frightening, though Harrison found it almost mystical: 'there was a God, and I could see him in every blade of grass. It was like gaining hundreds of years of experience in 12 hours.'[17]

So it was a member of the British professional class who introduced the Beatles to psychedelic drugs. And it was members of the cognitive elite in America and Britain who were at the fore-front of espousing experimentation with psychedelic drugs. In America in the early 1960s it was a Harvard professor, Timothy Leary. In England the case had been made in 1954 by Aldous Huxley in *The Doors of Perception*. And it was none other than that iconic figure of Victorian England, Sir Arthur Conan Doyle, who romanticised the use of cocaine, with a 7 per cent solution of which Sherlock Holmes injected himself using a syringe kept in a morocco leather case. And there were other eminent Victorian drug-takers, most famously Thomas De Quincey.

A critical turning point in Britain was a famous editorial in *The Times* on 1 July 1967, with the headline (taken from the poem 'Epistle to Dr Arbuthnot' by Alexander Pope, 1735) *Who breaks a butterfly on a wheel?* Mick Jagger and Keith Richards of the Rolling Stones had been arrested and charged with the possession of illegal drugs. The police wanted to make a strong public example of them, so as to send a warning to the younger generation that drugs were anything but harmless. They felt that unless harsh action was taken, a whole generation might fall into the habit. *The Times* editorial, however, argued that Jagger and Richards should be released, on the basis that they were being made scapegoats for the larger issue and the drugs they were using were essentially harmless.

The author of that editorial was the new editor of *The Times*, William Rees-Mogg, well on his way to becoming the epitome of the great and the good of Britain at that time. I was nineteen years old, and he was one of my heroes. He was an expert on everything from economics to poetry, and whatever he said carried with it the stamp of wisdom and authority. I remember the editorial clearly. It was a shaping moment of the sixties, and what he said seemed to make sense. Yet, watch the film *Beautiful Boy*, or read Alex Berenson's *Tell Your Children: The Truth About Marijuana, Mental Illness, and Violence*, and you will be shocked to the core. Even a new Charles Dickens would find it hard to describe what a catastrophe drug taking among the young has been. Britain and

America in 2019 are not the Victorian age with its coalmines and satanic mills, yet our children and young people are suffering in perhaps even more profound ways. Marijuana is not harmless, and the drug-taking epidemic begun in the 1960s has ruined hundreds of thousands of lives.

Hence the point of the old joke: think long and hard about the possible future consequences of our decisions. Things that seem harmless now may in retrospect be seen as very harmful indeed, fifty years from now. The belief that we can predict future outcomes is, said Hayek, the 'fatal conceit'.

*

Each year for the twenty-two years that I was Chief Rabbi, I was given the privilege by the BBC of making a television programme to be broadcast around the time of the Jewish New Year. The idea of the programme was to deliver as far as possible a universal message – obviously so, since the Jewish community in Britain is so small, and in any case a large section of the British public is not religious at all.

This presented a challenge each year. How do you translate religious concepts into a language and sensibility that is deeply secular? In particular, one year, I wanted to explain to viewers the important but difficult ideas of repentance and behavioural change that are at the heart of the Judeo-Christian ethic. How could you do so without religious terminology or iconography?

In the end, I realised that the best way of doing so was through the idea of addiction. We know how much harm we do to ourselves when we become addicted to alcohol, drugs or other such activity like gambling. But it is extremely difficult to wean ourselves away from such habits, however self-destructive they are.

What has to happen is something very like repentance. First, you have to realise you are doing something wrong. Second, you have to make something like a public admission of this. Third, you have to commit to behavioural change, however hard that may be.

Weaning yourself off addiction to drugs was the nearest I could come to weaning yourself from bad habits and wrong deeds.

So I spent a day with a group of eighteen-year-old heroin addicts. It was a wrenching experience. Most of them came from broken and abusive homes. They had not had a fair chance in life, and my heart went out to all of them. If I had been in their situation, I am not sure I would have had the strength to avoid falling into some kind of drug- or alcohol-induced oblivion.

The director of the centre was an amazing young woman who seemed to be able to inspire behavioural change in these wounded but lovely individuals. I asked her, simply, 'What is it that you give them that gives them the strength to change?' I will never forget her reply. 'We are the first people they have met who give them unconditional love,' she began. That was something I expected: that is what faith is about, religious or otherwise. It was her next statement that shook me. 'We are the first people they have met who care enough about them to say, "No."' A shiver went down my spine. Sometimes the fate of a life depends on the ability to say and hear the word No.

Years later, faced with the extraordinary spread of drug use, abuse and addiction among millions of young people in the West, I think of the lives that might have been saved if figures of authority and influence had cared enough to say No more firmly.

*

It has taken fifty years for the full extent of the drug problem to become apparent, reaching the numbers affected now. It took a similar length of time for the breakdown of families and communities to generate the social problems we have been considering. What is happening now that will have serious consequences in fifty years' time? There are several such issues, each of which is far too large to be dealt with adequately here. But to mention just one, and that far too briefly, the most significant challenge of our time is climate change. Fifty years from now people will look back and wonder why we failed to take decisive action. The Hayek principle applies here. Look back, not forward. We have enough evidence of massive environmental destruction almost wherever human beings have set their feet. The potential for harm is enormous in both scale and scope, and much of it will be irreparable once it has happened.

Unless we have resolve in the present, we will be bequeathing future generations a planet with rising temperatures, more extreme weather patterns, longer and more extreme droughts, warmer ocean temperatures, more intense tropical storms, melting sea ice, shrinking glaciers, rising sea levels, plastic-polluted oceans, air-polluted cities, low-lying coastal regions rendered uninhabitable, and extinctions of animal and plant species on an almost unprecedented scale.

Giving testimony in the British House of Commons on 9 July 2019, the naturalist Sir David Attenborough called for a moral transformation in attitudes to the natural environment similar to the one that took place in relation to slavery in the nineteenth century. There was a time when slavery was considered normal, then it became unacceptable. The same has to become true, he said, about the human degradation of the environment.[18]

What makes climate change so significant in this context is that it highlights the fatal weakness of an I-centred culture, where the major institutions of the market and the state are the only recognised authorities. The market is predominantly focused on short-term profit, not long-term responsibility. There are market-based solutions to environmental problems, but they involve government intervention. They are rarely arrived at by the market left to its own devices.

As for the state, this too tends to be limited, in this case by the time horizons of the government; in other words, up to and not much beyond the next election. Governments have thus far often been disinclined to impose a significant cost on the electorate for the sake of a benefit in the distant future.

As for the self-interested individual: what responsibilities do I have for a future so distant that I will not live to see it? All three, the market, the state and the individual, operate on the basis of a localised rationality, into which global environmental responsibility is hard to translate. That, it seems to me, is why, despite all the knowledge of environmental catastrophe of one sort or another that has been accumulating since the 1960s, we still have not enacted the policies or taken the actions that would have prevented a further acceleration of global warming and the other symptoms of climate change.

Hence the fundamental importance of the 'We' dimension involved in moral thinking, a 'We' that extends in both time and space. I am responsible for the good of others, including those who will come after me. I am, among other things, a guardian of the future for the sake of generations not yet born. Therefore, I may not morally act in ways that benefit me, here, now, if, as a result, future generations will have to pay the price.

This is a point made by Robb Willer of Stanford University. People, he says, are generally reluctant to undertake costly political actions even for a beneficial cause. 'People think quite differently, however, when they are morally engaged with an issue. In such cases people are more likely to eschew a sober cost–benefit analysis, opting instead to take action because it is the right thing to do.'[19] Morality makes a difference to the way we think about problems and their solution. It shifts us from self-interest to concern for the common good, and from a narrow focus on immediate gain to more distant horizons. We need to be able to think in this collective, long-term way if we are to avoid the short-sightedness that led people to think that you could abandon morality without paying a momentous price.

The long journey from 'We' to 'I', from shared moral code to 'morality is what I choose it to be', seemed to make sense in the 1960s. Hart won, Devlin lost. We can't rewrite that history. But we live with the consequences, and some of those are very bad indeed: drug addiction, markets without morals, the consumerisation of happiness, the fracturing of the family, and other phenomena we will encounter in chapters to come. What the philosophical, legal and moral voices of the time failed to factor in was the law of unintended consequences. Things never turn out the way we think they will. Too often, Western thought has been short-sighted – we might even say, time-blind.

It needs moral courage to say No to the things that are tempting in the present but ruinous in the long run: drugs, cheap plastic goods, cars for all, and the other ways in which we enjoy our present at the cost of our children's future. We need space in our lives to gather collective wisdom about the common good, and to consider sacrifice now for the sake of benefit in generations to come.

PART THREE

Can We Still Reason Together?

II

Post-Truth

Beginning in April 2007, an email began circulating on the Internet, and quickly spread around the English-speaking world. It announced that, 'Recently, this week, the UK removed the Holocaust from its school curriculum because it "offended" the Muslim population, which claims it never occurred.' It continued: 'This is a frightening portent of the fear that is gripping the world and how easily each country is giving into it.' Holocaust denial, so the message suggested, was rampant and it had achieved a significant victory in Britain. It was important, said the email, to let others know what was happening, so it urged anyone who received it to pass it on to others with the aim of it being seen 40 million times.

The story was false. It was based on a report that a single school among the tens of thousands in Britain was not teaching the Holocaust, for a reason quite different to the one suggested. The Holocaust Education Trust in Britain issued a denial as soon as it became aware of the email, but whereas the first went viral, the second, the correction, did not. So contagious was the fear that it begat another false story. Misreading the abbreviation UK (United Kingdom) for the University of Kentucky, a new message went out that this university had removed Holocaust material from its history curriculum. The university was forced to issue its own denial.

The initial email circulated widely among American Jews, many of whom received it multiple times. So powerful was the impression it created that I was asked by the Anti-Defamation League to go on a lecture tour around the United States simply to convince American Jews that Britain was not succumbing to 1930s-style antisemitism or Islamist radicalism. To what extent

I succeeded, I am not sure. So great is the power of fear that even assuring people that the facts are otherwise does not altogether banish the original suspicion. That was when I discovered the extent to which the Internet has given new life to the old saying that 'A lie will go round the world while the truth is pulling its boots on.'

In 2016 the *Oxford English Dictionary* announced *post-truth* as its 'word of the year', an adjective defined as 'relating to or denoting circumstances in which objective facts are less influential in shaping public opinion than appeals to emotion and personal belief'. In 2017, three political journalists, James Ball, Matthew d'Ancona and Evan Davies, all published books entitled *Post-Truth*,[1] suggesting perhaps a lack of imagination but certainly also the depth of the idea's penetration as a significant phenomenon of our time. D'Ancona noted that the term itself had been used as early as 1992 in an essay by the playwright Steve Tesich in *The Nation* magazine. Speaking about the Iran-Contra scandal and other events in which the public was misled, he suggested that 'we, as a free people, have freely decided that we want to live in some post-truth world'.[2] But use of the term spiked in 2016 in the context of the American presidential election and the British Brexit vote.

Both these campaigns were marked by extensive use of social media to influence public opinion, along with a host of assertions and allegations that were at best misleading and at worst downright lies. The Brexit campaign was marked by some highly misleading propositions, most notoriously that Britain would regain £350 million weekly, claimed as the cost of membership in the European Union, which they could dedicate solely to the National Health Service. The years that have passed since then have made it clear how little any of the campaigners on either side actually knew what the consequences would be. They are still unclear now. The American presidential campaign was characterised by wild assertions whose relationship with the truth seemed to be thoroughly flexible.[3]

More significantly, there was dark manipulation by social media companies – Facebook in particular – of what should have been private and protected. In the Cambridge Analytica scandal the personal records of 87 million people, 70 million of them in the United States, were accessed and used for political purposes without their knowledge or agreement. We now know that there was also Russian involvement in both the American presidential election and the Brexit referendum in 2016, seemingly with the intention of destabilising the politics of the West. During the American election, the Russian Internet Research Agency, an organisation of more than a thousand people in St Petersburg operating behind undercover identities, reached more than 126 million Facebook users and 20 million on Instagram with polarising material.[4] This augurs ill for the future of democracy.

The extent of the problem can be judged by two recent reports from America. A Brookings survey found that 57 per cent of those questioned had been exposed to fake news during the 2018 mid-term elections. Nineteen per cent thought that this had influenced their vote. Forty-two per cent believed that there is more fake news now than in 2016.[5] A 2019 report of the Pew Research Center revealed the depth of public concern about this. A majority of Americans now view fake news as a more serious national problem than terrorism, illegal immigration, racism or sexism. Almost seven in ten say it undermines confidence in government. Fifty-four per cent say it damages people's confidence in one another. Fifty-six per cent believe the problem will become worse over the next five years and only one in ten believe that progress will be made in reducing it.[6]

Speaking in London in 2019, Lord Hall, director-general of the BBC, warned that the world is facing 'the biggest assault on truth since the 1930s'. Comparing the spread of fake news to Nazi propaganda in the build-up to the Second World War, he said that 'An assault on truth is an assault on democracy.'[7]

In the previous chapters I have described the consequences of a moral revolution whose origins can be traced across the centuries,

as far back as the Reformation. This revolution became radical-
ised in the nineteenth century and then became a shared, public,
taken-for-granted reality in the 1960s. In the next few chapters
I want to look at further phenomena that owe their trajectory
to more recent developments, in particular to information and
communication technology. What happens to truth when we get
our information less from books and newspapers than from social
media? And why should we care about truth in the first place?

Almost from the birth of civilisation there has been a conflict
between truth and power – what is in fact the case, and what those
who wield it wish people to believe is the case. Ancient history
provides a vivid example: Egyptian reports about the victory of
Ramesses II over the Hittites at the Battle of Kadesh (1274 BCE).
It so happens that there are alternative contemporary accounts
that suggest that in fact the Egyptian ruler fell into a trap set by
the Hittites, who sent one of their number, pretending to be a
defector, to tell Ramesses that the Hittites had fled the city. Thus
emboldened, the Egyptian pharaoh advanced with his army, only
to discover that they had walked into an ambush by the opposing
army. Bewildered and outsmarted, the Egyptian force managed to
survive only because reinforcements arrived in the nick of time.

The battle itself was inconclusive, and Ramesses retreated.
However, he then had his own account recorded in temples
throughout Egypt, declaring the result a momentous victory for
Ramesses and his troops. This was history as written by would-
be victors. Those who have the power to do so, do their best to
ensure that the tale told by future generations is one in which they
emerge as the heroes.

George Orwell, writing in 1942 about the Spanish Civil War,
says something strikingly similar about the success of Fascist
propaganda: 'This kind of thing is frightening to me, because it
often gives me the feeling that the very concept of objective truth
is fading out of the world. After all, the chances are that those
lies, or at any rate similar lies, will pass into history ... So for
all practical purposes the lie will have become the truth.'[8] Power

seeks to impose its own interpretation of events – of the world – on people's minds, a spectre that haunts Orwell's novel, *1984*.

Yet for most of the history of the West there has been a countervailing principle, derived from religion on the one hand, philosophy on the other, that valued truth as an end in itself. It must not be bent, distorted, disguised or compromised for the sake of other ends. The prophets of the Hebrew Bible spoke truth to power. The New Testament declares that the truth will set you free. Philosophers, inspired by Socrates, engaged in a lifelong pursuit of truth (though admittedly, in *The Republic*, Plato developed the concept of a noble lie told for political purposes). Where there is a strong moral arena independent of the pursuit of wealth or power, the market or the state, then truth stands a chance of surviving intact against the assaults that will from time to time be made against it. Telling a lie will be a disqualification, whether you are a scientist, business-person or politician. A reputation for truth-telling will be an essential test of character.

A world of truth is a world of trust, and vice versa. In it, there is something larger than individuals seeking their own interest. Truth becomes the intellectual equivalent of a public space that we can all inhabit, whatever our desires and predilections. It was only when science developed ways of testing the truth of hypotheses by experiment, evidence and evaluation that knowledge became more than opinion and real progress could be made in this arena. Where there is honesty – truth and truthfulness – there tends to be law, order and prosperity. A respect for truth is essential for authority, collaborative endeavour and human graciousness. But it requires humility. I have to be able to recognise that certain facts are true even though they challenge my convictions. I have to acknowledge that there is something larger than me.

What has happened in recent years is that the shrinking of the moral arena and the move from 'We' to 'I' has converged with the new technologies of communication to damaging effect. What was once a public respect for truth has been replaced by the noise of social media and the absence of any form of quality control on the Internet. Back in 1995, even before the birth of Google, the journalist John Diamond wrote that the real problem about the Internet is that 'there is no real way of discerning truth from lies'.[9] Everything is to be found there: the true, the false, whether accurate, distorted, well researched, invented, balanced or tendentious, and there is no clear-cut way of telling one from the other. Besides which, when politics plays itself out in the new media and becomes less like campaigning and more like marketing, it becomes progressively less about facts, policies and rational debate than about emotions and moving people viscerally.

So, though alternative facts, fake news and post-truth are not new, what has changed is the speed and scope with which they are communicated, via the Internet, YouTube and social media. Everyone has access to these channels of communication, and those who seek to spread rumours and unattested allegations can now do so with unprecedented ease and power. Quality journalism has its own internal principles of ethics. 'Comment is free', said C.P. Scott of the *Manchester Guardian* in 1921, 'but facts are sacred.' 'Everyone is entitled to his own opinion,' said Daniel Patrick Moynihan, 'but not to his own facts.' But for some time now, a large proportion of the population has received its news not directly from the press but via social media, where there is no immediate way of checking accuracy or selectivity even of ostensibly journalistic sources. The Internet has not yet developed a reliable ethic of truth.

Two factors make this particularly dangerous. The first is known as the *confirmation bias*, that is, our tendency to believe those accounts that accord with our own image of the world and to discount others. Social media algorithms multiply this effect by showing us items they know we are likely to agree with. As of 2018, some 68 per cent of Americans get at least some of their news via social media, and social media tends to ensure that the items we see represent views we agree with.[10] Fifty-seven per cent of Americans say that the news they see on social media is largely inaccurate, but they continue to use it as a news source anyway, because of its convenience.[11] The resultant filtering out of opposing views leads to a mistrust and deepening lack of understanding of those whose opinions are not like ours. Differences become divides. We begin to inhabit disconnected islands of the likeminded.

The second is the fact that our *attention is selective*. We are far more likely to notice things that arouse our fear. This engages the most primitive and rapid-response part of the brain, sometime known as the reptilian brain, that is hardwired to ensure our survival. This governs our flight, fight or freeze reactions. It registers fear, and its operation is so fast and automatic that it can be hard to override. That is why the 'Holocaust denial' story with which I began had such widespread traction, while the correction was hardly noticed. By the time we get around to checking whether our fears are justified, the terror itself, often compounded by memories of previous traumas, has already done its work.

The spread of post-truth, then, has much to do with the new media of instantaneous global communication. But it also has a wider intellectual context. The first relates to the work of Marx, Nietzsche and Freud, given a generic name by Paul Ricœur as *the hermeneutics of suspicion*.[12] This was the idea that beneath any apparent communication, something else is going on. There is a subtext beneath the text. For Marx it was the powerful concretising their power. For Nietzsche, it was the weak taking their revenge against the strong. For Freud it was the subterranean currents of unconscious drives. But for all three, what was said was less important than what was *beneath* what was said. 'Truth' was a mere mask, concealing the realities of power.

The second, arising in part because of the first, was the philosophical movement that flourished between the 1960s and 1980s known as *postmodernism*. As the name implies, however, it arose in conscious opposition and succession to modernism. Modernism was the project of the Enlightenment. Reason and observation – represented respectively by philosophy and science

– would establish objective truth with none of the dogmatic presuppositions of religion.

It was precisely this idea, that there are foundational truths, that postmodernists rejected. It isn't so, they said. There is a fundamental difference between reality itself, and the way we talk and think about reality. The latter is a phenomenon of language, and there are many languages. Philosophy is no more and no less than the way a specific culture, or an individual thinker, interprets reality. History depends on the bias of the historian. A literary text is as much dependent on the reader as on the writer.

Even science is not objective, the postmodernists claimed. A key text here was an influential book by T.S. Kuhn, *The Structure of Scientific Revolutions*, in which he argued that in any given age, the way science interprets the evidence depends on the prevailing theory, what he called the 'paradigm'.[13] Evidence that conflicts with the paradigm is explained away until it accumulates to the point where a new theory emerges – relativity, for example, or quantum physics – and the paradigm shifts. Putting all this together, we arrive at the conclusion that reality is 'socially constructed'. It is not out there in the world. It is 'in here', in the mind. There is no such thing as truth. There are truths, plural, each of which is to a large degree subjective. That is how academic discourse collectively arrived at the proposition put forward by Nietzsche a century earlier, that 'There are no facts, there are only interpretations.'

Postmodernism was a deeply obscure movement. Its leading protagonists had a habit of speaking in sentences whose meaning was almost impossible to fathom. A joke at the time said that the difference between the mafia and a postmodernist was that the mafia makes you an offer you can't refuse; a postmodernist makes you an offer you can't understand.

Not everyone read these masters of obscurity, Lyotard, Baudrillard, Derrida, Lacan, Irigaray, Latour, Virilio, Deleuze, Guattari and the rest, superbly skewered by Alan Sokal and Jean Bricmont in their *Intellectual Impostures*,[14] but they were part of a mood, and their precursors – Marx, Nietzsche and Freud – were hugely influential. So they made it possible on an intellectual level to believe that there is no such thing as truth, even though that proposition is fraught with self-contradiction.

In one study, undertaken in 2015, the reactions of liberals and conservatives to certain kinds of news story were tested. It was found that 'just as conservatives discount the scientific theories that run counter to their worldview, liberals will do exactly the same'.[15] Science becomes what vindicates your prejudice, history is mere 'narrative', and the story you tell about the past depends on which side you are on. All morality is relative, dependent entirely on personal choice. Thus was the intellectual climate prepared for the assault on truth made possible by the new technologies of communication. In a world without truth, fake news and alternative facts flourish because there is nothing else, nothing that stands above the conflicting voices and clashing narratives. Truth was defeated in theory long before it was destroyed by social media.

The result is inevitable. Where truth dies, there dies trust. A mere 10 per cent of Generation Z, born in or after 1995, trusts politicians to do the right thing. Indeed, the loss of trust is systemic, as we have seen. People do not trust journalists, or international corporations, or anyone else for that matter. They assume that they, the public, are being misled as a matter of course. In the absence of accountability to the truth, all that is left is spin, obfuscation, denial, and the manipulation of public opinion.

It was Nietzsche who foresaw what was likely to happen. When people gave up their faith in religion, it would not be religion alone that they would lose. They would lose morality, and with it a concern for truth, and then even science would lose its authority. Science, he said, can only function if we bring to it a prior conviction: 'The question whether *truth* is needed must not only have been affirmed in advance, but affirmed to such a degree that the principle, the faith, the conviction finds expression: *Nothing* is needed more than truth, and in relation to it, everything else has only second-rate value.'[16] Why not, after all, deceive? Why not allow oneself to be deceived? The pursuit of truth has many advantages, but so does deception. A candid look at human existence would tell us, he says, that life is 'aimed at semblance, meaning error, deception, simulation, delusion, self-delusion'. History has always favoured the masters of deception. When, therefore, we speak of a commitment to truth, *'we stand on moral ground'*. He continues:

> Thus the question, 'Why science?' leads back to the moral problem: *Why have morality at all* when life, nature, and history are not moral? . . . It is still a metaphysical faith upon which our faith in science rests – that even we seekers after knowledge today, we godless anti-metaphysicians still take our fire, too, from the flame lit by a faith that is thousands of years old, that Christian faith which was also the faith of Plato, that God is the truth, that truth is divine.[17]

Nietzsche fearlessly faced the conundrum he saw before him. He was adamant that religion was false, but he nonetheless acknowledged that its flame inspired great human endeavour. The question he could not help but ask, therefore, resonates even more strongly: 'What if this should become more and more incredible?' His point is simple and stark: take away the moral imperative, which he believed to be ultimately a religious/metaphysical one, and human beings would have no reason to tell the truth if deception and manipulation were to our advantage, which they often are.

Nietzsche, the most profound atheist of recent centuries and himself the inspiration for postmodernism, maintained a fierce honesty with his readers. In a world without an agreed basic moral code, do not expect truth to survive. That is our world today. The manipulative use of social media in the interests of economics and politics, wealth and power, has led us directly into a post-truth era in which trust in public institutions is at an all-time low. This is what happens when we try to run a society based on the market and the state alone.

Without moral commitment, the still small voice of truth is inaudible beneath the cacophony of lies, half-truths, obfuscations and evasions. Without truth, no trust; without trust, no society. Truth and trust create a world we can share.

12

Safe Space

I was the first member of our family to attend university. My father had left school at the age of fourteen, my mother at the age of sixteen. For me, university was an immense culture shock. For the first time I met people from the upper classes; for the first time I met people from the industrial working class. My own personal views were challenged every day, and in every way.

To be a philosopher in those days was almost by definition to be an atheist – though one student had scribbled some graffiti in the Cambridge University Library: 'God exists; it's just that He doesn't want to get involved.' When I began my doctorate, my supervisor Bernard Williams, himself a formidable atheist, suggested that I spend a year in Oxford under the supervision of Philippa Foot who, though she was also an atheist, was at least more sympathetic to religious ethics than most other philosophers of the time – she was really an Aristotelian, the forerunner of the kind of virtue ethics that Alasdair MacIntyre would later practise so influentially.

Nothing in my education thus far had prepared me for this. Yet it was a glorious experience, thrilling, bracing, mind-expanding. I loved every moment of it, and learned some of the most important truths I ever encountered. I discovered that university was a place where you listened respectfully to views radically opposed to your own, in the knowledge that others would listen respectfully to yours.

The late Abba Eban, Foreign Secretary of Israel, was educated at Cambridge, and on one occasion, when he returned to speak there, began: 'It was here that I learned the integrity, honesty and love of truth . . . that have been such a disadvantage to me in my political career!' He was right, at more than one level. But that is the real gift of a university education – a willingness to hear ideas quite different from those that you have heard until now, the courage to take them seriously, not necessarily agreeing with them but at least entering the mindset of those who think that way, the willingness also to expose your own ideas to critical scrutiny, and not feel threatened thereby, but rather enlarged. Certainly that is what I felt.

That was safe space, protected space, space where there were clear intellectual ground rules, where you spoke civilly, argued rationally and listened respectfully, and where you emerged at the end of the day knowing that you could face all the challenges adult life would throw at you, without flinching and without fear. This was and is the collaborative pursuit of truth.

So I was deeply disturbed when in 2001 our youngest daughter, then studying at the London School of Economics, came home one night in tears. She had attended an anti-globalisation rally that quickly degenerated into an assault first against America, then against Israel, then against Jews. She said to me, 'Dad, they hate us.' That this could happen in the twenty-first century was deeply shocking.

Since then, university campuses throughout the West have become places of swirling intolerance of a kind I never thought I would see in my lifetime. Take Balliol College Oxford, a college that has provided Britain with three prime ministers, five Nobel laureates, and such famous thinkers as Adam Smith, Gerard Manley Hopkins and Aldous Huxley.

In October 2017 its students decided to ban the Christian Union from its Freshers' Fair, on the grounds that the presence of a Christian might be 'alienating' for members of non-Christian faiths and, as such, constitute a 'micro-aggression'. The organiser of the fair said that Christianity's historic use as 'an excuse for homophobia and certain forms of neo-colonialism' meant that students might feel 'unwelcome' in their new college if the Christian Union had a stall. The presence of a representative from the Christian Union could cause 'potential harm' to the incoming students. So great was the outcry that the decision was reversed within days, but the fact that the ban was mooted in the first place is deeply shocking.

In 2019, the vice-chancellor of Cambridge University defended the decision of the Divinity Faculty to rescind its offer of a visiting fellowship to Canadian psychologist Jordan Peterson. The reason, as I noted earlier in the introduction to this book, was that a photograph had surfaced of Professor Peterson putting his arm around a man wearing a T-shirt bearing the words 'proud Islamophobe'. The photograph had been taken to signal Jordan Peterson's endorsement of that slogan.

This was an absurd proposition. Anyone who has given a public lecture under circumstances such as those at which the photograph was taken knows that at the end of the evening, dozens of people, sometimes hundreds, want to be photographed with the speaker. In this case, many had paid to do so. The speaker is barely aware of what is going on, and certainly has no time to take in what particular slogan appears on which particular T-shirt. Selfies taken under such circumstances are not endorsements. They are certainly not grounds for dis-inviting a scholar like Peterson, whose work is dedicated to exploring the roots of hatred through the study of archetypes, religious narratives and Jungian psychoanalysis. It felt to me like a regression to the time when, in 1745, David Hume was denied the Chair in Moral Philosophy at Edinburgh University on the grounds that he was suspected of being an atheist. I had hoped we had moved on since then.

A cluster of concepts that has invaded Western university campuses has had the cumulative effect of putting at risk academic freedom and the role of the University as the arena of intellectual diversity, reasoned argument, civil debate, respectful listening and the collaborative pursuit of truth.

One of these concepts is that of *micro-aggression* – meaning a slight, trivial, inconsequential piece of speech or behaviour that might cause offence, even though it was not intended to. As Bradley Campbell and Jason Manning point out in their book *The*

Rise of Victimhood Culture, this is a curious concept. On the one hand it involves a liability to take offence, which belongs traditionally to an *honour* as opposed to a *dignity* culture (responding to insults is a feature of honour cultures; dignity cultures encourage people not to take things personally). On the other, it is not the person who feels slighted who takes action. Instead, he or she puts pressure on the university authorities, a third party, to do so; a feature of a *dignity* as opposed to an *honour* culture.[1] In any case, it is hard to see how the concept of micro-aggression can be made morally coherent. If I do not intend to offend you, how can I be held guilty for disturbing your hypersensitivity that reads into my words something that was neither meant nor would have been so understood by most people?

Another key concept is *safe space*, that is, a place where one will not have to confront views that you might find personally distressing. Some universities go to extremes. In an essay in the *New York Times* Judith Shulevitz described one such case: the environment created for students at Brown University attending a debate on whether or not the United States constitutes a 'rape culture'.[2] The organisers of the debate were concerned that some of the students might be distressed by the feminist Wendy McElroy's argument, so they organised a space where anyone who felt distressed could recuperate. They equipped a room with cookies, colouring books, bubbles, Play-Doh, calming music, pillows, blankets, and a video of frolicking puppies, together with staff members trained to deal with trauma. One student who sought out the safe space explained, 'I was feeling bombarded by a lot of viewpoints that really go against my dearly and closely held beliefs.'[3]

Clearly there is something caring and therapeutic about this, but it is not without its dangers. As Shulevitz herself noted, 'Once you designate some spaces as safe, you imply that the rest are unsafe.' If so, you can claim that they should be made safer by banning views that are coherent but controversial and outside the consensus. There is 'concept creep' at work here: from self-defining groups seeking a protected space in which to meet, to imposing their standards on the university as a whole, to the university administration centrally enforcing those standards.[4] One student at Columbia University, Adam Shapiro, refused to take part in a university-wide safe space exercise, arguing that 'kindness alone won't allow us to gain more insight into truth', and 'I don't see how you can have a therapeutic space that's also an intellectual space.'

One practical result of these ideas is the growing practice of *no-platforming* – essentially, the banning of certain speakers from university campuses on the grounds that they hold opinions with which some or other group of students disagrees. Some of the most famous campaigners against prejudice in our time have, in the past decade, been banned from speaking at universities in Britain: feminists like Germaine Greer, Julie Bindel and Suzanne Moore, gay activist Peter Tatchell, anti-racist activist Nick Lowles, and Iranian communist Maryam Namazie. Their sin? Not to have embraced the particular cause-of-the-day, not least because it may conflict with the no-less-genuine cause of yesterday.[5]

To be sure, free speech has limits, and these are specified in the law of the land. Among the kinds of speech not protected by the First Amendment in the United States, for example, is speech that incites imminent lawless action. In *Chaplinsky v. New Hampshire* (1942) the Supreme Court held that under certain circumstances 'fighting words' were unprotected, that is, speech that would tend to provoke an immediate breach of the peace, i.e. violence. In Britain, Section 4 of the Public Order Act 1986 makes it an offence for a person to use threatening, abusive or insulting words or behaviour that causes, or is likely to cause, another person harassment, alarm or distress. Abusive, racist or inflammatory speech has no place on campus because it has no place in society as a whole. But the fact that a speaker may articulate, reasonably and respectfully, views with which some of the audience disagrees cannot be sufficient reason to deny such a person a platform. To do so is not only a clear and present danger to freedom of speech; it is a betrayal of the mission of the university itself. 'Universities have to be bastions of freedom of thought and research', writes Sir Anthony Seldon of Buckingham University, 'or they perish.'[6]

No-platforming, safe spaces and similar behaviours, isolated at first, have grown rapidly since around 2013, the point at which Generation Z (born in or after 1995) first started attending college. The irony is immense. In some respects, obviously, tolerance has won many important battles, in relation to respect for gender and sexual orientation in particular. Yet after several decades of non-judgementalism, moral relativism and expressive individualism, we now have in their place judgementalism and moral absolutism, based on something as primordial as group identity. The new intolerance is ugly and regressive.

Jeff McMahan, White's Professor of Moral Philosophy at Oxford, together with moral philosopher Professor Peter Singer of Princeton and Dr Francesca Minerva, a bioethicist at the University of Ghent, have come together to create *The Journal of Controversial Ideas*, an academic publication that will publish peer-reviewed articles, but will do so anonymously, so that their authors are protected against backlash, protest and dismissal. That such a journal had to be created is eloquent testimony to the mood of threat that academics feel at the highest level. In McMahan's own words, 'There is a real climate of intimidation at universities that makes people fearful of speaking out on controversial issues.' People are scared of doing so 'because they are frightened of threats to their career and even their physical well-being'.[7]

Gerard Baker, opinion columnist at *The Times*, recently wrote a fascinating piece about attending his daughter's graduation from Oberlin College in Ohio, famous for being the first college to admit women and black students in the mid-nineteenth century. Lamenting the current limiting of its horizons, he sensed 'a sharp narrowing in the willingness of students (and many academics) to think beyond what makes them comfortable'. He decried no-platforming and safe spaces, and intolerance of intellectual diversity. The combined effect, he wrote, 'is that American universities are producing battalions of automatons, barely human beings, programmed to think alike in their ambitions and in their ideas'.[8] Harsh words, yet all the more telling because they come from someone completely outside the world of academia.

How did this happen? The ideal of the university used to be of a moral community, collectively engaged in the collaborative pursuit of truth. To be sure, doubtless it often fell far below that standard. But the very idea of the university as a moral space has become attenuated, and in its place – as with society as a whole – come the values of the market (the university as a production-line of career-enabling qualifications) and the state (the university as the arena of a struggle for power).

When seen in terms of the market, the university ceases to be induction into the community of scholars and the intellectual heritage of humankind, and becomes a commodity to be purchased, a degree that will result in a better job and a higher salary. And since students pay the price, they can to some extent determine what is offered.

When seen in terms of power, the logic of the university is recalibrated. Now power lies in the hands of those who can mobilise the maximum amount of support in threatening to accuse university authorities of riding roughshod over students' sensibilities. Indignation becomes a potent political weapon when power prevails over the ethos of learning.

The whole cluster of values on which the university is built begins to seem fragile. One development in particular proved to be fateful: the idea that gained force between the 1930s and the 1960s that moral language is a disguised form of expression of emotion. Saying that something is good or that such-and-such an act is right meant no more than, 'I approve of this; do so likewise.'[9] This placed emotion at the heart of the moral life, and it is not surprising that it has reappeared in our time, with the inevitable corollary that if moral judgements are no more than statements of personal feeling, then there are no serious moral arguments to be had. You can't argue with an emotion. You either feel it or you don't. And emotions, since they can be assailed, need to be protected. Hence the entire vocabulary of safe space.

Greg Lukianoff and Jonathan Haidt have taken this idea further in their book on the threat to academic freedom: *The Coddling of the American Mind*. They have subtitled the book *How Good Intentions and Bad Ideas Are Setting Up a Generation for Failure*.[10] They take as their reference point Cognitive Behavioural Therapy, one of the most effective forms of therapy today.[11] They note that everything Cognitive Behavioural Therapy is designed to minimise, contemporary campus politics is designed to maximise, with great potential harm.

So, for example, students are encouraged to engage in *mind reading*, attributing thoughts to speakers who may have no such idea in mind. They *catastrophise*, believing that terrible events are about to happen. They *label*, seeing individuals in stereotyped form. They engage in *dichotomous thinking*: you are either on my side or the other side. There is no nuance, no complexity, just with-me or against-me. They *over-generalise*, seeing a universal law, instead of an isolated occurrence. And so on.

Cognitive Behavioural Therapy achieves extraordinary success because it teaches the exact opposite. Don't mind-read: don't think you know what others are thinking. Don't catastrophise: it isn't that bad. Don't label: everyone is different. Don't dichotomise: life isn't always either/or. Don't over-generalise: this may be an exception, not the rule. So for Lukianoff and Haidt there is bad psychology at work, not just a threat to academic freedom. It will, they say, damage students' ultimate capacity to function in the world.

I must confess, though, that I am yet more disturbed than Lukianoff and Haidt, because I see what is happening on British and American campuses not merely in terms of emotions but also in terms of its historical precedents. In 1927 a French intellectual, Julien Benda, published a book entitled *La Trahison des Clercs*, 'The Treason of the Intellectuals'. In it he said that Western civilisation had once lived by high ideals, always falling short, to be sure, but always aspiring to them. Now, he said, 'our age is indeed the age of the *intellectual organisation of political hatreds*. It will be one of its chief claims to notice in the moral history of humanity.'[12]

In 1933, all Jews were summarily dismissed from all German university positions. Notoriously, Martin Heidegger, one of the most original and important philosophers of the twentieth century, enthusiastically put this ruling into place, including dismissing one of his own most respected teachers.[13] There seems, as far as I can see, to have been no public protest by non-Jewish intellectuals or academics.

The Jews were excluded because it was believed that Jews and Judaism had corrupted German culture. More than eighty years earlier, Richard Wagner had published a pamphlet along these lines, 'Das Judenthum in der Musik' ('Jewishness in Music', 1850), in which he spoke of 'the involuntary repellence possessed for us by the nature and personality of the Jews, so as to vindicate that instinctive dislike which we plainly recognise as stronger and more overpowering than our conscious zeal to rid ourselves thereof'. Jews offended German sensibilities. This became the politically correct line in German artistic and intellectual circles, and none dared speak out.

Heidegger himself was an enthusiastic member of the Nazi Party, for which he never subsequently expressed remorse. Various attempts were later made to whitewash, explain away or minimise his antisemitism, but these were refuted by the publication in 2014 of his 'black notebooks', which revealed, in the words of the *Guardian*, 'Antisemitism at the core of his philosophy'.[14] Heidegger himself, in 1929, before Hitler's rise to power, wrote that the fight against Jewishness was the defining struggle of the age: 'either we will replenish our *German* spiritual life with genuine native forces and educators, or we will once and for all surrender it to the growing Judaisation in a broader and narrower sense'.[15]

In Frankfurt, until 1811, there was a ghetto in which all Jews were required to reside. They were confined to the ghetto every Sunday and Christian holiday, in case, catching sight of one on the way to or from church, their presence might offend a Christian. The connecting factor in all three instances, of Wagner, Heidegger and the Frankfurt ghetto, is the idea that even the existence in my space of someone-not-like-me is offensive and threatening, whether to German music, German culture or the German Sunday. That is what happens when we exercise our right not to be offended. Our safe space is created by confining someone else to the ghetto, or worse.

Here we come to the heart of the matter, because safe space to some is very unsafe space to others. As Santayana said in slightly different words: what we forget, we repeat.

Antisemitism, sad to say, has returned to British and American campuses. In a 2017 survey undertaken by the National Union of Students, 28 per cent of Jewish students said they had experienced personal abuse, and of these, two-thirds believed that there was an antisemitic element involved. Almost half said they would feel uncomfortable attending an event of the National Union of Students, and 65 per cent believed that the Union would not respond appropriately to allegations of antisemitism if they arose.[16] This is a significant breakdown of trust in an institution that should be representing all students.

In 2010, speaking at the Oxford Union, Israel's Deputy Foreign Minister Danny Ayalon was interrupted with shouts of 'Slaughter the Jews'.[17] In 2018 a Jewish student centre in Oxford was twice targeted with racist messages.[18] In 2019 a Jewish medical student at the University of Dundee who had asked not to be forced to take an examination on the Sabbath was told by a professor that she was 'not doing your people any favours, as we will think twice about taking anyone with a Jewish name in future'.[19]

In a 2019 article Cathy Elliott, a teacher at University College London, reported that, of Jewish students who responded to a question from the college's Jewish Society, 72 per cent had experienced antisemitism on campus, including 'racial slurs, antisemitic tropes and conspiracy theories, hurtful remarks and "jokes" about the Holocaust and Nazis, remarks about their appearance, and physical and verbal aggression and bullying'.[20] Classic antisemitic myths, from the Blood Libel to the Protocols of the Elders of Zion, are being updated and recycled. A university environment in which some of the worst prejudices in history can reappear is not a healthy one, morally or intellectually.

The Greek city state of Athens was the first human experiment in democracy. Yet barely a century later, as mentioned earlier, the worthy citizens of Athens sentenced Socrates to death for corrupting the young by teaching them to ask questions. That was an early example of what can happen when a group exercises a right not to be offended. Their rights are purchased at the expense of someone else's right, or in Socrates' case, his life.

Democracy in and of itself is no guarantor of freedom of thought or speech. That is why academic freedom is so important – and that means freedom for all, equally.

*

There are many factors at work in the present assault on academic freedom, but undoubtedly one, as we have seen, is the loss of truth as a value. There is no such thing as truth, goes the postmodern mantra: there are only interpretations. There is no such thing as history; there are only narratives. The university, like every other social institution, is recast. It is no longer seen as a community of scholars in pursuit of truth; instead it is viewed as a system of power. In the past – so the theory goes – the strong exercised hegemony over the weak by teaching them to see the world in ways that perpetuate the existing hierarchy and its injustices. That hegemony must be exposed for what it is. In the new dispensation, there are only victims and oppressors, and if you are not on the side of the victims, you must be an oppressor. That is the moral blackmail currently used to curtail freedom of speech.

One of the scariest books I have ever read is Ed Husain's *The Islamist*.[21] Husain is a former member of the radical Islamist group Hizb ut-Tahrir. In the book, he gives a graphic description of how a handful of radicals were able to intimidate an entire college in East London, with thousands of students. It should be required reading for all of us. It turns out to be disturbingly easy to blackmail college authorities by threatening to expose them – in this case as racists or Islamophobes – and to ostracise and ultimately oust anyone who resists. The radicals were able to cast themselves as victims. Anyone who opposed them could therefore be portrayed as an oppressor, guilty therefore of our present culture's unforgiveable sin.

To take a different example: two professors at Yale, Erika and Nicolas Christakis, found themselves at the centre of controversy for suggesting that the university should not be directly engaged in regulating what costumes students might wear for Halloween, presumably holding that since Halloween celebrations were not formal university activities but voluntary events organised by the students themselves, it should be for the students to decide. Erika, a lecturer at the Yale Child Study Center, specifically invited the students to deliberate on the matter themselves. 'Talk to each other,' she said. 'Free speech and the ability to tolerate offence are the hallmarks of a free and open society.' She was encouraging students to take responsibility, but a small group took her remarks the wrong way, reading them as suggesting that she was in favour of racist costumes. Having failed to understand the sensitivities of those who saw themselves as victims, it seemed to follow that she must be an oppressor. She and her husband Nicolas were eventually forced to resign as heads of one of Yale's residential colleges, and Erika Christakis left Yale entirely.[22]

Nietzsche rightly warned that when truth dies, all that is left is the will to power. The first place where this comes to light is the university, the home if not of truth itself then at least of the pursuit of truth. There are indeed injustices in society; there are prejudices; there are disadvantaged minorities. Their case must be heard and their battles fought. But that belongs to the domain of politics. It is not, and should not be, the domain of academia. There is a difference between truth and power. They have different logics and different homes.

The university must be the guardian of open debate, courteous argument, civil speaking and respectful listening. It must provide space for dissenting minds and for voices that challenge our comfortable assumptions. It must teach us to distinguish truth from falsehood, cogent argument from sophistry, the presentation of evidence from mere passion and persuasion. Never must it fall into the 'intellectual organisation of political hatreds' that reduced European universities to moral bankruptcy in the 1920s and 1930s, for if it does so it will have betrayed its mandate to protect our political freedoms by defending intellectual freedom.

The Talmud tells the following story about the third-century sages, Rabbi Yochanan and Resh Lakish. Resh Lakish had originally been a robber or highwayman, but was persuaded by Rabbi Yochanan, the leading sage in Israel at the time, to devote his life to Talmudic study. One day, in the house of study, they had a forceful disagreement on a point of legal interpretation. In his anger, Rabbi Yochanan said something demeaning to Resh Lakish, who was wounded by the jibe, became ill and eventually died.

Rabbi Yochanan grieved for him so much that the other sages feared for his sanity. They decided that he needed another study partner, and sent him Rabbi Elazar ben Pedat, known for his expertise in Jewish law. The passage then says:

> Whatever Rabbi Yochanan said, Rabbi Elazar said, 'There is a source that supports you.' Rabbi Yochanan said, 'Do you think you are like Resh Lakish? Whenever I would state something, Resh Lakish would raise twenty-four objections, to which I would respond with twenty-four rebuttals, with the result that we more fully understood the tradition. But all you say is, "There is a source that supports you," as if I did not know on my own that my view was correct!'[23]

Here in all its depth and pathos is the rabbinic ethic of the pursuit of knowledge as an extended argument between differing views within a fellowship of learning. The text is candid about the dangers. In the heat of the moment, Rabbi Yochanan said something he subsequently regretted, with devastating consequences. But he remained insistent that the search for truth is no less important than the truth itself, that scholarship thrives on challenge, that, as the sages put it, 'rivalry between scribes increases wisdom'. Merely to be reassured that you are correct adds nothing. Understanding comes from the willingness to be challenged.

Against the outer wall of the BBC's new Broadcasting House in London there stands a statue of George Orwell, and engraved above is a sentence he wrote, in very much the same spirit: 'If liberty means anything at all, it means the right to tell people what they do not want to hear.'[24]

There is a fundamental principle of Roman law, which states that justice requires *audi alteram partem*: 'Hear the other side.' No institution that denies a hearing to the other side can be a vehicle for justice, the furtherance of knowledge or the pursuit of truth.

13

Two Ways of Arguing

Speaking to young leaders at a seminar in Chicago on 29 October 2019, Barack Obama launched an unusually fierce attack on the political culture that has developed in the West in recent years, particularly the use of social media as a political weapon. He criticised its use by people to show how 'woke' they are – how ultrasensitive to social justice issues – by condemning others online.

'This idea of purity, and that you're never compromised, and you're always politically woke – you should get over that quickly,' he said, and continued: 'The world is messy. There are ambiguities. People who do really good stuff have flaws. People who you are fighting may love their kids, and share certain things with you.'[1] In other words, social and political issues are complex and multifaceted. Not every issue is a clash between right and wrong. Sometimes it is between right and right, between two strong but incompatible ideals. Something similar applies to people, too. Even the good have failings; even the bad have saving graces.

Obama said,

> I do get a sense sometimes now among certain young people, and this is accelerated by social media – there is this sense sometimes of the way of me making changes is to be as judgemental as possible about other people, and that's enough.
>
> If I tweet or hashtag about how you didn't do something right or used the wrong verb, then I can sit back and feel pretty good about myself. Did you see how woke I was, I called you out . . . That's not activism. That's not bringing about change. If all you're doing is casting stones, you're probably not going to get that far.

Obama was speaking here from experience. Genuine political activity demands direct personal involvement. His own earliest political engagement was as a community organiser in Chicago.

The reaction to these remarks was significant. Inevitably some approved, some didn't. What was interesting was that the divide did not coincide with political orientation. It had to do with age. By and large the boomers (born between 1946 and 1964) and Generation X (born between 1965 and 1980) tended to agree with the former president, while Millennials (born between 1981 and 1994) and Generation Z (born from 1995 onward) did not. For the younger age group, social media is a natural forum of politics and a genuine mode of engagement. As one writer in the *New York Times* put it, 'Old, powerful people often seem to be more upset by online criticism than they are by injustice.'[2] For young people, social media represent 'the only platform many of us have, to talk about the causes we care about'.

As for Barack Obama himself, he is clearly sympathetic to many of the causes taken up by those who see themselves as 'woke': the plight of the poor, the unemployed, ethnic minorities and LGBT communities. What he was saying, though, is that you cannot bring about change in a free society by indignation, condemnation, character assassination and self-righteousness, all communicated by social media. You change the world by changing people, and you change people by engaging with them, recognising that they too are people with values and ideals of their own.

That is what the change-agents themselves say. Simon Fanshawe, founder of Stonewall, stated that same-sex marriage was achieved 'by talking to people who don't agree with us'.[3] Patrisse Khan-Cullors, one of the founders of Black Lives Matter, wrote in *How We Fight White Supremacy*, 'People don't understand that organizing isn't going online and cussing people out or going to a protest and calling something out.' It is a matter of grassroots engagement.[4]

Loretta Ross, an African-American academic and activist on women's issues, racism and human rights, has also argued against the call-out culture of shaming by social media. There is, she says, a much more effective way to build social justice movements: 'they happen in person, in real life'. She cites the example of the work she did to de-programme incarcerated rapists in the 1970s. By talking about her own experience of being raped, she created an environment in which the men were able to open up about their own experiences of assaulting or being assaulted. They went on to create Prisoners Against Rape, America's first anti-sexual assault programme led by men.[5]

Janice Turner, writing in *The Times*, argued that 'lurid threats, fear-mongering, the bloody debris of ravaged reputations, only shuts mouths – it doesn't change minds'. It creates an environment of fear and intimidation not unlike those that have existed under totalitarian regimes. To be sure, your liberty is not at stake, but your name, your standing and your job may be. It can be thrilling, she says, to start a 'Twitter pile-on'. You begin a movement to denounce X or delegitimate Y and soon thousands join. 'It resembles solidarity and a mass movement: all those people agree with me! Yet each is sitting alone, atomised, pressing a "like" button. In a moment, this two-minute hate will be forgotten as another target hoves into view.'[6]

David Brooks in the *New York Times* has argued that the politics of wokeness is almost guaranteed *not* to bring about change. It encourages people to see injustice in maximalist terms, as something drastic, overwhelming. It leaves no room for nuance, subtlety, mitigating factors, other points of view. It is expressive but not practical. 'It doesn't inspire action; it freezes it. To be woke is first and foremost to put yourself on display. To make a problem seem massively intractable is to inspire separation – building a wall between you and the problem – not a solution.'[7]

What ultimately is at stake between those who agreed and those who disagreed with Barack Obama? It is about more than whether social media can bring about political change. It is about whether politics has space for ambiguity and complexity. Do I owe anything by way of respect to those who disagree with me?

Can we acknowledge that our allies have faults and our opponents have virtues? Is politics about I–Thou relationships, or is it only about power? Are we all, left and right, progressive and conservative, part of a single overarching moral community? Do we acknowledge the things that unite us or do we focus only on what divides us? How, in any complex society, do we structure disagreement?

I want in this chapter to make a fundamental distinction between two kinds of argument, and to suggest what it is to live graciously with those with whom we disagree. The case I make here comes from a Jewish perspective, but I am confident that other faiths and traditions will have their own way of arriving at a similar conclusion.

*

Judaism is unusual in that virtually all its canonical texts are woven through with arguments. In the Bible, Abraham, Moses, Jeremiah and Job all argue extensively with God. In Midrash, rabbis argue with one another on the basis of the principle that there are seventy 'faces' or interpretations of every text. In the Mishnah the rabbis argue about Jewish law and in the Gemara they argue about the arguments of the Mishnah.

Every later text comes with its commentaries and counter-commentaries. In the twelfth century Moses Maimonides did the most daring thing of all: he wrote a code of law with all the arguments removed. This generated more arguments than any other text for the next eight hundred years until today. Other people have conversations. Jews have arguments.

Inevitably, though, the rabbis reflected on the nature of argument itself. Were all arguments good? Were all equally valid? Were there some arguments that were destructive and dangerous? In clarifying their thoughts, they came up with a major distinction, between what they called an *argument for the sake of heaven*, and one that they held not to have been for the sake of heaven.

Their classic example of an argument for the sake of heaven was the relationship between the two rabbinical schools, those of Hillel and Shammai, in the first century BCE. Hillel in particular embodied the sages' ideal of a scholar. This is how they characterised the disputes between the two schools:

> For three years there was a dispute between the schools of Shammai and Hillel. The former claimed, 'The law is in agreement with our views,' and the latter insisted, 'The law is in agreement with our views.' Then a voice from heaven (*bat kol*) announced, 'These and those are the words of the living God, but the law is in accordance with the school of Hillel.'
>
> Since both 'these and those are the words of the living God', why was the school of Hillel entitled to have the law determined in accordance with their rulings? Because they were kindly and modest, they studied their own rulings and those of the school of Shammai, and were even so humble as to mention the teachings of the school of Shammai before their own.[8]

The concept of 'argument for the sake of heaven' allowed the sages to reframe disagreement as a unifying, not just divisive, force. That is implicit in the radical idea that each of two opposing opinions can represent 'the words of the living God'.

This suggests an alternative to the principle of Aristotelian logic, the 'law of contradiction' that states, 'Either p or not-p': either an assertion is true or false. Not necessarily so, say the sages. Two contrary propositions may both be true, from different perspectives, or at different times, or under different circumstances. That both are true follows from the fact that they are both interpretations of a biblical verse. Both therefore represent 'the words of the living God'. And because God grants his people the authority to interpret his word, both views are mandated, though only one can actually become law. God gives his blessing to a multiplicity of perspectives and thus creates the possibility of non-zero-sum disagreement. Several views may be true, even if only one is authoritative as law.

The yet deeper point is that the greatest minds know that theirs is not the only truth. The school of Hillel knew that more than one interpretation can be given. That is why they studied the views of their opponents alongside, and even before, their own. They were 'kindly and modest' because they realised that truth is not an all-or-nothing affair. It is a conversation, scored for a multiplicity of voices. The intellectual arrogance of knowing that you are right, your opponents wrong, is ruled out from the beginning. In the search to know what God wants of us, here, now, every voice is part of the argument, and the argument itself is as important as its outcome.

This therefore was the paradigm of an argument for the sake of heaven. What was the opposite, an argument not for the sake of heaven? Here the sages looked at the biblical episode in which Korach challenges Moses and Aaron's leadership of the people. Here is the text from the book of Numbers:

> Korah son of Izhar, the son of Kohath, the son of Levi, and certain Reubenites – Dathan and Abiram, sons of Eliab, and On son of Peleth – took men and rose up against Moses . . . They came as a group to oppose Moses and Aaron and said to them, 'You have gone too far! The whole community is holy, every one of them, and the Lord is with them. Why then do you set yourselves above the Lord's assembly?' (Num. 16:1–3).

Korach was a populist, one of the first in recorded history, and populism has re-emerged in the West, as it did in the 1930s, posing great danger to the future of freedom. What links populism on the one hand, and the phenomenon of 'wokeness' discussed by Barack Obama on the other, is that they are both binary, both extreme. Both divide the world into good and evil, black and white with no shades of grey. Both see themselves as the oppressed and their opponents as the oppressors. They see no saving grace on the other side.

Populism is the politics of anger.[9] It makes its appearance when there is widespread discontent with political leaders, when people feel that heads of institutions are working in their own interest rather than that of the general public, when there is a widespread loss of trust and a breakdown of the sense of the common good.

People come to feel that the distribution of rewards is unfair: a few gain disproportionately and the many stay as they are, or lose out. There is also a feeling that the country they once knew has been taken away from them, which might be because of the undermining of traditional values, or because of large-scale immigration.

Discontent takes the form of rejection of the current political and cultural elites. Populist politicians claim that they, and they alone, are the true voice of the people. The existing leaders are sharing out the rewards among themselves, indifferent to the suffering of the masses. Populists stir up resentment against the establishment. They are deliberately divisive and confrontational. They promise strong leadership that will give the people back what has been taken from them.

In 2017, support for populist parties throughout Europe was running at around 35 per cent, the highest level since the late 1930s. Parties of the far right gained power in Poland and Hungary, and made a strong showing in Austria, France and Holland. In Southern Europe, in countries like Spain and Greece, populism tends to be of the Left. Regardless of what form it takes, when populism is on the rise, tyranny is around the corner.[10] Human rights are dispensed with. The public grants the strong leader exceptional powers: so it was in the 1930s with Franco, Hitler and Mussolini. People are willing to sacrifice their freedom for the promised utopia, and to tolerate great evils against whichever scapegoat the leader chooses to blame for the nation's problems.

The Korach rebellion was a populist movement, and Korach himself an archetypal populist leader. Listen carefully to what he said about Moses and Aaron: 'You have gone too far! The whole community is holy, every one of them, and the Lord is among them. Why then do you exalt yourselves above the assembly of the Lord?' (Num. 16:3).

These are classic populist claims. First, implies Korach, the establishment, represented by Moses and Aaron, is corrupt. Moses has been guilty of nepotism in appointing his own brother as High Priest. He has kept the leadership roles within his immediate family instead of sharing them out more widely. Second, Korach presents himself as the people's champion. The whole community, he says, is holy. There is nothing special about you, Moses and Aaron. We have all seen God's miracles and heard his voice. We all helped build his Sanctuary. Korach is posing as the democrat – so that he can become the autocrat.

Next, he and his fellow rebels mount an impressive campaign of *fake news* – anticipating events of our own time. We have to infer this indirectly. When Moses says to God, 'I have not taken so much as a donkey from them, nor have I wronged any of them' (Num. 16:15), it is clear that he has been accused of just that: exploiting his office for personal gain. When he says, 'This is how you will know that the Lord has sent me to do all these things and that it was not my own idea' (Num. 16:28), it is equally clear that he has been accused of representing his own decisions as the will and word of God.

Most blatant is the post-truth-style claim of Datham and Aviram: 'Isn't it enough that you have brought us up out of a land flowing with milk and honey to kill us in the wilderness? And now you want to lord it over us!' (Num. 16:13). This is the most tendentious speech in the Torah. It combines false nostalgia for Egypt as a 'land flowing with milk and honey', replacing their slavery there with the image of God's promised plenty for them in the Holy Land, blaming Moses for the report of the spies, and accusing him of holding on to leadership for his own personal prestige – all three outrageous lies.

Nahmanides was undoubtedly correct[11] when he says that such a challenge to Moses' leadership would have been impossible at any earlier point. Only in the aftermath of the episode of the spies, when the people realised that they would not see the Promised Land in their lifetime, could discontent be stirred by Korach and his assorted fellow-travellers. They felt they had nothing to lose. Populism is the politics of disappointment, resentment and fear.

For once in his life, Moses acted autocratically, putting God, as it were, to the test:

> This is how you shall know that the Lord has sent me to do all these works; it has not been of my own accord: If these people die a natural death, or if a natural fate comes on them, then the Lord has not sent me. But if the Lord creates something new, and the ground opens its mouth and swallows them up, with all that belongs to them, and they go down alive into Sheol, then you shall know that these men have despised the Lord (Num. 16:28–30).

This dramatic effort at conflict resolution by the use of force (in this case, a miracle) failed completely in its aim of quelling discontent. The ground did indeed open up and swallow Korach and his fellow rebels, but the people, despite their terror, were unimpressed. 'On the next day, however, the whole congregation of the Israelites rebelled against Moses and against Aaron, saying, "You have killed the people of the Lord"' (Num. 17:6). God may have fulfilled Moses' plea, but in the eyes of the people, the plea itself was autocratic and wrong.

What is even more striking is the way the sages framed the conflict. Instead of seeing it as a black-and-white contrast between rebellion and obedience, they insisted on the validity of argument in the public domain. They said that what was wrong with Korach and his fellows was not that they argued with Moses and Aaron, but that they did so 'not for the sake of heaven'. The schools of Hillel and Shammai, however, argued for the sake of heaven, and thus their argument had enduring value.[12]

What matters in Judaism is why the argument was undertaken and how it was conducted. What is the fundamental difference between an argument for the sake of heaven and one that is not? Following Meiri and other medieval commentators, the sages were distinguishing between an argument for the sake of *truth* and one for the sake of *victory*. Hillel and Shammai were arguing for the sake of truth, the determination of God's will. Korach, who challenged Moses and Aaron for leadership, was arguing for the sake of victory: he wanted to be a leader too.

In argument for the sake of truth, if you win, you win, but if you lose, you also win, because being defeated by the truth is the only defeat that is also a victory. We are enlarged thereby. As Rabbi Shimon ha-Amsoni said: 'Just as I received reward for the exposition, so I will receive reward for the retraction.'[13] In an argument for the sake of victory, if you lose, you lose, but if you win, you also lose, for by diminishing your opponents, you diminish yourself. Moses won the argument against Korach, but only at the cost of invoking a miracle in which the earth opened up and swallowed his opponents. Yet this did not end the argument. In this kind of confrontation, there is no benign outcome. You can only aim at minimising the tragedy.

The entire thrust of postmodernism, inspired by Marx, Nietzsche and Freud, is to develop a 'hermeneutics of suspicion' in which there is no truth, only victory. Every argument is a (concealed) exercise of power, an attempt to establish a 'hegemonic discourse'. Judaism rejects this idea, not because it is never true – in the case of an argument not for the sake of heaven, it is – but because we can tell when it is and when it isn't. There is such a thing as truth, and collaborative argument in pursuit of it. That is the basis of trust on which all genuine communication depends.

In his excellent short book, *What Is Populism?*, Jan-Werner Muller argues that the best indicator of populist politics is its delegitimisation of other voices. Populists claim that 'they and they alone represent the people'. Anyone who disagrees with them is 'essentially illegitimate'. Once in power, they silence dissent. Wokeness has the same argumentative structure. Those who hold attitudes or make remarks or use terminology outside the received woke norms are to be denounced, shamed, 'called out' or 'cancelled'. That is why the silencing of unpopular views on university campuses today, in the form of 'safe space', 'trigger warnings' and 'micro-aggressions', is so dangerous. When academic freedom dies, the death of other freedoms follows.

The divisiveness of modern politics and modern culture flows directly from the fact that we seem to have lost the sense of moral community that allowed people to feel that though their political views might be opposed, nonetheless they were part of the same nation, heirs to its history, sharing its fate, responsible for one another, engaged collectively in pursuit of the common good. This did not stop politics being abrasive, sometimes brutal. But it did mean that people recognised the humanity of their opponents, listened to them and recognised that other viewpoints had integrity.

It was that appeal to moral community, and ultimately to a common humanity, that made Martin Luther King Jr, Nelson Mandela and Yitzhak Rabin the great leaders they were. They sought not power but truth; not victory but healing. They recognised that argument is not a zero-sum game. It is not a matter of winners and losers but of collectively moving forward in our recognition of the injustices, hardships and prejudices that still exist, and of the humanity of those who suffer from them. It is not necessary to delegitimise, call out or cancel your opponents. It is better, simply, to persuade them.

Hence the power of Judaism's insistence on the legitimacy of 'argument for the sake of heaven'. Judaism does not silence dissent: on the contrary, it dignifies it. This was institutionalised in the biblical era, in the form of the prophets who spoke truth to power. In the rabbinic era it lived in the culture of argument evident on every page of the Mishnah, Gemara and their commentaries. In the contemporary State of Israel, argumentativeness is part of the very texture of its democratic freedom, in the strongest possible contrast to much of the rest of the Middle East.

A free society depends on the dignity of dissent. Judaism itself is predicated on this principle. That is what is happening in the biblical dialogues between heaven and earth, and the rabbinic dialogues between Hillel and Shammai and their descendants. Dismiss a contrary view and you impoverish the entire culture. The book of Job is not about whether Job is right or wrong in his complaint about the injustice he feels has been done to him. Its purpose is to show that he has the right to speak, to challenge God, to be heard and (in some sense) to be answered. William Safire, a political journalist, perceptively called his book on Job *The First Dissident*.

A healthy culture protects places that welcome argument and respect dissenting views. Enter them and you will grow, others will grow, and you will do great things together. But resist with all your heart and soul any attempt to substitute power for truth. And stay far from people, movements and parties that demonise their opponents. As Barack Obama said: 'If all you're doing is casting stones, you're probably not going to get that far.'

14

Victimhood

On 11 August 2017, the world's oldest man passed away, just a month short of his 114th birthday – making him one of the ten longest-lived men since modern record-keeping began. If you knew nothing else about him than this, you might expect to discover that he had led a peaceful life, spared of fear, grief and danger.

The actual truth is the opposite. The man in question was Yisrael Kristal, Holocaust survivor. Born in Poland in 1903, he survived four years in the Lodz ghetto, and was then transported to Auschwitz. In the ghetto, his two children died. In Auschwitz, his wife was killed. When Auschwitz was liberated, he was a walking skeleton weighing a mere 37 kilos. He was the only member of his family to survive.

He was raised as a religious Jew and stayed so all his life. When the war was over, with his entire world destroyed, he married again, this time to another Holocaust survivor. They had children. They moved to Israel and settled in Haifa. There he began again, setting up in the confectionery business, as he had done in Poland before the war. He made sweets and chocolate. He became an innovator. If you have ever had Israeli orange peel covered in chocolate, or liqueur chocolates shaped like little bottles and covered with silver foil, you are enjoying one of the products he originated. Those who knew him said he was a man with no bitterness in his soul. He wanted people to taste sweetness.

In 2016, at the age of 113, he finally celebrated his bar mitzvah. A hundred years earlier, this had proved impossible. At that point, his mother was dead and his father was fighting in the First World War. With an almost poetic sense of fittingness, Yisrael died on the eve of the Sabbath when we read in synagogue the eleventh chapter of Deuteronomy, with its commands to wear tefillin (phylacteries) and teach Torah to your children, 'so that you and your children may live long in the land that the Lord swore to your ancestors'.

Yisrael Kristal faithfully did both. On his bar mitzvah he joked that he was the world's oldest tefillin-wearer. He gathered his children, grandchildren and great-grandchildren under his tallit and said, 'Here's one person, and look how many people he brought to life. As we're all standing here under my tallit, I'm thinking: six million people. Imagine the world they could have built.'

This was an extraordinary man. His life sheds light on one of the most tantalising verses in the Pentateuch. Describing the death of Abraham, the text says that he 'breathed his last and died in good old age, old and satisfied' (Gen. 25:8). His is the most serene death in the Torah. Yet consider his life, fraught as it was with trial after trial.

To pursue the call of God, he had to say goodbye to his land, his birthplace and his father's house and travel to an unknown destination. Twice, famine forced him into exile, where his life was in danger. Promised countless children – as many as the dust of the earth and the stars of the sky – he nonetheless remained childless until old age. Then God told him to send away the son he had had by Sarah's handmaid Hagar. And if that trial were not heart-breaking enough, God then told him to sacrifice his only son with Sarah, Isaac, the one whom God had told him would be his spiritual heir and bearer of the covenant into the future.

Seven times promised a land, when Sarah died Abraham owned not a single square inch of territory in which to bury her, and had to entreat the Hittites to let him buy a field and burial cave. His was a life of disappointed hopes and delayed fulfilment. What kind of man was this that the Torah can say that he died 'in good old age, old and satisfied'?

I learned the answer to this question through a series of life-changing encounters with Holocaust survivors. They were among the strongest, most life-affirming people I have ever met. For years

I wondered how they were able to survive at all, having seen what they saw and known what they knew. They had lived through the deepest darkness ever to have descended on a civilisation.

Eventually I realised how they had done it. Almost without exception, when the war was over, they focused with single-minded intensity on the future. Strangers in a strange land, they built homes and careers, married and had children and brought new life into the world.

Often they did not talk about their experiences during the Shoah, even to their spouses, their children and their closest friends. This silence lasted, in many cases, for as long as fifty years. Only then, when the future they had built was secure, did they allow themselves to look back and bear witness to what they had suffered and seen. Some of them wrote books. Many of them went around schools, telling their story so that the Holocaust could not be denied. First they built a future. Only then did they allow themselves to remember the past.

That is what Abraham did. He had received three promises from God: children, a land, and the assurance that he would be the father, not of one nation but of many nations (Gen. 17:4–5). At the age of 137, he had one unmarried son, no land and no nations. Yet he uttered not a single word of complaint. It seems that he realised that God wanted him to act, not to wait for God to do the work for him.

So, when Sarah died, he bought the first plot in what would become the Holy Land, the field and cave of Machpelah. Then he instructed his servant to find a wife for Isaac, his son, so that he might live to see the first Jewish grandchildren. Lastly, in his old age, he married again and had six sons, who would eventually become progenitors of many nations. He did not, except briefly, sit and mourn the past. Instead he took the first steps towards building the future.

That, in his own way, is what Yisrael Kristal did – and that is how a survivor of Auschwitz lived to become the world's oldest man. He too died 'in good old age, old and satisfied'. This is a transformative idea. *To survive tragedy and trauma, first build the future. Only then, remember the past.*

There are real victims, and they deserve our empathy, sympathy, compassion and care. But there is a difference between being a victim and defining yourself as one. The first is about what happened to you. The second is about how you define who and what you are. The most powerful lesson I learned from these people I have come to know, people who are victims by any measure, is that, with colossal willpower, they refused to define themselves as such.

So when it came to making a series of programmes for the BBC entitled *Morality in the Twenty-First Century*, I felt I had to travel to Toronto to have a conversation with someone I had not met before but have mentioned already, Canadian psychologist Jordan Peterson, because of his resolute opposition to a victim culture, and his insistence – sadly rare these days – on young people taking responsibility for their own lives. He has become an iconic intellectual for millions of young people, as well as a figure of caricature and abuse by others who should know better. The great popularity of his podcasts – hours long and formidably intellectual – suggests that he has been saying something that many people feel a need to hear and are not adequately hearing from other contemporary voices.

During our conversation there was a moment of searing intensity. Peterson was talking about his daughter Mihkaila. At the age of six, she was found to be suffering from severe polyarticular juvenile idiopathic arthritis. Thirty-seven of her joints were affected. During her childhood and teen years, she had to have a hip replacement, then an ankle replacement. She was in acute, incessant pain. Describing her ordeal, Peterson's voice wavered, on the verge of tears. Then he said:

> One of the things we were very careful about and talked with her a lot about was to not allow herself to regard herself as a victim. And man, she had reason to be, to regard herself as a victim . . .

[but] as soon as you see yourself as a victim . . . that breeds thoughts of anger and revenge – and that takes you to a place that's psychologically as terrible as the physiological place. And to her great credit I would say this is part of what allowed her to emerge from this because she did eventually figure out what was wrong with her, and by all appearances fix it by about 90 per cent. It's unstable but it's way better because of the fact that she didn't allow herself to become existentially enraged by her condition . . . People have every reason to construe themselves as victims. Their lives are characterised by suffering and betrayal. Those are ineradicable experiences. [The question is] what's the right attitude to take to that – anger or rejection, resentment, hostility, murderousness? That's the story of Cain and Abel, [and] that's not good. That leads to Hell.[1]

When I heard this, I understood the connection that had led me to this man. His words immediately recalled the Holocaust survivors I had come to know. They were victims of one of the worst crimes against humanity in all of history. *Yet they did not see themselves as victims.* The survivors I knew looked forward with almost superhuman courage, built a new life for themselves, supported one another emotionally, and only many years later told their story, not for the sake of revisiting the past but for the sake of educating today's young people on the importance of taking responsibility for a more human and humane future.

How is this possible, I used to ask myself? How can you be a victim and yet not see yourself as a victim, without being guilty of denial, or deliberate forgetfulness, or wishful thinking?

The answer is that, uniquely – this is what makes us *Homo sapiens* – in any given situation we can look back or we can look forward. We can ask: 'Why did this happen?' That involves looking back for some cause in the past. Or we can ask, 'What then shall I do?' This involves looking forward, trying to work out some future destination, given this as our starting point.

There is a fateful difference between the two. I can't change the past. But I can change the future. Looking only back, I will see myself as an object acted on by forces largely beyond my control. Looking forward, I see myself as a subject, a choosing moral agent, deciding which path to take from here to where I want eventually to be. Both are legitimate ways of thinking, but one leads to resentment, bitterness, rage and a desire for revenge. The other leads to challenge, courage, strength of will and self-control. That is what Mikhaila Peterson and the Holocaust survivors represent: the triumph of choice over fate.

There *are* victims. There is injustice and oppression, inequality and exclusion, and in the past whole groups – Jews, blacks, gypsies, women, homosexuals, transsexuals – have found themselves subjugated, marginalised, ill-treated and ignored. Those injustices must be fought and ended. That is a given. Compassion, the emotion we feel towards victims, is among the constitutive elements of the moral sense. It defines what is best in the great ethical and religious traditions. Nothing should be taken as qualifying this emotion and the acts for good it evokes.

What is dangerous, though, is the *politicisation* of victimhood: its transfer from individuals to groups, and from there to the public square. In every age there are victims, and we must help them. 'Do not stand idly by the blood of your neighbour,' says the Bible. 'Learn to do right,' says Isaiah. 'Seek justice. Relieve the oppressed. Defend orphans. Plead for the widow.' What is new and dangerous is the *culture* of victimhood. It involves the blurring of the boundaries between the personal and the political. It has to do with what Philip Rieff called 'the triumph of the therapeutic'.

Recall that the liberal revolution of the 1960s was undertaken in the name of the individual. It was the individual who had rights; the individual who should be free to live as he or she chooses so long as there is no harm to others. Liberal politics at its best is, or aspires to be, class-, colour-, gender-, race- and religion-blind. The dominant strand in Western thought is that our ultimate focus is on the individual as such, prior to the identification of any attributes: male, female, black, white, rich, poor, Jew, Christian, believer, non-believer, it is the individual who has rights, freedom, a claim to dignity and access to justice.

Then came the 1970s when, at least in Britain, the dominant force was the trade union movement, and the 1980s, when Thatcherism, Reaganomics and economic liberalism held sway. Subsequently, though, class and wealth divisions became less prominent in politics. Other issues increasingly took their place. At first these were construed in terms of the individual, but eventually they came to be framed in terms of groups: first Jews, then African Americans, then women, then gays, now transgender individuals. Each sought equal rights before the law, which was entirely justified. The significant change, though, was that they defined themselves as targets of prejudice or victims of oppression. This was a fundamental shift from classical liberalism to something more like neo-Marxism: a worldview that sees the human condition as entirely defined by structures of power, and humanity itself divided into oppressors and victims. Rather than seeking recognition as individuals, they sought it as groups, defined now not in terms of socio-economic class, but in terms of primordial markers such as race, gender and sexual orientation. That became the basis of the identity politics we have discussed previously.

In the liberal state, individuals negotiated for the right to live as they choose so long as they do no harm to others. In the contemporary state, groups campaign for something never before held to be the business of politics: recognition, regard, self-esteem. Culture has become political. So has self-image. The traditional curriculum of canonical texts – the Bible, Shakespeare and the rest – is held to represent the hegemony of dead white males, and must therefore be set aside. This body of literature leads excluded groups to have a negative self-image, and this impacts on their life-chances. Marx had spoken about economic oppression. His latter-day successors speak about psychological oppression: our group underachieves because it is discriminated against, if not explicitly then implicitly. This is an offence against the right of each group to self-esteem. We are the victims, not of a crime, but of a culture. We are the new oppressed.

All this leads to a politics of competitive victimhood. We have been wronged. We are looked down on. We have a claim to what Bertrand Russell once called 'the superior virtue of the oppressed'. All this has truth to it. But it cannot become political without destroying the very basis of liberal democracy, which is built on the threefold separation between nation, group and individual: between state, civil society and private life. When individual feelings (negative self-image) become part of the self-definition of the group, and when groups call for remedial action by the state, then *identity politics* or *the politics of recognition* is born. This is at the heart of contemporary multiculturalism and constitutes its greatest danger. As Michael Walzer has written:

> The members of oppressed groups have been encouraged – mistakenly, I think – to believe themselves injured above all by the disrespect of the dominant others and to seek the signs of proper regard. But a permanent state of suspicion about the demeaning or malicious things that are about to be said or done is self-defeating. It leads too often to a dead-end politics of anger and resentment.[2]

A decent society is one in which people work to redress disadvantage and deprivation. There are marginalised groups; there are groups that have suffered greatly in the past. There is everything to be said for a politics that strives for equal opportunity and human dignity. But there is a great difference between a future-oriented politics and one that focuses on grievances of the past; between a culture that emphasises responsibility and one constructed around an ever-expanding notion of rights; between one that defines people as victims and one that helps genuine victims to recover their capacity for action and self-determination. Politics is about power and the distribution of resources. It is not about the psychology of self-esteem or the allocation of blame. When these boundaries are blurred, the result is deeply damaging to the good group-relations on which an ethnically and religiously diverse society depend.

*

In May 1944, at the age of sixteen, Edith Eger, together with her mother, father and sister Magda, and 12,000 other Jews from her town, Kosice, in Hungary, were first interned and then taken to Auschwitz. Her parents were killed immediately. When she asked an inmate of the concentration camp when she would see her mother again, the woman pointed to the smoke rising from a chimney in the distance, and said, 'She is burning there. Talk about her in the past tense.' Somehow Edith survived not only the horrors of Auschwitz but also the death march that killed almost all her companions. When she was eventually discovered by American GIs, lying beneath a pile of corpses, she had typhoid fever, pneumonia, pleurisy and a broken back.

She married a fellow patient at the hospital where she was recovering. Eventually she moved with her family to the United States, where she became a psychologist. But the trauma of Auschwitz remained, until at the age of fifty-three she returned there to confront her demons. Much later, at the age of ninety, vigorous and life-affirming, she wrote her autobiography, *The Choice*, which appeared in 2017 and became a bestseller. She is living testimony to the powerful assertion of Viktor Frankl, another survivor of Auschwitz, who said that in the death camps they took away every freedom except one: the freedom to decide how to respond. As Edith Eger's mother said to her as they were being transported to Auschwitz: 'Just remember, no one can take away from you what you've put in your mind.'

Suffering, Eger says in her book, is universal, but victimhood is optional.[3] 'There is a difference', she says, 'between victimisation and victimhood.' All of us are likely to be victimised at some stage. We will suffer abuse, injury, ill fortune or failure. We live exposed to forces beyond our control. Victimisation comes from the outside. But victimhood comes from the inside. 'No one can make you a victim but you.' We develop a particular kind of mindset, 'a way of thinking and being that is rigid, blaming, pessimistic, stuck in the past, unforgiving, punitive, and without healthy limits or boundaries'. We become 'our own jailors'.

Eger is emphatic in not blaming the victims – among them her own parents. As she says, victimisation comes from the outside, often in the form of forces we cannot control. But healing comes when we refuse the self-definition of victim. It was that refusal that kept her alive and that she tries to help her patients discover within themselves. Hence the title of her book. There is always a choice. Often we cannot choose what happens to us, but we can always choose how to react. We are never defined by events. To allow ourselves to be so defined is to hand sovereignty over our own lives to others. Eger, in contrast, asked how her own sufferings could enable her to help other sufferers. She used her own strength to inspire strength in them. She helped them on their own personal walk through the valley of the shadow of death. That was her *tikkun*, the word in Jewish mysticism that refers to the redemption of the past, the healing of a fractured world.

That, in large measure, is what morality is about.

I have used the word 'morality' throughout this book as if there were only one way for this key word to be understood. Clearly it isn't quite so. Their differing definitions of morality illustrate perhaps the single greatest difference between the Judeo-Christian mindset on the one hand, and the culture of ancient Greece on the other (though in truth both hold multiple potential definitions of the word). The Greeks believed in *moira* or *ananke*, blind, inexorable fate, often foretold by an oracle. Hence the story of Oedipus. Laius, Oedipus' father, is told by the Oracle that he will be killed and his place usurped by his son. To avoid this fate, the infant Oedipus is left chained to a rock to die. He is found, rescued and brought up by a humble family, not knowing who his true father is. He is told by the Oracle that he will kill his father and marry his mother. To avoid this, he leaves home. He meets a stranger. They argue, fight, and the stranger dies. The stranger is, of course, Laius. The power of the drama lies in the fact that everything the characters do to circumnavigate fate only brings them closer to its realisation. That is the essence of Greek tragedy. Human freedom is an illusion destined to be shattered on the unyielding rock of inevitability.

The Judeo-Christian ethic, by contrast, is about *guilt* and *responsibility*. Towards the end of his *God: A Biography* Jack Miles makes a fascinating distinction between Greek and Shakespearean tragedy. In Greek tragedy fate is determined by factors external to the agent, outside his or her control. In Shakespearean tragedy those factors are internal. They form a struggle in the mind of the hero. That is what makes Hamlet quite unlike Oedipus. In the case of Hamlet, the conflict lies within: between 'the native hue of resolution' and 'the pale cast of thought'. As Miles puts it: 'It is precisely the profound effect of the Bible on European society that explains why Shakespearean tragedy is as unlike Greek tragedy as it is.'

Shame and necessity give rise to a culture of *tragedy*. Guilt, repentance and responsibility give rise to one of *hope*. If we have free will, we are not slaves to fate. If at the heart of reality there is a forgiving presence, then we are not condemned by guilt. 'Penitence, prayer and charity avert the evil decree', goes one of the most famous Jewish prayers. There is no fate that is inevitable, no future pre-determined, no outcome we cannot avert. There is always a choice.

There are tragic cultures and there are hope cultures, and, though some combine elements of both, the two are ultimately incompatible. In hope cultures, we are agents. We choose. All depends on what we decide, and that cannot be known in advance. In tragic cultures, we are victims. We are acted on by forces beyond our control, and they will eventually defeat even the strongest. The only redemption of victimhood is to refuse that self-definition. In the long run no good can come of it, for it belongs to a world of tragedy. It divides us into victims and oppressors – and we are always the victims, while the others are the oppressors. Look at any conflict zone in the world and you will find that both sides see themselves as the victims, therefore innocent, and the others as the wrongdoers. That is a recipe for perpetual conflict and perennial disappointment. There is only resentment, rage and desire for revenge, all of which achieve nothing since all they do is provoke a reaction of attempted retaliation.

The choice of freedom brings the defeat of victimhood and the redemptive birth of hope.

15

The Return of Public Shaming

In 2015, Sir Tim Hunt, winner of the 2001 Nobel Prize in Physiology for his work on cell division, gave a talk at the World Conference of Science Journalists at Seoul, South Korea. Asked to speak about the contribution of women to science, he decided to begin with a joke: 'Let me tell you about my trouble with girls. Three things happen when they are in the lab. You fall in love with them. They fall in love with you. And when you criticise them, they cry.' He made it reasonably clear at the time that he was speaking in a spirit of levity. Immediately after these words, he said, 'But seriously . . .' and went on with his talk, focusing positively on the contribution of women to science.

However, his remarks were tweeted and went viral. The response was angry and negative. Hunt was forced to resign his position as honorary professor at University College London's Faculty of Life Sciences and as a member of the Royal Society's biological sciences awards committee. He was told that if he did not resign immediately, he would be sacked.

Several scientists subsequently came out in his defence. Women scientists spoke of how helpful he had been to them in their careers. His own wife, Mary Collins, was herself a distinguished scientist. But amid the firestorm caused by the viral media, it was impossible for either of them to fight back. Almost overnight he had become a pariah.

In his book *So You've Been Publicly Shamed*, Jon Ronson tells the story of Justine Sacco, director of corporate communications for the Internet firm IAC.[1] On 20 December 2013 she was on a flight from New York to Cape Town. During her layover at Heathrow, she sent out a series of Tweets intended to be humorous. One of them read, 'Going to Africa. Hope I don't get AIDS.

Just kidding. I'm white.' She waited half an hour for replies, but none came. The flight itself took eleven hours, during most of which she was asleep.

When she arrived, she discovered that during that time she had become the number-one trending topic on Twitter. She had lost her job. She had been denounced by media bloggers and celebrities throughout the world. During the eleven days between then and the end of December, she was Googled 1,220,000 times.

The new social media environment has made almost any kind of public comment exceptionally hazardous. As one journalist told Ronson, 'I suddenly feel with social media like I'm tiptoeing around an unpredictable, angry, unbalanced parent who might strike out at any moment. It's horrible.'[2]

Social media has, in effect, brought back public shaming, the kind of rough justice that occurred before the modern age, or may still occur in places where law enforcement is felt to be ineffective and vigilante groups enforce community norms without any formally constituted legal authority.

In one respect this new form of shaming can be important and positive. It allows people who might otherwise not have had the time, money or resources to bring to public attention behaviour that ought to be condemned. The cases of sexual harassment and paedophilia, following allegations against individuals such as film producer Harvey Weinstein, or priests in the Catholic Church, are a case in point. Both the public exposure and the shaming have been appropriate.

What the social media have done in such cases is to provide a voice for those who otherwise might not have had it, or who might have been intimidated by people or institutions with power and access to strong legal representation. Here the effect has been positive, empowering and morally consequential.

The problem with vigilante justice is that it follows no legal norms. There is no due process. The accused has little chance of presenting his or her case. There is no impartial procedure for deciding whether a wrong has been committed and, if so, what should be the appropriate punishment. Instead, there is mob rule. And once the mob has been let loose, it becomes difficult to distinguish between genuine cases of wrongdoing, and other accusations motivated by malice, or a desire for revenge, or some other less than fully moral cause.

David Brooks tells the story of Emily, part of the hard-core punk music scene in Richmond, Virginia. She was the girlfriend of a band member, travelling with him to a concert in Florida, when they received a call telling them that the concert had been cancelled because the boyfriend had been accused of sending a sexually explicit photograph to someone who had objected to him doing so. Eventually Emily herself turned against him and wrote a Facebook post denouncing him. He was dismissed from the band, lost his job and was thrown out of his apartment. Sometime later, in an unrelated incident, Emily herself was denounced for an act of cyber-bullying that had taken place ten years earlier, when she was at high school. Now she became the object of hate, was banned from the punk scene, and found herself traumatised and alone. Her whole life, she said, felt as if it were 'done and over' and as if she were 'a monster'. When the person who wrote the denunciation was asked whether he regretted it, he said that, to the contrary, it gave him a rush of pleasure. She deserved it, he said. 'I don't care if she's dead, alive, whatever.' When the interviewer began probing into his mind-set, he revealed that he had been abused by his father as a child.

Brooks's comment on this entire episode is that it shows how 'zealotry is often fuelled by people working out their psychological wounds'. When denunciation is done through social media, rather than by face-to-face encounter, 'you can destroy people without even knowing them'. He adds that 'there is no personal connection that allows apology and forgiveness'.[3]

That is very much the point. We can easily forget some of the most important distinctions in the moral life: between guilt cultures and shame cultures, and between retribution and revenge. The difference between them is fundamental and turns on the question: is justice personal or impersonal?

Shaming is an ancient response to wrongdoing that began long before the establishment of courts of law and judicial procedures. The primary unit in early times was not society as a whole but clans, groups, tribes. The logic of tribal conflict is that when a member of one group wrongs a member of another, the shame – the assault on the honour of the group – must be avenged. The second group takes revenge by harming a member of the first. This then starts a cycle of retaliation that is potentially without end. It may have been just such a cycle that demolished life on Easter Island. Recall the Montagues and the Capulets, the Corleones and the Tattaglias. To be sure, there were laws and courts in the eras of both of these imaginary conflicts, but they show how tribal loyalties can prove stronger than the power of impartial legal process. According to the French scholar René Girard, in *Violence and the Sacred*, religion began as a way of deflecting violence within the group, applying it to someone outside the group who then became the sacrificial victim, restoring in-group harmony.

That revenge culture is what the Hebrew Bible seeks to bring to an end, with what Albert Einstein called its 'almost fanatical love of justice'. People sometimes contrast what they call the Old Testament God of justice with the New Testament God of forgiveness. This is a regrettable error. The forgiveness in Christianity has its origins in the forgiveness set out in the Hebrew Bible. The first recorded instance of interpersonal forgiveness is Joseph's reconciliation with his brothers, who had earlier sold him as a slave. The most sacred day in the Hebrew calendar, Yom Kippur, the Day of Atonement, is the festival of divine forgiveness. Forgiveness and retribution belong together. They are not contrasts, but two aspects of the same moral vision.

Revenge is personal. I and my group have been wronged, therefore I and my group must do wrong to you in return. Retribution is impersonal. That is what justice is. It means that justice is no longer the Montagues against the Capulets but both of them under the impersonal, impartial bar of justice. Verdict and punishment are no longer the domain of the family of the victim, but rather of judges, the courts and the administration of justice.

So the reappearance of revenge as a force, courtesy of social media, is a massive social regression. So too is the re-emergence of a shame culture – public dishonouring without trial, due process, pleas in mitigation, proportionality and the possibility of forgiveness. The distinction between shame and guilt takes us back to a fascinating chapter in the intellectual history of the twentieth century.

After the Japanese attack on Pearl Harbor in 1941, the Americans realised that they were about to be forced into a war with a country whose culture they did not understand. So they asked one of their leading anthropologists, Ruth Benedict, to explain the Japanese to them. She did so, and her work was published after the war as *The Chrysanthemum and the Sword*.[4] One of the key distinctions she made was between the guilt culture of America, and a shame culture like Japan.

Guilt cultures conceive of morality as *a voice within* – the voice of conscience that tells us whether or not we have done wrong. Shame cultures think of morality as *an external demand* – what other people expect of us. To feel shame is to experience or imagine what one looks like in the sight of others who pass judgement on us. Shame cultures are other-directed. Guilt cultures are inner-directed.

Guilt cultures make a sharp distinction between the sinner and the sin. The act may be wrong, but the agent's integrity as a person remains intact. That is why guilt can be relieved by remorse, confession, restitution, and the resolve never to behave that way again. In guilt cultures there is repentance and forgiveness. Shame is not like that. It is a stain on the sinner that cannot be fully removed. A shame culture does not provide forgiveness; it offers something similar but different, namely appeasement, usually accompanied by an act of self-abasement. In a guilt culture it makes sense to confess your sins. In a shame culture it makes no sense at all – instead it becomes all-important to cover up your wrongdoing by any means possible. As Herbert Morris puts it: 'With guilt, we are disposed to confess; with shame to hide. We seem to rid ourselves of guilt, when we are fortunate enough to do so, by restoration; we seem to rid ourselves of shame by changing ourselves.'[5]

Bernard Williams, my doctoral supervisor, in his outstanding book *Shame and Necessity*, makes another important distinction. The most primitive experiences of shame are 'connected with sight and being seen', but it has been interestingly suggested that 'guilt is rooted in hearing, the sound in oneself of the voice of judgement; it is the moral sentiment of the word'.[6]

It has long seemed to me that this is the real meaning of the story that has been given so many other interpretations, namely the sin of Adam and Eve in the garden. It is my view that the story is not primarily about forbidden fruit, or sex, or original sin. It is about the respective roles in the moral life of seeing and hearing.

The story begins with Adam and Eve naked and 'unashamed'. Note that this is the first reference to shame in the Bible, albeit in its absence. The serpent tells the woman that if she eats from the fruit 'her eyes will be opened' (Gen. 3:5). Note the significance of this. They had not been blind until now. In what respect will their eyes be opened? This seems to be an explicit reference to a mode of moral judgement, 'knowing good and evil', that has to do with sight rather than sound. The woman looks at the tree and sees that it is 'intensely desirable to the eyes'. The text also adds that it was 'attractive as a means of becoming wise', but Robert Alter in his new translation renders this as 'lovely to look at', following a suggestion by Amos Funkenstein and by the classic Aramaic translations.[7]

The couple eat, their eyes are opened, they know that they are naked, and they seek to cover their nakedness. Every element of this is visual, from beginning to end. Far and away the most interesting line is the one that reads: 'They heard God's voice walking in the garden with the wind of the day. The man and his wife hid themselves from God among the trees of the garden' (Gen. 3:8).

Everything about this verse is strange. Voices don't walk. And you can't hide from God. The point, however, is that Adam and Eve have become utterly sight-oriented. That is why they think you can hide. That is why they experience a voice walking as if it were itself something to be seen rather than to be heard.

Judaism, with its belief in an invisible God who created the world with words, is an attempt to base the moral life on something other than public opinion, appearance, honour and shame. As God tells Samuel, 'The Lord does not look at the things people look at. People look at the outward appearance, but the Lord looks at the heart' (1 Sam. 16:7). Hence the ethic of the divine word; hence the key term in Judaism, *Shema*: 'hear' or 'listen'. Hence the importance of the inner voice, of conscience, of guilt rather than shame; of repentance, not rejection; of forgiveness rather than appeasement; of the integrity of the individual regardless of his or her deeds. This was, and remains, one of the most revolutionary shifts in the history of ethics, and Western civilisation owes a great deal to it.

The return of public shaming and vigilante justice, of viral videos and tendentious Tweets, is not a move forward to a brave new world but a regression to a very old one: that of pre-Christian Rome and the pre-Socratic Greeks. There are other and better ways of ensuring that justice is done.

16

The Death of Civility

There were five of us, sitting facing one another, and we were to be together for the next eight hours. Across the aisle were Prime Minister John Major and Foreign Secretary Malcolm Rifkind. Opposite me sat the leader of the opposition, Tony Blair, and next to me, Paddy Ashdown, leader of the Liberal Democrats, Britain's third party. It was Sunday 5 November 1995, and we were on a plane of the Queen's Flight to attend the funeral of Israeli Prime Minister Yitzhak Rabin, who had led the Oslo peace process with the Palestinians, and had been assassinated the previous night by a Jewish religious-nationalist zealot while attending a peace rally in Tel Aviv.

A normal commercial flight from London to Ben Gurion Airport takes no more than four and a half hours, but this plane of the Queen's Flight, like an antiquated but very dignified limousine, travelled slowly, though in immense style, and needed to land halfway to refuel. I had been invited, as Chief Rabbi, to represent the Jewish community. The atmosphere was sombre. We all knew that a great man had given his life for the sake of peace in the Middle East, much as had Anwar Sadat, president of Egypt, in retaliation for his peace deal with Israel in 1979. War often turns ordinary people into heroes, while the pursuit of peace can make genuine heroes look like traitors to their own more nationalistic countrymen.

Half an hour into the flight, Paddy Ashdown turned to John Major and said, 'John, here we are, leaders of three opposed parties, but we probably have more in common with one another than we do with the extremists in our own parties. We've never sat together before like this. Let's talk honestly and openly about what we really believe regarding the biggest issues today.' John

Major, with a smile, willingly agreed, and for hour after hour all four politicians talked together as candid friends. It was possibly the only time such an extended conversation took place between the party leaders. For eight hours, I sat and listened to the closest British politics came to a team of rivals, sharing their deepest convictions with total openness and friendship. I cherish the memory of those hours because it showed me politics at its best.

An American historian, Doris Kearns Goodwin, wrote a book about Abraham Lincoln called *Team of Rivals*, about how Lincoln had brought together the candidates who stood against him in the presidential election, turning them into a team, to face together the divisive issue of slavery that had brought the nation to civil war.

In an earlier age, there used to be a phrase for this kind of thing: 'dining with the opposition'. This was *civility* in its deepest sense. It was as if politicians were playing for different teams, but with the same love of the game, respect for one another's abilities, and an absolute conviction that the team is bigger than the player, and the game is bigger than the team. That private encounter left its mark on the tone of British politics in the public square. Thereafter these leaders may have argued passionately, but they were never less than respectful, they spoke about issues not personalities, and what united them was more than good manners. It was a conviction they shared about politics: that it exists to reconcile the conflicting desires and aspirations of people within a polity, and to do so without violence, through reasoned and respectful debate, listening to, while not agreeing with, opposing views, and trying as far as possible to serve the common good.

Yitzhak Rabin, whom I had come to know, believed in the same kind of civility, and his assassination was a symptom of its breakdown in Israel. In the previous months I had been urging him to spend more time with the extreme elements of the religious Zionist camp who, in quite violent language, were vehemently opposing the peace process, but he told me not to worry. In a letter he wrote to me shortly before his death he spoke of his conviction that 'compromise and tolerance are essential if peace is to be achieved'. He believed in speaking to all sides, and did so with great humility and respect.

That day I could not escape the memory of another great man who was assassinated, and who had likewise remained calm in the face of conflict, Martin Luther King Jr. Four hours after King's death on 4 April 1968, in an impromptu speech that was one of the finest he ever gave (he too would be assassinated, just two months later), Robert F. Kennedy spoke directly to the pain of African Americans, to his own grief at his brother's assassination, and to the larger grief of a nation divided. He urged his listeners not to choose 'violence or lawlessness, but love and wisdom, and compassion toward one another, and a feeling of justice toward those who still suffer within our country, whether they be white or they be black'. He ended by quoting Aeschylus on the task of politics: 'To tame the savageness of man and make gentle the life of this world.'

Civility is more than good manners. It is a recognition that violent speech leads to violent deeds; that listening respectfully to your opponents is a necessary part of the politics of a free society; and that liberal democracy, predicated as it is on the dignity of diversity, must keep the peace between contending groups by honouring us all equally, in both our diversity and our commonalities. All politics is about the pursuit of power, but liberal democratic politics carries with it a special responsibility to use that power for the dignity of each and the good of all.

There can be little doubt that in both Britain and America, civility in the public domain is at, or close to, an all-time low. In Britain the think-tank Policy Exchange recently published a paper called *An Age of Incivility*.[1] It speaks bluntly of a definitive shift in the tone and character of British politics. There has been a coarsening of language. Insult, rage, vicious attacks on opponents, intimidation and abuse have all become commonplace. A 2017 paper published by the Committee for Standards in Public Life argued that the extent of intimidation now prevalent in British politics posed a threat to the very nature of representative democracy. The poison appears to be currently spreading in all directions, with plentiful examples of misogyny, homophobia, anti-Muslim prejudice, antisemitism, personal invective, the attribution of malign motives to opponents, routine comparison between one's political opponents and the Nazis, conspiracy theories, threats of violence and accusations of treachery. There have even been instances of dehumanisation: people on the Left calling Conservatives, and even Labour moderates, 'lower than vermin'.[2]

Something similar has been happening in American politics likewise. In 2019 the Center for the Study of the Presidency and Congress produced a report on the state of political civility in the United States. It spoke of 'ever greater partisanship, zero-sum governing, and tribal gridlock'.[3] In addition, trust in the political process has been deeply undermined by the manipulation of social media and the result has been, to quote the Center, a political discourse of 'surpassing crudeness and incivility'.

The 2016 presidential election in particular was marked by deep divides and angry discourse. Donald Trump attacked his opponent, delivering a stream of *ad hominem* attacks whose relationship to truth often seemed more accidental than essential, while Hillary Clinton derided her opponents as 'the deplorables: racist, sexist, homophobic, xenophobic, Islamophobic – you name it'. According to a January 2017 Reuters/Ipsos poll, one in six Americans had stopped talking to a family member or close friend because of the election.[4]

To be sure, many elections in the past have been raw, rude and raucous in their rhetoric. That is part of the competitive spirit of electoral politics. But something new *is* happening: the sense that the other side is less than fully human, that its supporters are not part of the same moral community as us, that somehow their sensibilities are alien and threatening, as if they were not the opposition within a political arena, but the enemy full stop. This is the result of four independent but mutually aggravating causes.

The first is the development we have been tracking throughout this book: the deepening individualism of Western societies since the 1960s. After both world wars, there was a strong persisting sense of togetherness born during the war itself and lasting for some time thereafter. So powerful is the feeling of unity in the face of an enemy that many non-democratic leaders will deliberately conjure up the spectre of an external threat simply to unify the population and dampen down any opposition to his or her leadership. This is a deeply encoded instinctive reaction that goes back to the hunter-gatherer stage in human evolution.

Any country that has been at peace for as long as the Western nations have been – essentially since the end of the Second World War – will find that their sense of togetherness has atrophied. In place of this togetherness our respective populations feel themselves mere assemblages of atomic particles connected by no strong sense of identity and kinship. This is, historically, a very dangerous point, and we can understand why simply by going back a century. The Edwardian age, which, like ours, had been largely spared the reality of war, led many people throughout Europe to feel that the general culture had become individualistic and decadent. Intellectuals, in Britain, France and especially Germany, held that going to war would have a morally cleansing effect. Even Martin Buber, instinctively a pacifist, was at the very beginning of the war convinced that it represented a 'world historical mission' for Germany, along with Jewish intellectuals, to civilise the Near East. Be wary of an age in which people find war a solution to the decadence of peace.

Second comes the entire phenomenon of the Internet, which has changed the nature of communication and the way we acquire our information about the world. Until relatively recently, the main way in which people discovered what was going on was through newspapers or television networks. These generally represented a broad range of opinions and held to journalistic standards that offered reassurance of balance and truth in reporting. Even media with a distinct partisan bias nonetheless gave some voice to dissenting views. Besides which, they informed their readers and viewers of events that might not fall directly within their zone of interest, but which inevitably gave them a general sense of what was happening elsewhere. The name for this kind of communication is broadcasting.

This has been replaced by narrowcasting: news filtered to reflect our given interest and political stance. The result is that we see the world the way other people like us see the world, and the commentary we read is one that is already in line with our own take on events. This hugely intensifies the confirmation bias that leads us to register and remember facts that support our view, and dismiss and forget those that do not. This tendency is a dangerous flaw in our cognitive capacities – useful when we were facing predators or rival tribes on the savannah, but hardly relevant to the global twenty-first century. But once social media's algorithms have taken this and amplified it, it becomes very dangerous indeed. As Professor Cass Sunstein has shown in *Going to Extremes: How Like Minds Unite and Divide*,[5] if you associate with people who share your views, you will all become progressively more extreme. Thus a tendency to extremism is built into the way we now acquire information about the world.

Third, there is the un-civilising impact of the new media themselves, generally described as the *disinhibition effect*. As anyone who has read the comment thread of an online newspaper article or followed a Twitter storm will know, it is the equivalent of handing thousands of people megaphones and inviting them to shout their loudest, rudest and crudest commentary on anyone and anything, a cacophony of noise in place of true communication.

Those who have studied this phenomenon attribute it to five features of social media:

- First, it is anonymous. You don't have to give your true name, or reveal your real identity.
- Second, it is invisible. You don't see the people you are insulting, and they don't see you.

- Third, it is not done in real time. It is asynchronous. There is a time gap between your saying what you have to say and others hearing it.
- Fourth, it is unregulated. There are no ground rules.
- Fifth, and most important, it is not face to face, the mode in which all our most important communications are governed by everything that we have inherited in terms of interpersonal skills and conventions.

The factors that normally inhibit our being rude to someone are thus absent. The end result is that I can simply say what I feel better for having said, without consideration or restraint. This is not the normal logic of communication, which is to inform, persuade or convince. Rather, this is communication as primal therapy, and it helps create the anger it then expresses and amplifies.

Finally comes the great and substantive divide itself: what David Goodhart in his book *The Road to Somewhere* calls the division between the Somewheres and the Anywheres.[6] In Britain, the Somewheres are people attached to a particular place and local loyalties. Goodhart notes that despite vast increases in mobility, 60 per cent of British people still live within twenty miles of where they lived when they were fourteen.[7] In America, these are the people in the 'flyover states' away from the main urban centres, who have tended to feel that they have done badly in the past several decades. In both countries, these people's standard of living has been static or declining. Their jobs are no longer assured. They feel ignored by the elites. They feel that they have been the losers in the social contract. And they feel thoroughly resentful, not least because their voice is so seldom heard. These are the ones who tended to vote to make America great again, and who voted for Brexit.

Then there are the Anywheres, the urban elites who are essentially cosmopolitan. Having achieved educational and career success, they have 'portable identities' that allow them to move confidently to new places and challenges. They tend to value autonomy, mobility and novelty above loyalty to a particular group or tradition, and they often have more in common with cosmopolitan individuals from other countries and cultures than they do with the people in the towns and villages physically closer but psychologically further away. David Brooks put this pointedly in the *New York Times*, when he noted that the top three bestselling motor vehicles in the United States are all pickup trucks. How many of you, he asked his *New York Times* readership, know someone with a pickup truck? Somewheres have them, Anywheres don't.

This division between Somewheres and Anywheres runs right through the politics of Europe likewise, and it is this unacknowledged gap that has empowered the resurgent nationalists of the far right, and the rest. The up-in-arms Somewheres are derided as populists, xenophobes, racists and so on, but their grievances are real, as is their sense of having been betrayed by self-serving elites. Both in the US and Europe they feel that their jobs, wages and social services have all been put at risk by an unprecedented and sustained level of immigration. They feel that they have been pushed to the back of the queue. Likewise they feel that the outsourcing of employment overseas, whether in manufacturing or service industries, has been done for the advantage of international corporations, to the disadvantage of local populations.

There may be counter-arguments – outsourcing has kept consumer prices down and massively increased our choice of goods to buy – but these feelings are real, and cannot be ignored.

Taken together, these four tendencies combined threaten a genuine risk of political breakdown.

Given these vast challenges, why should mere civility matter? Stephen Carter calls civility 'the sum of the many sacrifices we are called to make for the sake of living together'.[8] Edward Shils calls it 'a belief which affirms the possibility of the common good; it is a belief in the community of contending parties within a morally valid unity of society'.[9] Civility is more than good manners. It is an affirmation that the problems of some are the problems of all, that a good society presupposes collective responsibility, that there is a moral dimension to being part of this nation, this people, this place. We speak to one another because we feel bound to one another in a shared enterprise in which we each have a part to play. I would add three insights from Jewish thought that I think are relevant in understanding the importance of civility.

There is no doubt that Judaism is not strong on the *civil* element – polite, well-mannered, mild – of civility. The prophets were passionate, not polite. The rabbis were argumentative rather than agreeable. But Judaism does have three important things to say about why we should 'reason together' – the favourite phrase of Harvard political philosopher Michael Sandel, taken from the prophet Isaiah (1:18).

The first is the truly remarkable passage in Genesis 18 in which God discloses in advance to Abraham what he is about to do to Sodom and Gomorrah.

> 'Shall I hide from Abraham what I am about to do ... For I have chosen him, that he may command his children and his household after him to keep the way of the Lord by doing right-eousness and justice, so that the Lord may bring to Abraham what he has promised him.' Then the Lord said, 'Because the outcry against Sodom and Gomorrah is great and their sin is very grave, I will go down to see whether they have done altogether according to the outcry that has come to me. And if not, I will know' (Gen. 18:19–21).

The passage offers no conceivable reason why God would wish to seek Abraham's opinion on the matter. In fact, by the very terms of the biblical narrative, there can be no conceivable reason. There is nothing Abraham might know that God does not know, nor could Abraham possibly have a better sense of justice than God himself. Yet God is clearly inviting a response from Abraham, and indeed it comes, in one of the most radical passages in all religious literature:

Then Abraham drew near and said, 'Will you indeed sweep away the righteous with the wicked? Suppose there are fifty righteous within the city. Will you then sweep away the place and not spare it for the fifty righteous who are in it? Far be it from you to do such a thing, to put the righteous to death with the wicked, so that the righteous fare as the wicked! Far be that from you! Shall not the Judge of all the earth do what is just?' (Gen. 18:23–5)

What is going on here? It seems that we have in this passage a biblical version of the Roman axiom of justice that I have already mentioned: *Audi alteram partem*, 'Hear the other side.' There cannot be justice if there has been no speech in defence of the accused. That is what Abraham provides here. Even God himself must submit to this rule. There can be no justice in which all sides have not had a hearing. Abraham must defend his neighbours as far as he can, even though their way is not his. That is the first rule of a just society.

The second is an equally radical rabbinic passage, about a debate in the mind of God before he came to create *Homo sapiens*:

Rabbi Shimon said: When God was about to create Adam, the ministering angels split into contending groups. Some said, 'Let him be created.' Others said, 'Let him not be created.' That is why it is written: 'Mercy and truth collided, righteousness and peace clashed' (Psalms 85:11).

Mercy said, 'Let him be created, because he will do merciful deeds.'

Truth said, 'Let him not be created, for he will be full of falsehood.'

Righteousness said, 'Let him be created, for he will do righteous deeds.'

Peace said, 'Let him not be created, for he will never cease quarrelling.'

What did the Holy One, blessed be He, do? He took truth and threw it to the ground.

The angels said, 'Sovereign of the universe, why do You do thus to Your own seal, truth? Let truth arise from the ground.'

Thus it is written, 'Let truth spring up from the earth' (Psalms 85:12).

This is an audacious theological interpretation. God, it suggests, was in two minds before creating mankind. Yes, humanity is capable of great acts of altruism, but it is also endlessly at war. Human beings tell lies and their lives are full of strife. God takes truth and throws it to the ground: for life to be liveable, truth on earth cannot be what it is in heaven. Truth in heaven may be platonic – eternal, harmonious, radiant. But man cannot reach to such truth, and if he does, he will create conflict not peace. Men kill precisely because they believe they possess the truth, while their opponents are in error. In that case, says God, throwing truth to the ground, let human beings live by a different standard of truth, one that is conscious of its limitations. The divine word comes from heaven, but it is interpreted on earth.[10] The divine light is infinite, but to be visible to us it must be refracted through finite understanding. Truth in heaven transcends space and time, but human perception is bounded by both space and time.

What is more, when two propositions conflict it is not necessarily because one is true, the other false. It may be, and often is, that each represents a different perspective on reality, an alternative way of structuring order, no more and no less commensurable – nor contradictory – than a Shakespeare sonnet, a Michelangelo painting and a Schubert sonata.

God, wrote Rabbi Abraham Kook, 'dealt kindly with his world by not putting all the talents in one place, in any one man or nation, not in one generation or even one world'.[11] Each culture has something to contribute to the totality of human wisdom. The sages said: 'Who is wise? One who learns from all men.'[12] This is the Jewish equivalent to the story of Socrates. The Delphic Oracle proclaimed Socrates the wisest in Athens because although he knew nothing, everyone else also knew nothing, whereas

Socrates alone *knew* that he knew nothing. The Jewish variant states that we all know something, and the wisest is the one who *knows* that we all know something, and is therefore willing to learn from everyone, for none of us knows all the truth, but each of us knows some of it.

Finally, there is a line in the Hebrew Bible that is almost never correctly translated. It refers to the first two human children: Cain and Abel. Each brings an offering to the Lord. God accepts that of Abel and rejects that of Cain – for what reason, we do not know. However, God senses that Cain is resentful towards his brother and warns him against doing harm to Abel. We then read: 'Cain said to his brother Abel . . . and when they were in the field, Cain rose up against his brother Abel and killed him.'

The text cannot be translated literally because it is syntactically ill-formed. It says that 'Cain said', but it doesn't say *what* he said. The text's fractured syntax forces us in the most dramatic way to focus on the fractured relationship between Cain and his brother – and then spells out the consequence: *when words fail, violence begins*.

Hence the three principles of civility:

1. For there to be justice, all sides must be heard.
2. Truth on earth cannot aspire to be truth as it is in heaven. All truth on earth represents a perspective, and there are multiple perspectives.
3. The alternative to argument is violence. That is why the argument must continue and never cease.

Those are the conclusions I have reached since that long plane journey when I listened to three party leaders arguing together as they flew to attend the funeral of a brave politician, assassinated by a zealot who did not believe in the democratic argument, and believed instead that politics can be dictated by the barrel of a gun.

*

I have argued that the loss of shared moral community means that we find it difficult to reason together. Truth gives way to power. Uncomfortable views are excluded from campuses. To win support, people start defining themselves as victims. Public shaming takes the place of judicial establishment of guilt. Civility – especially respect for people who oppose you – begins to die. The public conversation slowly gives way to a shouting match in which integrity counts for little and noise for much. This is not a culture whose survival can be taken for granted. It is one that is fraying at the seams.

Now we must consider the question of morality itself: what does it have to tell us about the human person and the dignity and meaning of our lives?

PART FOUR
Being Human

17

Human Dignity

In his novel *Zadig*, Voltaire described humans as 'insects devouring one another on a little atom of mud'. The late Stephen Hawking, meanwhile, stated that 'the human race is just a chemical scum on a moderate-size planet, orbiting round a very average star in the outer suburb of one among a billion galaxies'. The philosopher John Gray declared that 'human life has no more meaning than that of slime mould'.[1] In his book *Homo Deus*, despite its bold title, Yuval Harari reaches the conclusion that, 'Looking back, humanity will turn out to be just a ripple within the cosmic data flow.'[2]

Humans are, on this view, not distinctive at all. We are part of nature, nothing more. There is nothing corresponding to the soul in this view, nor is there anything in the rich repertoire of works of the human spirit that truly differentiates us in kind from other forms of life. Our hopes, dreams and ideals arise from electrochemical brain processes; that is all they are. Striking is the sheer loss of the sense of grandeur and possibility that drove Renaissance humanism. This loss of dignity is deeply embedded in popular science today. We have become 'the naked ape',[3] 'a gene's way of making another gene',[4] a data-processing algorithm, an organism among organisms, without freedom or virtue, neither sacred nor unique. Reviewing this history of the descent of man it is hard not to feel that we have lost more than we have gained. For what does it profit humanity if it gains the world and yet loses its soul?

How did this happen?

The descent of man is a drama in several acts, extended over several centuries. First came Copernicus's discovery that the earth was not the centre of the universe. The sun did not revolve around

235

man's habitation. On the contrary, it was the earth that cycled the sun. In the fullness of time that initial paradigm shift has been repeated many times over. The solar system is not the centre of the galaxy and our galaxy is only one of more than a hundred billion others. Set in space, this wide earth of ours turned out to be a speck of dust on the surface of infinity.

What applied to space applied to time also. Newton, in the seventeenth century, could still believe that the earth was some six thousand years old, and spent a fair amount of time trying to work out the exact date of its birth. Yet as rock strata began to be understood, and fossils were found, the birth had to be pushed back further and further, to hundreds of thousands of years, then to millions, and finally to 4.54 billion, in a universe 13.8 billion years old. If so, then the entire history of humanity was an eyelid's blink in eternity, if that. The universe had survived for billions of years without *Homo sapiens*. How then could we claim to be the ultimate purpose of creation?

Then came Spinoza, who taught us that to the extent that we are physical beings we are subject to physical laws, all of which have the character of necessity. Therefore freedom – God's gift to humanity, that separated us from the animals – is an illusion. There is, in fact, only one form of freedom: the consciousness of necessity. The philosopher grows wise by knowing that things could not have been otherwise.

Spinoza's discoveries set the stage for a whole series of determinisms of different kinds, each finding the course of history in some other shaping force, but all agreed that we are what we are because we could not be otherwise than we are, and that all thoughts to the contrary are mere illusion.

Marx argued that the whole of human history was shaped by economic forces, and by the desire of a dominant class to maintain hegemony. Religion, which taught otherwise, was itself the tool of the ruling classes, used by them to teach the poor to accept their fate as the will of God, and to live with suffering in this world in the hope, even promise, of reward in the world to come.

Then came Darwin, with the shocking revelation that human beings were not even *sui generis*, a class on their own. Not only were they not the image of God, they were just one branch of the primates, close cousins to the apes and chimpanzees. There might be differences in degree between humans and others, but not of kind. Other animals, said Darwin and his followers, had feelings, used language, experienced some form of consciousness.

Then came Freud, with the revelation of a subterranean channel of dark instinctual drives running beneath the surface of our minds. We are driven by Eros and Thanatos, the sex instinct and the death instinct. We all want to murder our father and marry our mother. In fact, this was the source of religion itself. Long ago the younger males of the tribe gathered together to murder their father, the alpha male. Having done the deed, they then experienced overwhelming remorse – the return of the repressed emotion. That is what God and the voice of conscience are.[5] Religion, said Freud, is the obsessional neurosis of humankind.[6]

Finally – at least thus far – came the neo-Darwinians, with their assault on the one thing humans could still pride themselves on, their altruism, their willingness to sacrifice themselves for the sake of others. Not so, argued the evolutionary psychologists. The human person is, after all, just a gene's way of making another gene. Whatever stories we tell ourselves, our apparently altruistic acts are only ways of ensuring our genetic survival into the next generation. We only really help kin, and we do so in precise proportion as they share our genes. 'Scratch an altruist,' said Michael Ghiselin, 'and watch a hypocrite bleed.'[7]

Nor was this all. What riveted the neo-Darwinians was the implication that evolution proceeded by mere chance, random genetic mutation, which produced the variety on which natural selection could work. Steven J. Gould drew the conclusion that if the tape of evolution were to be replayed there would be no certainty that *Homo sapiens* would have emerged.[8] So not only were human beings not made by an act of special divine creation. Their very existence was pure accident.

So: we are nothing, our planet is insignificant, our existence is a mere caesura in time. Our noblest thoughts conceal base intentions. There is no freedom, only necessity or worse, mere random chance. There is no truth, just hegemonic narrative. There is no moral beauty, just a sordid struggle to survive. The historian Will Durant has a fine characterisation of this cluster of attitudes, this prevailing mood, which he sees as common to all civilisations at a certain point in their development. There is a clash between religion and science. Science wins. Scepticism increasingly becomes the norm:

> The intellectual classes abandon the ancient theology and – after some hesitation – the moral code allied with it; literature and philosophy become anticlerical. The movement of liberation rises to an exuberant worship of reason, and falls to a paralyzing disillusionment with every dogma and every idea. Conduct, deprived of its religious supports, deteriorates into epicurean chaos; and life itself, shorn of consoling faith, becomes a burden alike to conscious poverty and to weary wealth. In the end a society and its religion tend to fall together, like body and soul, in a harmonious death.[9]

Our view of humanity becomes like Hamlet's: 'To me, what is this quintessence of dust?'[10]

*

Yet human dignity matters to us a great deal. As Michael Rosen, Professor of Government at Harvard University, points out in his study of dignity,[11] the first sentence of Article 1 of the United Nations Universal Declaration of Human Rights (1948) states: 'All human beings are born free and equal in dignity and rights.' Article 1 of the Basic Law of the Federal Republic of Germany (1949) reads, 'Human dignity is inviolable. To respect it and protect it is the duty of all state power.' But where does the idea of human dignity come from?

238

Leon Kass of the University of Chicago finds one source in ancient Greece, in the figure of the hero who 'draws honour and prizes by displaying his worthiness and noble and glorious deeds'. Following the Socratic turn in Greek thought, the ideal of heroism was supplanted by the virtue of wisdom. Human excellence was no longer forged on the battlefield but in the pursuit of truth. However, as Kass goes on to note, 'the Greek exemplars are of little practical use in democratic times'. Dignity, for the Greeks, was possessed by some people, not all.[12]

Rosen argues that the first person to think of dignity as something possessed by all human beings as such was the Roman statesman and philosopher, Cicero. In his work *De Officiis* (On Duties), Cicero invites his readers to remember always 'how vastly superior is man's nature to that of cattle and other animals: their only thought is for bodily satisfactions . . . Man's mind, on the contrary, is developed by study and reflection.' We are different, and dignified, because we can think.

There is, however, an entirely different source, noted by Kass and in passing by Rosen, namely the Hebrew Bible, which speaks of a free God, not constrained by nature, who, creating man in his own image, grants him that same freedom, commanding him but not compelling him to do good. The entire biblical project, from beginning to end, is about how to honour that freedom – in personal relationships, families, communities and nations. Biblical morality is the morality of freedom, its politics are the politics of freedom, and its theology is the theology of freedom. On this view, we have dignity because we can choose. Dignity is inseparable from morality and our role as choosing, responsible, moral agents.

The figure who did more than anyone else in the modern world to develop this idea was Immanuel Kant. As I have shared, I am critical of elements of his philosophy, but his account of human dignity is exemplary. In *The Groundwork to the Metaphysics of Morals* he writes that 'morality, and humanity in so far as it is capable of morality, is that which alone has dignity'.[13] Michael Rosen sums up his position thus:

Only morality has dignity and only human beings carry the moral law within themselves, so it would be wrong to think of human beings as part of the natural world in the way that rivers, trees, or dogs are. Yet Kant's conception of dignity is at the same time deeply egalitarian. Dignity is something that all human beings have in common.[14]

Morality and human dignity go hand in hand. Lose one, and we will lose the other.

*

There is – and this is my point – a glaring contradiction at the heart of contemporary thought. On the one hand there is the unprecedented emphasis on human dignity as exemplified by the opening of the Universal Declaration of Human Rights. On the other, our self-image as human beings has fallen so low that serious scientists could speak of us as chemical scum or slime mould. Over the course of the same period that human self-image has diminished, human powers of understanding, explanation and control have expanded beyond all previous imaginings and at an ever-faster rate. How is it that the higher human achievements become, the lower our self-image sinks?

On this, the most insightful observer is Nietzsche:

Has not man's self-deprecation, his *will* to self-deprecation, been unstoppably on the increase since Copernicus? Gone, alas, is his faith in his dignity, uniqueness, irreplaceableness in the rank ordering of beings, – he has become *animal*, literally, unqualifiedly and unreservedly an animal, man who in his earlier faiths was almost God ('child of God,' 'man of God') . . . since Copernicus, man seems to have been on a downward path, – now he seems to be rolling faster and faster away from the centre – where to? into nothingness? into 'piercing sensation of his nothingness'?[15]

Nietzsche called this a 'laboriously won *self-contempt* of man', describing it as humanity's 'last, most serious claim to self-respect', as if to say that even if everything else is nothing, humans alone know that they are nothing. This is the new religion, of which scientists are the new priesthood, offering salvation from humankind's ever more drastically fallen state. Nietzsche wrote *On the Genealogy of Morality*, from which this quote was taken, in 1887. Yet scientific self-abasement – the systematic insistence that we are 'nothing but' reproductive units blindly replicating ourselves – has continued unabated ever since.

It is totally unwarranted. The fact that we occupy a small space in the universe and a small stretch of the totality of time says nothing about our significance or lack of it. Yes, we have dark drives, but we also have high ideals, and the force of the latter can lift us above the pull of the former. There is no logic that forces us to accept the 'hermeneutics of suspicion'[16] of the Marxists, Freudians and neo-Darwinians, that we don't really mean what we say, that all human communication is either deception or self-deception. In plain language, this is mere cynicism, and its effect is to undermine the trust on which human relationships and institutions depend.

*

No blame can be levelled at Marx, Darwin and Freud for what others made of their ideas. Yet the doors that they opened have led us to a place that is very dangerous. Why?

First, there is something intrinsically dehumanising in the scientific mindset that operates in detachment, driven by analysis, the breaking down of wholes to their component parts. The focus is not on the particular – this man, that woman, this child – but on the universal. Science per se has no space for empathy or fellow feeling. That is not a critique of science, but it is an insistence that science is not the sum total of our understanding of humanity.

So much of what is unique about humanity – our imagination, our ability to conceptualise and imagine worlds that have not yet been, our capacity to communicate deeply with others, to bridge distances and orchestrate our differences – cannot be analysed scientifically, but is nonetheless essential to who we are and what we are about.

That is not to say that scientists are not compassionate and loving human beings: surely they are. But when science is worshipped and everything spiritual dethroned, then a certain decision has been made to set aside human feelings for the sake of something seemingly higher, nobler, larger. That is how idolatry begins.

Second, as Nietzsche rightly asked: 'Why morality at all, when life, nature, history are "non-moral?"'[17] There is no morality in nature. No good, right, duty or obligation are written into the fabric of things. There is no way of inferring from how things are to how things ought to be. The Talmud says that had God not revealed the commandments, 'we could have learned modesty from the cat, industry from the ant, marital fidelity from the dove, and good manners from the rooster'.[18] But equally we could have learned savagery from the lion, pitilessness from the wolf and venom from the viper.

Every civilisation has a way of identifying and pre-empting disastrous patterns of behaviour, some way of establishing boundaries, of saying, 'Thou shalt not.' In mythological societies the work is done by the concept of taboo. In the Judeo-Christian heritage there is the divine command. There are certain things you do not do, whatever the consequences. That is what was lost in the modern age. Hayek, as we have seen, called it 'the fatal conceit': that we know better than our ancestors, that we can calculate the consequences better than them, circumvent the prohibitions they observed, and achieve what they did not achieve.[19]

By undermining the classic conceptions of humanity, Marxist, Darwinian and Freudian accounts tragically removed the great constraints on human behaviour. They did this in different ways, but all three subverted the force of the 'Thou shalt not.' When nothing is sacred, then nothing is sacrilegious. When there is no Judge, there is no justice. There is only effectiveness and the pursuit of desire.

There is a third point, no less significant. Science cannot, in and of itself, give an account of human dignity, because dignity is based on human freedom. Freedom is a concept that lies outside the scope of science. Science cannot locate freedom, because the scientific world is one of causal relationships. A stone is not free to fall or not to fall. Lighting does not choose when and where to strike. A scientific law links one physical phenomenon to another without the intervention of will and choice. To the extent that there is a science of human behaviour, there is an implicit denial of the freedom of human behaviour. That is precisely what Spinoza, Marx and Freud were arguing: that freedom is an illusion. But if freedom is an illusion, then so is the human dignity based on that freedom. Science cannot but deconsecrate the human person, thereby opening the gate to a possible desecration.

At this point, the voice of morality – the very voice that has been progressively weakened over the past fifty years – has to intervene, and explain explicitly what is unique about humankind, and what we must cultivate and protect in the coming years.

*

One way of seeing how this works is to look at what seems to me to be a set of philosophical errors in the conclusion of Yuval Harari's *Homo Deus*. Harari argues that a new way of looking at the world, a new religion, if you will, is beginning to emerge. He calls it *dataism*. This sees organisms as algorithms, ways of processing data. You may not agree, he writes, 'with the idea that organisms are algorithms, and that giraffes, tomatoes, and human beings are just different methods for processing data. But you should know that this is current scientific dogma, and that it is changing our world beyond recognition.'[20]

According to dataism, says Harari, human experiences are not sacrosanct, nor are human beings the apex of creation. They are 'merely tools for creating the Internet of all things, which may eventually spread out from planet Earth to cover the whole galaxy and even the whole universe. This cosmic data processing system would be like God; it will be everywhere and will control everything and humans are destined to merge into it.'[21] This sounds very much like a twenty-first-century version of Laplace's view of the universe as a field of forces in which human choices and meanings play no part.

Harari ends by asking three questions:

1. Are organisms really just algorithms, and is life really just data-processing?
2. What's more valuable – intelligence or consciousness?
3. What will happen to society, politics, and daily life when non-conscious but highly intelligent algorithms know us better than we know ourselves?[22]

All three questions are arresting, but all are intrinsically misleading. The first is an instance of reductivism. When someone says 'X is really just Y', you know to look out for oversimplification. Is a painting really just an assemblage of pigments on canvas? Is a Beethoven quartet really just a series of vibrating sound waves in the air? The words 'really just' are used too often by scientists venturing into amateur philosophy, to claim that they alone understand the nature of reality: they are the new Gnostics, possessors of the secret wisdom. The claim is exaggerated and misleading. Reality is always bigger than 'really just'.

The third question is likewise unhelpful. Non-conscious but highly intelligent algorithms will never know us better than we know ourselves, because they do not 'know' anything at all. Some person *using* such algorithms might theoretically do so. Even so, there is a difference between the way someone else knows us (from the outside) and the way we know ourselves (from within).

As philosopher David Pears has argued, someone else can *predict* what we are going to do, but only we can *decide*.[23] That power of decision is what makes us moral agents, and humans will always have it in a way that mere algorithms as such do not.

This brings us to the key second question, sandwiched between the other two. As Harari demonstrates, in some respects computers are already more intelligent than we are. So, if we seek to preserve our humanity, the answer is not to elevate intelligence, but – and this is Harari's error – neither is it consciousness. Not only human beings are conscious. Animals are likewise. It should be clear to all of us that the fact that animals are conscious imposes a duty upon us not to inflict unnecessary pain on animals, a moral principle that has grown considerably in force as we have better understood our biological kinship with them.

It is neither intelligence nor consciousness, but rather *self-consciousness* that makes human beings different. That self-consciousness comes from the fact that we are capable of experiencing the world in two different ways – what George Herbert Mead calls 'I' and 'Me'.[24] On the one hand, I experience the world through my own direct consciousness. In this respect, I stand at the centre of my reality.

On the other hand, I also can stand apart from my own imme-diate subjective perceptions and see the world, as Adam Smith put it, from the perspective of an impartial observer. This is what Mead called the 'Me', the socialised self that emerges through my dialogue with significant others, parents, teachers, peers, and the various shaping influences of the culture into which I have been born. Freud developed a similar theory, calling this aspect of consciousness the superego, the internalised voice of conscience. It is this ability to see the world in two different ways that allows us to have what Harry Frankfurt calls *second-order desires* and make what Charles Taylor calls *strong evaluations*.

Like other beings, we as 'I' have drives, desires, passions, but unlike any other, we as 'Me' can ask ourselves whether it is right to pursue or satisfy them. What if satisfying my desires means that you will go hungry? What if my pursuit of passion means putting you in a distressing situation? That judgement is what makes us moral beings, and it is not reducible to algorithms. Algorithms can predict, but only human beings can decide, and that is a crucial distinction.

That self-consciousness which makes us all moral agents defines the responsibility and freedom that we have, and it is this that we will have to apply to the development of artificial intelligence, among other things, and that we must continue to nurture, because it is what makes us unique among all life forms currently known to us. Morality lies at the very heart of human dignity.

It is also important to point out two directly opposed errors, both of them widely held, about the nature of morally responsible freedom. The first, born in the 1960s, was the claim that we are the freest generation in history, free to do things, go places and experience phenomena of which our parents let alone grandparents could not even dream. We cherish that freedom, not only to do what we like, but to take institutions on our own terms, turning even religion into a consumer-friendly leisure-time activity. Robert Bellah, in his great work on contemporary society, *Habits of the Heart*, called this expressive individualism. That freedom is embodied in words like authenticity, autonomy, self-expression and self-realisation, to which we claim to have unfettered rights. As Supreme Court Justice Anthony Kennedy stated, 'At the heart of liberty is the right to define one's own concept of existence, of meaning, of the universe, and of the mystery of human life . . .'[25]

At the same time, neuroscientists, as well as the Darwinian biologists, have been telling us that freedom, in the sense of personal free will, is a complete illusion. What we are, what we do, what we fail to do, what we eventually become – all these are written in our DNA. We have no choice in the matter. Our acts and attributes are pre-determined. Spinoza was probably the first in the modern age to say so, but Marx and Freud added their own forms of determinism, economic for one, psychological for the other.

How then can we construct an entire culture, not to mention an economic and political context, that will give us maximal freedom, when at the other end of the room, the scientists are telling us that this freedom that we are pursuing is an illusion? These two contemporary dogmas are in flat contradiction with one another.

I put this point to Professor Colin Blakemore of Oxford in a television programme once. He told me he was a strict determinist: he believed that we have no choice whatsoever. Free will is simply a fiction we tell ourselves. I said to him, 'In that case, why have laws, courts, judges, trials and punishments? All these things are predicated on the fact that we have free will, that we could if we so chose have resisted doing what we did, that we have moral and legal responsibility. Since these are, for you, false beliefs, why go through the charade of the pursuit of justice? Instead, take the offender to a hospital and perform neurosurgery, or at the very least, ensure he is permanently injected with psychotropic drugs that render him malleable and harmless.'

Blakemore said, 'Well, I can see that some extremists might think that way.' I told him I thought this was a really bad answer. On his account of human psychology, we are not different in kind to an artificially intelligent robot, whose behaviour is only driven by the algorithms we put into it in the first place. That, according to Harari and others, is what DNA, genetics and neuroscience tell us: that we are no more than the hardware driven by the various algorithms that constitute human biology.

Speaking personally, I would not want to trust the defence of a free society to the hands of those who believe not only that there is no such thing as a genuinely free society, but that there is no such thing as a free human being either. That is what created the kinship between Pavlovian psychology and the Soviet Union. Pavlov believed that human beings could be behaviourally conditioned the way dogs were trained to salivate at the sound of a whistle. The denial of personal and political freedom went hand in hand.

It is our ability to see the world not only from our own perspective, but from that of others, that gives us our privilege and responsibility as moral agents, the only such known to us in the entire universe. There are other social animals. Some animals have, in basic ways, developed tools. Others have developed some form of language. But none so far have approached anything near what we would describe as moral agency.[26]

It is our existence as moral agents, our ability to stand outside our own desires and drives, our capacity to refrain from doing what we can do and want to do because we know it might harm others, our very experience of choice itself as both the challenge and glory of the human situation, that makes us different and confers dignity on human life. We are not insects, scum, slime mould, a ripple in the cosmic data flow. We may be the dust of the earth but there is within us, says the Bible, the breath of God. We have immortal longings. We are the moral animal.

18

Meaning

In November 2018, the Pew Research Center published the results of a survey of how Americans find meaning in life. Predictably, the most important source was family. Others included career, money, friends, hobbies, activities and religious faith. But as David Brooks noted in an article on the survey in the *New York Times*, a number of respondents testified to lives of quiet despair. These were some of the responses:

> It would be nice to live according to my being rather than my blackness. I will never know how a totally worthwhile life will feel because of this.

> Drugs and alcohol are the only shining rays of light in my otherwise unbearable existence.

> I no longer find much of anything meaningful, fulfilling or satisfying. Whatever used to keep me going has gone. I am currently struggling to find any motivation to keep going.[1]

Brooks himself argues that 'there is some sort of hard-to-define spiritual crisis across the land', which shows itself in a lowering of expectation and aspiration.[2] Only 11 per cent of the people surveyed said that learning was a source of meaning in their lives, and only 7 per cent mentioned helping other people. Philosophers have traditionally identified the search for a meaningful life with service to a moral cause, a community, a country, or God. People in the 2018 survey, by contrast, tended to describe moments when they felt good about themselves. It is as if they have lost the sense of vocation, the pursuit of meaning, a calling to something larger than the self.

The Pew report confirms a tendency already identified by the American Freshman Survey tracking attitudes of college students since the 1960s. In the late 1960s, their top priority, mentioned as essential or very important by 86 per cent, was 'developing a meaningful life philosophy'. By the 2000s, a mere 40 per cent cited this as their main goal, while the majority said their priority was 'being very well off financially'.[3] It is as if, in a world of 'I', the search for meaning has become less meaningful – which is problematic, because we are meaning-seeking animals.

I argued in the previous chapter that there is an essential connection between morality and human dignity. Remove the one, and we find it hard to make sense of the other. In this chapter I want to argue for a broadly similar connection between morality and the meaningfulness or otherwise of a life. John Steinbeck puts it strongly in *East of Eden*:

> Humans are caught – in their lives, in their thoughts, in their hungers and ambitions, in their avarice and cruelty, and in their kindness and generosity too – in a net of good and evil. I think this is the only story we have and that it occurs on all levels of feeling and intelligence. Virtue and vice were the warp and woof of our first consciousness, and they will be the fabric of our last . . . A man, after he has brushed off the dust and chips of his life, will have left only the hard clean questions: Was it good or was it evil? Have I done well – or ill?[4]

My own view is that the connection between meaning and goodness is slightly less tight. My doctoral supervisor Bernard Williams argued that the case of Gauguin, who abandoned his family in Paris to go and paint in Tahiti, showed among other things that moral considerations do not always override all others.[5] You can be a great artist while being a less-than-great human being. Not everyone who finds a meaning in life does so in consciously moral terms. But they almost always do so in terms of some project involving challenge, dedication, commitment and effort that takes them beyond themselves. A world dominated by the self leads ultimately to meaninglessness. As American philosopher Susan Wolf argues, if you are devoted only to your own happiness, you fail to realise that things other than yourself have value. It is as if, for you, you are the only valuable thing in existence.[6] Meaning involves the acknowledgement of a world beyond the self. An individualistic, I-centred culture will be one in which people struggle to find meaning.

*

David Foster Wallace, the author of the outstanding novel *Infinite Jest* (1996), was considered by many to be the finest American writer of his generation. On 12 September 2008, at the age of forty-six, he committed suicide. He had suffered for many years from depression, for which he had been treated by electro-convulsive therapy and antidepressant medication. We must not minimise the seriousness of this condition, which can be genetic, and has both physical and neurological dimensions. Yet there was something about the way he spoke about his life that convinced two distinguished American philosophers, Herbert Dreyfus and Sean Dorrance Kelly, that there was something of wider significance about the cultural discontent that Wallace articulated and embodied in his life and death.[7]

'It manifests itself,' Wallace once said, 'as a kind of lostness.' He said about himself and his friends that they were 'white, upper-middle-class, obscenely well-educated' and more successful than they could legitimately have hoped for. 'Some of them were deeply into drugs, others were unbelievable workaholics. Some were going to singles bars every night.' They were 'adrift'. As he told a magazine in 1993, 'This is a generation that has an inheritance of absolutely nothing as far as meaningful moral values.'

For Dreyfus, an expert on existentialism, and Kelly, chair of the Department of Philosophy at Harvard, Wallace's suicide struck home as a judgement on an entire generation. For them, David Foster Wallace was perhaps the greatest mind of their time. If such as he could experience the kind of devastating nihilism that led to his suicide, what did this say about those who remain?

Wallace found mere existence in the contemporary world almost overwhelmingly empty. The postmodernism that constituted his worldview favoured highly intellectualised, complex and aestheti-cised principles instead of embracing simplicity. He said that the postmodern aversion to simplicity is 'one of the things that's gutted our generation'. His belief was that if one could only open oneself to the apparently prosaic, like a queue at a supermarket checkout, you could experience just that situation as 'sacred, on fire with the same force that made the stars: love, fellowship, the mystical oneness of all things, deep down'.

This was, perhaps, a little optimistic. Few have felt the world as sacred, on fire with the same force that made the stars, without intense spiritual discipline and focus. That is what the great reli-gious mystical traditions were about, and none of them assumed that you could achieve this kind of experience without years of training, discipleship, meditation, reflection, and all the other things that go with mysticism. You can't press a button and arrive at such a state; you can't just invent a personal theology that will take you there; and you can't get there the way the previous generation arguably did, through psychedelic drugs, without also paying the heavy price that they paid, in terms of addiction and other forms of harm.

Kelly and Dreyfus are fascinating in both the seriousness with which they consider a case like David Foster Wallace's, and the response they offer, which is, as they term it, a call for a return to polytheism, that is to say, to multiple sources of ecstasy, and what Émile Durkheim called collective effervescence, through such experiences as watching a great tennis player or an outstanding ballet dancer. It may well be that this is what we are seeing today. The secular equivalents of religious ecstasy are sports events and rock concerts. But these are disconnected, one-off events, with no underlying unity. They are momentarily thrilling but not ultimately fulfilling. They offer distraction but not meaning, escape but not engagement. The big issues of life have been replaced by entertainment. Is that enough?

Tellingly, in his 2019 book *The Second Mountain*, subtitled *The Quest for a Moral Life*, David Brooks comments on Wallace's novel *Infinite Jest*. He says that it is a sustained description of 'the distracted frame of mind' that comes about when you have spent years pursuing open options. When everything is available, every lifestyle on offer, when all you have is freedom, but nothing to guide you in that freedom, 'it's not so much that you lose the thread of the meaning of your life, you have trouble even staying focused on the question'.

It is at least possible that what Wallace eventually discovered and found ultimately unbearable was the emptiness that Nietzsche foresaw would be the condition of a world without God. I mentioned in an earlier chapter how, in *The Gay Science*, Nietzsche placed in the mouth of a madman the famous words 'God is dead.' Less well known is his continuation of the passage:

'Whither is God?' he cried; 'I will tell you. We have killed him – you and I. All of us are his murderers. But how did we do this? How could we drink up the sea? Who gave us the sponge to wipe away the entire horizon? What were we doing when we unchained this earth from its sun? Whither is it moving now? Whither are we moving? Away from all suns? Are we not plunging continually? Backward, sideward, forward, in all directions? Is there still any up or down? Are we not straying, as through an infinite nothing? Do we not feel the breath of empty space? Has it not become colder? Is not night continually closing in on us? Do we not need to light lanterns in the morning? Do we hear nothing as yet of the noise of the gravediggers who are burying God?'[8]

Dreyfus and Kelly gesture towards the problem: 'our focus on ourselves as isolated, autonomous agents has had the effect of banishing the gods – that is to say, covering up or blocking our sensitivity to what is sacred in the world. The gods are calling us but we have ceased to listen.' But what Nietzsche and perhaps Wallace felt was something deeper than this: that the gods were *not* calling them, because for them there were no gods. What they heard was what terrified Blaise Pascal: 'The eternal silence of these infinite spaces.'

I once had a very amusing exchange with the prominent atheist Richard Dawkins on just this point. I said, 'Richard, you are just tone deaf. You can't hear the music beneath the noise.' Richard replied, 'You are right, I am tone deaf. But there is no music.' How, if you are tone deaf, can you know that there is no music? For some, the negative certainties of the modern world have removed the very possibility of hearing the divine music, the call, the voice of the beyond-within. But *All Things Shining*, Dreyfus and Kelly's book, is important for its honesty and openness about the difficulty of finding meaning in life without a dimension of the sacred.

Another contemporary intellectual conscious of living with meaninglessness is the historian Yuval Harari, whose *Homo Deus* I mentioned in the previous chapter. In his subsequent book, *21 Lessons for the 21st Century*, he dismisses all attempts to find meaning in human life as no more than a series of stories, and thus mere human artefacts, with no substantive reality beyond the effort and energy with which they have been invested.[9] 'The answer,' he says, 'isn't a story.'

Harari himself is drawn to a Buddhist perspective, according to which 'the universe has no meaning, and human feelings too carry no meaning'. They are no more than 'ephemeral vibrations, appearing and disappearing for no particular purpose'. He adds: 'That's the truth. Get over it.' Harari exemplifies perfectly Philip Rieff's contention that pagan cultures experience meaning as *fate*. Axial cultures, such as the great monotheisms, Judaism, Christianity and Islam, experience it as *faith*. Postmodern cultures, though, dismiss it as *fiction*.[10] Fiction has no reality outside the self, they say, which is why it can provide us with distraction but not with meaning. It can allow us to escape enjoyably from the world, but it is not in itself a mode of engagement with the world. That, it seems to me, is an impoverished view of the nature of stories and the unique human gift of narrative understanding.

*

In the context of a life, a story is not merely fiction. It is the pursuit of meaning. As I put it in my book *The Great Partnership*, the human mind has two primary modalities: science, which takes things apart to see how they work, and religion, which puts things together to see what they mean. Jerome Bruner talks of 'two modes of cognitive functioning', each of which 'provides distinctive ways of ordering experience, of constructing reality'. One is logical argument, the other is telling a story. The word 'then' means something different in the two cases: 'If X then Y' is not the same kind of connection as 'The king died, then the queen died.' The first is a timeless proposition, while the second is intrinsically set in time. The first is a logical connection, but the second is contingent. It belongs to the world of possibility, not necessity.[11]

The two modes function in different ways. One aims to convince us of its absolute truth, the other of its lifelikeness, its verisimilitude. Narrative is how we construct meaning out of the flow of events, and the fact that it does not have simple criteria of verification or refutation, the way science does, does not mean that it is mere fiction. On the contrary, storytelling is of the essence of who we are as meaning-seeking animals.

As Barbara Hardy put it, 'we dream in narrative, we daydream in narrative, remember, anticipate, hope, despair, believe, doubt, plan, revise, criticise, construct, gossip, learn, hate and love by narrative'.[12] Alasdair MacIntyre famously made this case in his masterwork, *After Virtue*, where he states: 'Man is in his actions and practice, as well as in his fictions, essentially a storytelling animal.' He draws the corollary: 'Deprive children of stories and you leave them unscripted, anxious stutterers in their actions as in their words.'[13]

We are, in large measure, the story we tell about ourselves, which means that we are always a work in process. Nor do we construct our story out of nothing. Our lives, our culture, our faith, all shape the narrative which, in itself, then reshapes our life. What interests me here is a particular *type* of narrative that has a profound resonance in the West, namely that of *the redemption of suffering*. I want to focus on the stories of two famous individuals. As it happens, both told their life story in the course of receiving an honorary doctorate, and both speeches are available as YouTube videos; they are the late Steve Jobs and J.K. Rowling, the creator of Harry Potter.

In his widely viewed address at Stanford in 2005 – the video has been seen by more than 40 million people – Steve Jobs told the poignant story of his early childhood. His mother was an unmarried college graduate who was determined to put her child up for adoption. She was insistent, however, that the adoptive parents be college graduates. She had made all the arrangements, but when Steve was born, the couple changed their mind and decided that they wanted a girl. Another family who had expressed their willingness to adopt a child were contacted and agreed immediately to take him. However, they were not college graduates, and Steve's mother would only accept their offer to adopt if they made a solemn pledge that they would ensure that he would go to college.

All of the complexities of Jobs's character can be seen embedded in that narrative – of well-educated individuals with sophisticated provisos, and of the actual couple who adopted Steve, who were not well educated but whose humanity shines through. What Jobs does in this powerful retrospective of his life is to speak about three crises in his life and what he learned from them.

The first occurred at college. After six months, Steve was struck by how much his college was costing his adoptive parents, at a simple financial level. He decided that he could not in good conscience continue his degree and be such a drain on their finances. He dropped out. For the next few years he lived on practically nothing, sleeping on the floors of friends' dorms, making a few dollars by returning Coca-Cola bottles for the deposit, and walking across town once a week to get a free meal at the Hare Krishna Temple.

This strange studenty half-life allowed him to go to lectures that were not part of his degree course but that simply interested him. One of them was a course in calligraphy, the aesthetic side of which fascinated Jobs. The result was that when he and Steve Wozniak built their first computers, they incorporated the choice of multiple fonts, which gave an element of beauty to the documents composed on these machines, and became a standard feature of computers ever since. So the first crisis allowed him to discover something he would never have done had he kept to the standard parameters of a degree course.

The second, life-altering crisis was when he was dismissed from Apple, the company that he and Steve Wozniak had built from nothing in his parents' garage, and which they had grown into a company with 4,000 employees and a value of $2 billion. Anyone else might have given up in despair at this point, but Jobs did not. Instead, he created a new computer company called NeXT, and bought another one, Pixar Animations, which under the genius of John Lasseter, allied with the perfectionism of Jobs, became the first maker of fully computer-animated films and produced – starting with *Toy Story* – a string of works of imaginative genius.

His third, heart-breaking, story was of being diagnosed with pancreatic cancer, which made him focus on a clear vision of what really mattered. 'Your time is limited, so don't waste it living someone else's life.' The prospect of death gave him focus. All external considerations of pride or fear, embarrassment or failure, fall away in the face of death, leaving only what is truly important.

In the course of relating these stories, Jobs described what seems to have been an ongoing feature of his life: he called it connecting the dots. 'You can't connect the dots looking forward;

you can only connect them looking backward. So you have to trust that the dots will somehow connect in your future. You have to trust in something – your gut, destiny, life, karma, whatever. This approach has never let me down.'

This is exactly what made Steve Jobs different from David Foster Wallace. Jobs was constructing a narrative. He was focusing on what made his life a story and on what kind of story it was. It was a redemptive story, a story of hope, a tale of how you can lack much, from financial resources to a relationship with your biological parents, and yet still emerge with head high, having made life better not just for yourself but for others also.

It would be hard to imagine three more crushing blows then than being given away by your mother, being fired from the company you started, and eventually contracting cancer. Yet what narrative does is to show us how the future can redeem the past, how what seems like a disaster now can turn out to have been a turning point in the journey whose final destination is more remarkable than might have been otherwise.

J.K. Rowling's story, which she told while accepting an honorary degree at Harvard, is about how she chose a different life from the one her parents wished her to. Both of her parents came from impoverished backgrounds and they saw university as a sure-fire way for their daughter to achieve financial stability. Instead of pursuing the degree in German they had agreed upon as fitting her for the working world, Rowling pursued her passion for Greek myths and immediately switched to Classics. Her lifelong passion, as we know, was for writing. There is a key moment in her talk when she describes herself, seven years after graduation, with a failed marriage, a young daughter, 'jobless, a lone parent, and as poor as it is possible to be in modern Britain without being homeless'. She was, within her parents' parameters, a failure.[14]

At this point, without pretending that failure was fun, she discovered nonetheless that it 'meant a stripping away of the inessential'. She went on, 'I stopped pretending to myself that I was anything other than what I was, and began to direct all my energy into finishing the only work that had mattered to me.' This gave her 'an inner security that I had never attained by passing examinations'. It taught her things about herself that she would not have discovered otherwise: that she had a stronger will and more discipline than she had suspected. She found that she had real friends. And 'the knowledge that you have emerged wiser and stronger from setbacks means that you are, ever after, secure in your ability to survive'.

These stories, of Steve Jobs and J.K. Rowling, are powerful contemporary examples of a form of narrative described by Dan McAdams, Professor of Psychology and Human Development at Northwestern University. His *Stories We Live By* is one of the key texts on the role of narrative in the discovery and formulation of a meaningful life. In a later book, *The Redemptive Self*, he tells of how he was giving a presentation of his work at a scientific conference in the Netherlands, when a woman in the audience responded by saying that his work was very interesting but 'These life stories you describe, they seem so, well, *American*.' He took this initially as a criticism, but eventually he realised there was a measure of truth in the comment. The stories we tell are influenced in part by the culture or cultures we inhabit. Just as there are national styles in music, literature, even humour, so there are national styles in narrative.

Building on the Dutch woman's insight, the type of life-narrative that McAdams identified as typically American is what he calls the story of the redemptive self. This is its basic structure: 'Bad things happen to me, but good outcomes often follow. My suffering is usually redeemed, as I continue to progress, to learn, to improve. Looking to the future, I expect the things I have generated will continue to grow and flourish, even in a dangerous world.'[15] That is a highly specific kind of story, rooted in a Judeo-Christian view of time as a vehicle of growth, change, discovery, encounter and redemption. It does not represent the cyclical view of time that one finds in some of the Hellenistic writers. It is not Oriental mysticism rooted in the experience of me-here-now.

The redemptive self does not live in the moment; it lives in the future made possible by the present, and in the story that reveals itself only in retrospect. And it is deeply moral. It sees personal suffering as a prelude to growth and to alleviating the suffering of others. It focuses on the moral responsibility that is the product of our ability to imagine a world that has not yet been and to act in such a way as to help it into being. It is the same mindset of a George Bernard Shaw, who said, 'You see things and say, "Why?" But I dream things that never were, and say "Why not?"' It also reflects Einstein's understanding of the meaning of life: 'Strange is our situation here on earth. Each of us comes for a short visit, not knowing why, yet sometimes seeming to divine a purpose. From the standpoint of daily life, however, there is one thing we do know: that man is here for the sake of other men – above all for those upon whose smiles and well-being our own happiness depends.'[16] It is this redemptive understanding of time that made the West what it is and gave it the power that for four centuries transformed the world.

Life *is* a story. It is our response to the call of suffering in the world. Great lives respond to the reality of other people, for whom J.K. Rowling wrote her books, Steve Jobs made his technological masterpieces, and which each of us heeds when we stretch out a hand to the needy and turn strangers into friends.

19

Why Morality?

Why is morality so essential to our dignity, our happiness, the meaningfulness of our lives and the structures of grace that constitute a good society? One way of answering that question is through the story of two people who, in 1831, both set out on journeys that changed their lives and ours, enabling us to see the world differently and more deeply. They did not know one another. Their interests were completely different, as were their destinations, but in a strange way, looking back, we can see that their thoughts converged. They gave us a new way of understanding the role of morality in human society.

The two men – one twenty-two years old as he set out, the other twenty-six – were similar in many ways. They were both from well-established families but had an intense curiosity about the world around them. Superb observers, who saw what others missed, they had the ability to theorise about what they saw and hypothesise novel explanations. One was the young British naturalist on HMS *Beagle*, setting out on a journey that would eventually take him to the Galapagos Islands: Charles Darwin. The other was a young French aristocrat who set sail for the United States to explore their handling of politics: Alexis de Tocqueville.

Despite their quite different interests and fields of research, both were eventually struck by essentially the same thing. They both observed phenomena that profoundly puzzled them, and they came to the same conclusion, namely that in any form of collective life, there will be a need for both competition and cooperation. Morality is the domain of cooperation. It is the place where we set competition aside and say, explicitly or implicitly: let us work together for the common good. This is harder than it sounds because competition and cooperation call for two sets of completely different instincts, the one for aggression and the other for altruism. Darwin and de Tocqueville discovered, each in his own way, that somehow or other we have to manage both instincts. There must be arenas in which the competitive instinct predominates, but there have to be others where it does not; places where concern for the common good finds its home.

Let us begin with Charles Darwin. We know something of his journey and the discoveries it led to. Having formulated his evolutionary theory, Darwin noticed what appeared to be a glaring inconsistency with observed features of human and even some non-human life, and he was wise enough and honest enough to see it and say so. If natural selection were true, if the evolution of species was determined by competition for scarce resources, then you would expect only the most ruthlessly self-interested to survive. Selflessness has no place in the Darwinian system, and Darwin rightly acknowledged that. Altruists, especially people who risk their lives for the sake of others, would tend to die disproportionately young because of the risks they took, so they were more likely than others not to have had a chance of handing on their genes to the next generation. In short, altruists as a species should be extinct.

But it isn't so. Darwin realised that in virtually all human societies, altruism was valued. Those who took risks for the sake of the group were highly admired. To take some twentieth-century examples, Martin Luther King Jr, Mother Teresa, Nelson Mandela were respected not for their ruthlessness but for the opposite, their willingness to make sacrifices for the sake of others. How is this compatible with natural selection? Darwin saw the general form of a solution, which, put in today's language, is this: we hand on our genes to the next generation as individuals, but only survive as members of groups. A human being on his or her own cannot survive. This is the seeming paradox at the heart of natural selection. As he says in *The Descent of Man*:

> There can be no doubt that a tribe including many members who from possessing in a high degree the spirit of patriotism, fidelity,

obedience, courage and sympathy were always ready to give aid to each other and to sacrifice themselves for the common good would be victorious over most other tribes and this would be natural selection.[1]

This is the nearest Darwin came to the concept of group selection. What Darwin saw was that it is very difficult to work out how anyone could arrive at altruism in the first place. In his words: 'The problem, however, of the first advance of savages towards civilisation is at present much too difficult to be solved.'[2]

Unsure of how it originated, once Darwin arrived at this solution, he saw that it was essential to preserve and develop the habits of altruism. So on the one hand natural selection works on the basis of competition for scarce resources, but on the other hand it depends on cooperation, which is vital to the survival of the group, and the group is vital for the survival of the individual. As a result, a kind of transfiguration takes place. In natural selection, in all social animals but above all in *Homo sapiens*, the paradox is that selfish genes get together to produce selfless people. That was the insight towards which Darwin pointed us.

*

In the same year, Alexis de Tocqueville visited America to see the new phenomenon of a democracy built on the principled separation of church and state. What fascinated him was a paradox very similar to Darwin's, again of the interplay of competition and cooperation. His initial assumption was that the separation of church and state should mean that religion has no power, and therefore it should have no influence either. The logical conclusion was that in a country where church is separate from the state, religion should be a marginal phenomenon. Yet de Tocqueville found the opposite: a nation where religion played a central role, so central that he called it the first of America's political institutions.[3]

How did this happen? This was the problem de Tocqueville set himself to solve. How could a nation in which religion has no power yet be one in which it has enormous influence? And as a corollary: how did an institution that had such influence abstain from exercising political power? Through interviews with clergymen, de Tocqueville discovered that religion was influential in America precisely *because* of the separation of church and state, because religion never got involved in party political disputes. He writes in *Democracy in America*: 'When I came to enquire into the prevailing spirit of the clergy, I found that most of its members seemed to retire of their own accord from the exercise of power and they made it the pride of their profession to abstain from politics.'[4] When he asked the clergymen why they stayed out of politics, they said, in essence, 'Because all politics is intrinsically divisive. Therefore if we were involved in the political system we too would be divisive. We want to be a unifying rather than a divisive force. Therefore we avoid politics.' Instead, religious leaders in the 1830s were involved in strengthening families, building communities and starting charities. They inspired people to a sense of the common good, educating them in 'habits of the heart', and bequeathing them the 'art of association' that de Tocqueville called 'their apprenticeship in liberty'.

Americans did not leave everything to the state. To the contrary, in many areas they came together locally and voluntarily to do things for themselves. De Tocqueville was astonished by the proclivity of Americans of all ages and classes to form associations on the slightest provocation:

They have not only commercial and manufacturing companies, in which all take part, but associations of a thousand other kinds, religious, moral, serious, futile, general or restricted, enormous or diminutive. The Americans make associations to give entertainments, to found seminaries, to build inns, to construct churches, to diffuse books, to send missionaries to the antipodes; in this manner they found hospitals, prisons and schools. If it is proposed to inculcate some truth or to foster some feeling by the encouragement of a great example, they form a society. Wherever at the head of some new undertaking you see the government in France, or a man of rank in England, in the United States you will be sure to find an association.[5]

This was America's equivalent of Darwin's tribes that were 'always ready to give aid to each other and to sacrifice themselves for the common good'. Realising that in a democratic society there is an enormous weight that falls on families, communities and local groups of all kinds, de Tocqueville saw that the whole arena often called 'civil society' (the part that is not the state) is vital for the health of democracy. That is where we learn the logic of cooperation, not competition. In families and communities, we do things for one another because their very existence depends on reciprocal altruism.

De Tocqueville believed that this sphere of local activism and voluntary association was what protected Americans from the creeping tyranny of the state. This was not likely to be a cruel tyranny. It would be a benign one. He called it 'regular, quiet and gentle'. It would be 'well content that the people should rejoice, provided they think of nothing but rejoicing'. It would be a tyranny unlike any known before, created without a revolution, maintained without resistance, existing simply to relieve citizens of the burden of caring about anyone other than themselves and their immediate families.[6] But it would be a tyranny nonetheless. It would mean the invasion of the state into more and more areas of private life. When people leave everything to the state, everything becomes political, and liberty – the space free from politics and the pursuit of power – depends on there being something strong to stand between the individual and the state. This something is the moral arena, which is not exclusive to religious organisations but is heavily dependent on them. Liberty, writes de Tocqueville, 'cannot be established without morality, nor morality without faith'.[7]

In a strange way, therefore, the journeys of Darwin and Tocqueville, begun at a similar time, came to the same conclusion. They both recognised that although the struggle to survive involves competition, there must be protected space within the group where we learn and constantly enact the habits of cooperation, altruism and concern for the common as opposed to the individual good. That is the conclusion on which these two very different travellers converged.

*

Now, nearly two centuries after these two set out, we know at least in rough outline how this works. The answer comes at three levels, very different from one another. The first was indicated graphically by J.B.S. Haldane when he was asked whether he would jump into a river to save his brother. He replied, 'No, but I would do so to save two brothers or eight cousins.' On the face of it, it would never make sense to risk your own life to save someone in danger of drowning. Why endanger your posterity for the sake of others? Haldane's point, elaborated in the 1960s by William Hamilton and others, is that such self-sacrifice makes sense in proportion to the closeness with which the people you are trying to save are related to you. We share 50 per cent of our genes with our siblings, an eighth with our cousins, and so on. Thus, by saving the lives of close relatives we would still be handing on our genes to the future. This is the logic of *kin selection*, and it is determined by genetic similarity.

This makes intuitive sense. We know that the matrix of altruism is formed within the family. It is there that we hand on our genes to the next generation, there that we have our greatest chance of defeating mortality this side of heaven. It was Edmund Burke who said that 'we begin our public affections in our families', and Alexis de Tocqueville who wrote that 'as long as family feeling was kept alive, the antagonist of oppression was never alone'. Biology, morality and society coincide. Morality begins with kin.

How groups became wider – from kin to kith, from relatives to friends – remained a major problem in evolutionary biology until the late 1970s. How would any animal, let alone a human being, come to form an association with non-related others, if self-interest always defeats the common good? This was the starting point of Hobbes's famous account of life in a state of nature, in which there was 'continual fear and danger of violent death, and the life of man, solitary, poor, nasty, brutish, and short'. What stops people fighting one another for long enough to create an association?

Some brilliant work in the late 1970s and 1980s provided the answer. It used a scenario drawn from the branch of mathematics known as Game Theory, called the Prisoner's Dilemma. This exercise imagines two criminals, suspected of a crime for which the police lack adequate evidence to secure a conviction. Their best chance of doing so is to interrogate the two men separately, giving each an incentive to inform on the other. Rationally, not being able to confer, they should each betray the other in the hope of a reduced sentence or at worst a shared sentence. The result will be that both end up in prison with a longer sentence than they would have received had they both stayed silent.

This sounds like a minor curiosity, but it upset the major assumption on which economics had been based since Adam Smith's *Wealth of Nations*, namely that division of labour combined with individual self-interest would result in collective gain. The Prisoner's Dilemma shows that this does not work without one other ingredient: trust. What stops the two accused men from staying silent is that neither can trust the other to do likewise.

What mathematicians discovered was that the Prisoner's Dilemma yields a negative outcome if played only once. If played many times (with a nuanced system of penalty and reward) the two men eventually learn to trust each other, because they learn that they gain if they do and lose if they don't. A competition to find the most effective strategy for survival in multiple encounters was won in 1979 by a simple set of rules designed by Anatol Rapoport, a political scientist with an interest in nuclear confrontation who had once been a concert pianist. He called it Tit-for-Tat. It said: on the first encounter be nice, and on subsequent encounters repeat the other person's last move. If he is nice, so should you be, and if not, then respond in kind. This was the first moral principle whose survival value was shown by computer simulation. What it did was to show the gold in the Golden Rule. It said, in a world where people will probably do to you what you did to them, it pays to act to others as you would wish them to act to you – a basic principle of most cultures.

This solves the Darwinian dilemma of how non-genetically related individuals can cooperate to form groups. If you do to others what you expect them to do for you – share food, give warning of impending danger and the like – then the group will function effectively and survive. If not, you will be punished by reprisals and possible exclusion from the group. Biologists call this reciprocal altruism. Some deny that this is altruism at all. It is 'self-interest rightly understood', or what Bishop Butler called 'cool self-love'. But the terminology is neither here nor there. This is the simplest basis of the moral life. If you start with benevolence, then apply the rules of reciprocity, you create a basis of trust on which groups can form. For this you do not need religion. All social animals work this out, because those who do not, do not survive.

It depends, though, on repeated face-to-face encounters. I have to be able to remember what you did to me last time if I am to trust you now. This requires a fair amount of memory, which explains why animals like chimpanzees and bonobos live in small groups. One ingenious biologist, Robin Dunbar, worked out that there is a correlation among species between brain size and the average size of groups. On this basis he calculated that for humans, the optimal size is 150. That is why the first human groups, even after the domestication of animals and the invention of agriculture, were quite small: the tribe, the village, the clan. Associations larger than this were federations of smaller groups.

How then did humans successfully develop much larger concentrations of population? How did they create cities and civilisation? Reciprocal altruism creates trust between neighbours, people who meet repeatedly and know about one another's character. The birth of the city posed a different and much greater problem: how do you establish trust between strangers?

This was the point at which culture took over from nature, and religion was born – that is, religion in the sense of an organised social structure with myths, rituals, sacred times and places, temples and a priesthood. Recall that we are speaking in evolutionary, not theological terms. Regardless of whether we regard religion as true or false, it clearly has adaptive value because it appeared at the dawn of civilisation and has been a central feature of almost every society since.

The early religions created moral communities, thus solving the problem of trust between strangers. They sanctified the social order. They taught people that society is as it is because this is the will of the gods and the basic structure of the universe. The fundamental theme of the early religions in Mesopotamia and Egypt was the tension between cosmos and chaos, order and anarchy, structure and disarray. The universe began in chaos, a formless ocean or unformed matter, and if the rules are not followed, it will become chaos again.

Later, the monotheisms found moral order in divine wisdom, the divine will or the divine word. One way or another, though, there was an order that, if not adhered to, would bring disaster. Thus a moral community was created on a far larger scale than could have been achieved on the basis of kinship or reciprocal altruisms. The world religions have in fact created some of the largest moral communities ever known, though they are always at risk of internal fracture through schism and sectarianism.

There is no biological mechanism capable of yielding order on such a scale. Ants manage it because, within groups and roles, they are clones of one another. They operate by kin selection. Humans are different from one another. That is what makes cooperation between them so difficult, and so powerful when it happens. This is when something new and distinctively human emerges. Learned habits of behaviour take over from evolved instinctual drives. Rituals make their appearance. Socialisation becomes a fundamental part of the education of the young. There are roles, rules, codes of conduct. The habits necessary to the maintenance of the group become internalised. We are the culture-creating, meaning-seeking animal. *Homo sapiens* became *Homo religiosus*.

We need some kind of moral community for there to be a society as opposed to a state. States function on the basis of power. But societies function on the basis of a shared vision of what unites the people who comprise it. Societies are moral communities. That was Lord Devlin's argument at the beginning of the great liberalisation debate in 1957. You could not have a society without an agreed moral code. It was a point made by Tocqueville himself:

> Without ideas held in common there is no common action, and without common action, there may still be men, but there is no social body. In order that society should exist and, *a fortiori*, that a society should prosper, it is necessary that the minds of all the citizens should be rallied and held together by certain predominant ideas . . .[8]

That is what makes our current situation so unusual and hazardous. What emerged from the liberalising measures of the 1960s was something that has never been managed successfully before, namely sustaining a society *not* held together by certain predominant ideas, *not* bound by a shared moral code, *not* committed to substantive ethical 'ideas held in common'. How can there be a society in the absence of anything to bind its members in shared moral belief?

Even in the 1830s Tocqueville foresaw this possibility, and warned strongly against it. He thought that the greatest single threat to democracy in America was what he named *individualism*, a situation in which people living apart become 'strangers to the fate of all the rest'. Their families and private friends constitute 'the whole of mankind'. As for fellow citizens, the individualist is 'close to them, but does not see them; he touches them, but he does not feel them; he exists only in himself and for himself alone'. In such a situation, there is nothing standing between the individual and the state, and the result is that everything becomes politics, therefore a struggle for power, therefore divisive and abrasive. Hence the loss of civility we charted in the previous chapter.

What has happened in the past half-century has been precisely what de Tocqueville feared. It took a long time to appear, precisely because of the strength of the institutions on which he discerned American democratic freedom to rest: religion, community, family and the sense of the nation as a moral community. As these eroded from the 1960s onwards, individualism was left as the order of the day, and so it is today. The individual trumps society. The 'I' prevails over the 'We'. We have the market and the state, the two arenas of competition, one for wealth, the other for power, but nothing else, no arena of cooperation that would bridge the difference between wealthy and powerful and the poor and powerless.

No social animal lives like this. No society has ever survived like this for very long, not even the greatest: not ancient Greece, not the Rome of antiquity, not Renaissance Italy. In each of these three cases, the release from traditional moral restraints for a while unleashed a burst of energy and creativity, but was too quickly followed by decline and fall. A society of individualists is unsustainable. We are built for cooperation, not just competition. In the end, with the market and the state but no substantive society to link us to our fellow citizens in bonds of collective responsibility, trust and truth erode, economics becomes inequitable and politics becomes unbearable.

20

Which Morality?

Maurice Samuels (1895–1972) was born to Jewish parents in Romania and came to Manchester with his family at the age of six. There, growing up, he discovered the type of English school-boy literature – *Tom Brown's School Days* and other books written in a similar spirit – that introduced him to a world of values radically different from the religion-saturated Jewish pietism of his parents' tradition. He writes about their impact on him: 'While they held the youngster spellbound with stories of adventures and high jinks in public schools . . . they indoctrinated him powerfully with English ideals of fair play, honesty, respect for the throne and the country, nobility, pluck, cheerfulness, loyalty, and cricket.'

Cricket, Samuels discovered, was not just a game. It was an attitude to life, a moral code: 'a thing that wasn't cricket was of course shocking and shameful; but these adjectives do not convey the force or flavour of the condemnation to an outsider'. Something that 'wasn't cricket' earned the disapproval of 'decent fellows' – the heroes of the schoolboy literature – who were the only kind of people whose opinion mattered. These were the people who, when they wanted to emphasise the truthfulness of an assertion, said, 'Honour bright!' Saying those two words, writes Samuels, meant something other and more than, 'What I am saying is true.' It was 'a reminder of one's consciousness of the code, it was a salute, a Masonic signal'.

What the young Samuels was experiencing was the culture shock that happens when someone brought up in a righteousness-and-guilt morality encounters an honour-and-shame morality. The Judaism of Samuels' parents was a classic instance of the former, while the late Victorian British public-school ethic was a distinctive embodiment of the latter. The difference between them is not like that between two people within a single culture who disagree on specific moral judgements. Rather, they are two different ways of life.

There is more than one way of being moral. That is one of the objections that could be raised to the argument implicit throughout this book. Here is one way of putting it: I have argued for the importance of morality to the health of society and the individual. But it could be said that such a morality belonged to an era when societies were held together by a single religion, or at least a single moral code. Before modern forms of travel and communication, most people would have seen their own community as the boundary of their world. Now, however, we can travel to and communicate with the world, and the world has come to us, notably in the sheer cultural diversity of most cities in the West. We can sample other moralities in the same way we can visit other cities or taste other cuisines. Morality is no longer a code imposed on us by the culture in which we live. It has become instead a matter of personal choice. So the things of which I have been critical – emotivism, individualism, subjectivism, self-realisation and self-esteem – are simply a given of our cosmopolitan, pluralistic situation. In the past, people faced a choice of whether to be moral or not. Today they face a quite different choice: *which* morality, or combination of moralities, to adopt.

I want to argue that it is not quite so. But first, how are we to understand the multiplicity of moral systems?

*

The best metaphor through which to understand the way in which different cultures see the moral life in different ways is language. The world has many languages – an estimated six thousand – and they have certain features in common, reflecting what has been called a depth grammar, that shapes and is shaped by the human brain, specifically what Steven Pinker, one of the participants in my BBC radio series on morality, calls the language instinct. But languages, or better, families of languages, are also different, and lead us to experience and understand the world in different ways. You will encounter reality differently if you were brought up speaking Mandarin than if you grew up speaking New York American English.

The differences between Western and Eastern ways of seeing the world have been brilliantly set out by Richard Nisbett in his book *The Geography of Thought*.[1] For instance, shown a picture of fish in a tank, complete with plants, rocks and bubbles, then asked what they had seen, American and Japanese students all mentioned seeing the fish, but the Japanese made 60 per cent more references to the background objects.

Shown three objects, a chicken, a cow and a clump of grass, and asked, 'Which two go together?', American children chose the chicken and the cow – both members of the same class: animal. Chinese children chose the cow and the grass – where there are cows there is grass. American children learn nouns faster than verbs, but South Asian children learn verbs faster than nouns. Nouns are about classification; verbs are about relationships.

Americans look to resolve conflict by universal principles of justice. The Chinese prefer mediation by a middleman, whose goal is not fairness but the reduction of animosity and the mending of relationship. A famous American reading primer begins, 'See Dick run. See Dick play. See Dick run and play.' The corresponding Chinese primer reads, 'Big brother takes care of little brother. Big brother loves little brother. Little brother loves big brother.' Westerners tend to think in terms of either/or, Chinese in terms of both/and: yin and yang, feminine and masculine, passive and active, interpenetrating forces that complete one another.

Something similar was argued by Carol Gilligan in her *In a Different Voice*. Her thesis was that men and women used distinctive styles of moral reasoning. Men found their identity by separation, women by attachment. Men were more likely to feel threatened by intimacy, women by isolation. Men played competitive games in groups, regulated by rules. Women were less rule-oriented, formed smaller and closer groups, but had fewer resources for conflict resolution.[2]

When it came to thinking about moral dilemmas, she found men more likely to analyse situations in terms of the rights, women in terms of responsibilities. Men's moral thinking tended to be formal and abstract, women's contextual and based on telling stories. Men spoke about justice, women about relationships. Men valued detachment and achievement, women valued attachment and care. For men, morality was primarily about the public world of social power, for women, it was more about the private world of interpersonal connection. Men saw morality as a set of rules for the avoidance of violence. Women were more likely to think of it as a style of relationship based on empathy and compassion.

Gilligan's thesis proved controversial.[3] But whether or not there are gender differences, there are certainly cultural ones. How then can we map the moral landscape?

*

One place to begin is with Michael Walzer's distinction (echoing anthropologist Clifford Geertz) between *thick* and *thin descriptions*. Thin descriptions are abstract and general; thick descriptions are concrete and specific. A thin description of a 'third space', for example, would be 'a place that is neither private nor public'. A thick description might involve a story about the role of coffeehouses in eighteenth-century London as gathering places for scientists, journalists and the like and their role in facilitating the emergence of new social groupings.

Applied to morality, *thin* applies to the moral concepts that we use to make judgements between and across cultures. They tend to be highly universal and lacking in specificity. Justice is a thin concept insofar as we can recognise injustice in cultures remote from our own. *Thick* relates to those features that make this culture different from others: the ones, for example, that

Maurice Samuels discovered growing up in early twentieth-century Manchester. Morality always begins, Walzer says, with thick concepts. We learn what it is to be moral within our own highly localised and specific culture.

Morality does not begin with a high level of abstraction. We learn to do this, not that, because that is how things are done in our world. Only later on do we discover that other people do things differently. It is a caricature, but one of Philip Roth's Jewish characters has a meal with a gentile family and discovers for the first time that you can have a conversation in which words are not used as weapons, something of a shock for a particular kind of American Jew of Roth's generation. A visit to a strongly caste-based Hindu community makes you aware of how social hierarchies can structure everyday interactions in a way quite unlike a more egalitarian society. There are religious communities in Britain that maintain attitudes of respect for parents that have disappeared from the cultural mainstream. Children stand in the presence of their parents and only speak when given permission. To call one's parents by name is completely forbidden.

Enlightenment thinkers tended to suppose that Western rationality was a universal norm – rather like the Greeks when they dismissed all non-Greeks as barbarians. In fact, though, morality comes in myriad forms. The word itself comes from the Latin *mores*, meaning the customs and conventions of behaviour within a group. The related word 'ethics' comes from *ethos*, the Greek word for the character of a community.

Both words hark back to 'thick' description of the way things are in a specific time and place, and both are far broader than the terms 'moral'. They include matters of religion, such as rituals and taboos, as well as others we might regard as less than ethical, such as manners, protocol and etiquette. It is only under the influence of philosophy that a specific area is set apart from others and seen as moral.

In *The Righteous Mind* Jonathan Haidt includes an intriguing analysis of two types of morality. One is supremely thin, consisting of two principles only: the avoidance of harm, and justice as fairness. This is an approach to morality he associates with what he labels 'WEIRD' cultures: Western, Educated, Industrialised, Rich and Democratic. The other – most common in traditional cultures – has three different sensibilities: loyalty, reverence and respect. These are thick values. You can find both in contemporary America, he says, depending on the extent to which individuals and groups preserve the sensibilities of the past.

Loyalty has a difficult time in a society dominated by egalitarianism, universalism and rights, for I am loyal to this, not that; to these people, not those. Reverence means that there are some values that are non-negotiable. I hold certain things holy. That, for instance, is at stake in the debate about assisted dying or voluntary euthanasia. One side believes, on the basis of personal autonomy, that I have the right to decide whether I live or die. The other believes that life is sacred, we do not own it, and therefore it is not ours to dispose of as we choose. Respect means that there are hierarchies built into some relationships, between student and teacher for example, or parent and child. These are thick values because they are tied to specific cultures, codes, customs and conventions. They are not universal; they have no real thin equivalents. The thinness of WEIRD cultures does indeed make them seem weird to those from more formal and structured societies.

*

There is a huge variety of thick ethical cultures, and one way of describing them – I am indebted here to Harry Redner's *Ethical Life: The Past and Present of Ethical Cultures* – is to distinguish four basic visions of the ethical life in the history of civilisations.[4] One he calls *civic ethics*, the ethics of ancient Greece and Rome. Second comes the *ethic of duty*, which he identifies with Confucianism, Krishnaism and late Stoicism. Third is the *ethic of honour*, a distinctive combination of courtly and military decorum to be found among Persians, Arabs and Turks as well as in medieval Christianity (the chivalrous knight) and Islam. The fourth, shared by Judaism and Christianity, he calls simply *morality*. It is an 'ethic of love': love of God, the neighbour and the stranger. It also has a strongly internalised sense of conscience, guilt, sin and repentance. Buddhism is also based on love, somewhat differently inflected but based on a sense of kinship with all creation.

The civic ethic originated in the Greek city states of antiquity and its highest virtue is service to the polis. To live for it is virtue, to die for it a form of glory. Morality here is focused on the city and its welfare, on military and political engagement. Unlike the Judeo-Christian ethic, there is no morality of private life or sexuality. The civic ethic tends to be focused on virtue rather than specific codes of conduct, four virtues in particular: wisdom, prudence, temperance and courage.

The ethic of duty arose in the form of Confucianism in China, Krishnaism in India and late Stoicism in Rome. It tends to arise in highly hierarchical societies that see their social structure as mirroring a hierarchy in the universe and in nature – the Great Chain of Being – and sees morality as what F.H. Bradley called 'my station and its duties', the particular responsibilities I shoulder given my place in the social order. Personal feelings are eclipsed by service to the system, whose practitioners are marked by politeness, grace and the demands of propriety.

The ethic of honour has existed in many societies throughout the ages. Pre-Socratic Greece was a classic example. A similar culture existed in many military societies, especially among horse warriors, like the chivalrous knight and the noblewoman to whom he did service, later transformed into the figure of the gentleman and the lady. Honour cultures have to do with membership of and status within a group. As William Ian Miller writes, about the culture represented in the Icelandic sagas:

> In an honour-based culture there was no self-respect independent of the respect of others . . . Your status in this group was the

measure of your honour, and your status was achieved at the expense of the other group members who were not only your competitors for scarce honour but also the arbiters of whether you had it or not.[5]

In an important essay, 'On the Obsolescence of the Concept of Honour' (1970), sociologist Peter Berger argued that one of the most important transitions in Western modernity was the movement from honour to dignity.[6] The difference between them is that honour is something you occupy in virtue of your rank in society; dignity is something that attaches to you by the mere fact of being human. Honour presupposes hierarchy whereas dignity is an expression of a specific form of equality, namely equality of respect. That is one reason that honour cultures, so important even in our own past, seem archaic from the point of view of the contemporary West.

Another reason is that honour cultures tend to lend themselves to violence, whenever someone believes that their honour has been slighted. The desire to focus and confine this led in early modern Europe to the phenomenon of duelling, which lasted through to the nineteenth century. Duels took place because the offended party believed he could restore his honour by demonstrating his willingness to risk his life for it. Such a combination of honour and violence can still be found today in some forms of Islam (in honour killings, for example), and in urban gangs. The reason for such violence is that honour cultures tend to be dismissive of law and its processes. In them a person – almost always a man – must stand up for himself or his own, rather than rely on others to do so. Conflict resolution is seen in strictly personal, I–Thou terms. It is about, not retribution, but revenge.

In a landmark study, *Culture of Honor: The Psychology of Violence in the South* (1996), Richard Nisbett and Dov Cohen argued that (non-military) honour cultures are the product of frontier herding societies. Farmers might be able to rely on law enforcement agencies, but herdsmen lived in low-population, low-density areas. Their livestock was at risk from raiders, so they had to defend their herds themselves. It became important for them to develop a reputation for fearlessness and ferocity, because that reputation itself was a form of security. If, on the other hand, they were attacked successfully, this would become known and would invite further raids. The settlers in the American North tended to be farmers by background, while those in the American South were herdsmen from Scotland and Ireland. That is why, even today, those from the American South are more likely to react violently to slights to their honour than those from the North.

The fourth ethic, the morality of love of God, the neighbour and the stranger, owes its origin, at least in the form most familiar in the West, to the Bible, Judaism and Christianity, and exists in a slightly different form in Buddhism. What is very striking about this ethic in contrast with the others is that it is not linked to specific social structures. It is focused, not on the city or the system or the group, but on God, the universe and the human person. That has given it its remarkable persistence and resilience. It brings together, in a way that is very far from inevitable, religion and ethics, so that to love God and to love one's fellow human are indivisible. That is the burden of the prophetic message in the Hebrew Bible. Time and again the message comes: do not believe that you can win divine favour by offering sacrifices while practising injustices.

Harry Redner says about the biblical injunction for love of neighbour that 'It is a supremely altruistic love, for to love one's neighbour as oneself means always to put oneself in his place and to act on his behalf as one would naturally and selfishly act on one's own.'[7] It is also open-ended. It is not confined to any specific group, for it includes the stranger, the one-not-like-me. This is extended in Christianity even to the enemy. One of the great gifts of Buddhism, in the Rock and Pillar Edicts of King Ashoka (third century BCE), was to add the idea of respect for those whose religion is different from one's own: 'A man should not do reverence to his own sect by disparaging that of another man for trivial reasons . . . The sects of other people deserve reverence. By respecting another's sect one exalts one's own.'[8] Redner notes that no similar sentiment could be found in Western ethics until the liberal Enlightenment in the eighteenth century.

*

Beyond the difference between thick and thin moralities, and the four broad approaches to the moral life, lies the question of the kind of person to which different cultures give rise. This was the subject of an important study, *The Lonely Crowd* (1950), by three American sociologists, David Reisman, Nathan Glazer and Reuel Denney.[9] They argued that different eras in history produced their own distinctive character types. In an era of low growth and high death rates the primary concern is to survive. These times produce people who are oriented to the heritage of the past: *tradition-directed* individuals. Then there is the era of transition, in which there is innovation and high growth rates. Life expectancy expands. The hold of the past and its traditional ways of life are weakened. Key examples were the changes brought about by the Renaissance and the Reformation. These produce *inner-directed individuals*. Lastly, there is the era of slowing economic growth and incipient population decline. This tends to give rise to *other-directed individuals*.

For the tradition-directed individual, 'The culture controls behaviour minutely, and, while the rules are not so complicated that the young cannot learn them during the period of intensive socialisation, careful and rigid etiquette governs the fundamentally influential sphere of kin relationships.'[10] There are codes of conduct that are to be followed in every detail.

The inner-directed individual may still respect tradition, but the world is changing too fast for tradition to cover all eventualities. Instead, he or she is intensively educated to develop a kind of internalised satellite navigation system, one that has generalised instructions and a sense of destination but is more flexible and more capable of adapting to new situations than the detailed codes of tradition could envisage.

The other-directed individual lives at a time when fewer people are engaged in agriculture or industry. They are more affluent. They find themselves more often in contact with people of different races and cultures. For them, other people, rather than the material environment, are the challenge to be addressed. They mix more widely and become more sensitive to one another's opinion. Other-directed people look to their contemporaries for direction and approval.

The Lonely Crowd appeared in 1950 and its insights were rapidly recognised. However, recent technological developments have made it worthy of renewed attention. Specifically, the impact of smartphones and social media has dramatically intensified the sense of social life as being about the presentation of one's self to others, rather than of genuine social interaction. The contemporary West is other-directed as never before.

Particularly telling in this context are the distinctions made between the *emotions* people experience when they do wrong. Tradition-directed individuals feel *shame*. Inner-directed individuals feel *guilt*. Other-directed individuals feel *anxiety*. Anxiety, we know, is felt by heavy users of social media. A 2019 report from the Berkeley Institute for the Future of Young Americans suggests that the rate of university students with anxiety disorders has doubled since 2008, from 10 per cent to 20 per cent, and attributes this to increased time on digital devices, social media in particular, as well as financial stress. In particular, students who spent more than twenty hours of leisure time per week on digital devices were 53 per cent more likely to have anxiety than young adults who spent fewer than five hours a week doing so.[11]

*

There are, in short, different lenses through which to view morality wherever we look. There is the thin morality of liberal individualism, where the only constraints on behaviour are fairness and the avoidance of harm, and there is the thick morality of loyalty, reverence and respect. There are the four broad types of moral tradition: civic ethics, the ethic of duty, codes of honour and the morality of love. And there are the three different kinds of moral personality: tradition-, inner- and other-directed. What then is left for the individual faced with so many alternatives, but to think of morality as a matter of relative or subjective choice? But that conclusion, I think, would be a mistake.

The nature of that mistake was made beautifully clear by David Brooks in the conversation we had for the radio programmes I made for the BBC about morality. He was talking about the distinction between 'freedom from' and 'freedom to'. 'Freedom from' means the absence of constraints, but 'freedom to' is, in his words, 'choosing the right restraint'. If you want to have the freedom to play the piano well, you have to chain yourself to it and practise every day. You have to make a commitment, and that, says Brooks, is in part 'a choice to forgo a future choice'. Or as he put it slightly differently, 'commitment is falling in love with something and then building a structure of behaviour around it for the moment when love falters'.

Moralities, I suggested at the opening of this chapter, are like languages, and to communicate effectively we have to be articulate in at least one language. None of us, at any given moment, stands poised between the six thousand languages spoken today, free to choose between them all. We may be multilingual. We may acquire a small vocabulary to help us on a foreign trip. But for most of us, there is one language in which we think and best express ourselves. And since language exists for the purpose of communication, and communication involves a listener as well as a speaker, we are constrained by our human environment. We need to speak in such a way as to be understood. That means that we need to live in a community of fellow speakers of the same language. We may use language to express our innermost feelings, but that language has rules of syntax and semantics, and we must obey them if we are to communicate effectively. It is those rules that define the community of those who speak our language. There has to be a 'We' – a community united by that language – before there can be an expressive 'I'.

To become moral, we have to make a commitment to some moral community and code. We have to make a choice to forgo certain choices. We have to choose the right restraints. And having fallen in love with some moral principle or ethical ideal, we have to build a structure of behaviour around it, for the moment when love falters. Politics may give us 'freedom from', but morality gives us 'freedom to' – to dance the choreography of interpersonal grace and be part of the music of loving commitment to the lives of others.

We may be more aware than any other generation of the multiple ways of being moral, but that does not mean that we are endlessly poised between them all. Just as marriage is a one-to-one relationship between two people, so morality is a one-to-one relationship between a person and a way of life. It is a choice that precludes other choices. Only the willingness to make a choice allows you morally to grow.

In the 2000 film *Wonder Boys* (based on the novel of that name by Michael Chabon), Michael Douglas plays writer, English professor and marijuana addict Grady Tripp, who, having written a brilliant first novel seven years earlier, is unable to complete his next book, which has by now grown to gargantuan length but seems no nearer to an ending. Towards the end of the film, one of his students, Hannah Green, in a life-changing remark, suggests a reason for his inability to give structure and closure to the unfinished work:

> Hannah: Grady, you know how in class you're always telling us that writers make choices?
> Grady: Yeah.
> Hannah: And even though your book is really beautiful, I mean, amazingly beautiful, it's ... it's at times ... it's ... very

detailed. You know, with the genealogies of everyone's horses, and the dental records, and so on. And . . . I could be wrong, but it sort of reads in places like you didn't make any choices. At all.

Often contemporary life can seem like that. We seem to be making choices all the time, but too often they are choices not to choose, not to foreclose future options. We resist commitment. We are, in Zygmunt Bauman's phrase, tourists not pilgrims. We prioritise 'freedom from' over 'freedom to'. But like marriage, morality involves commitment. And like a book, it involves the ability to edit out passages that may seem beautiful but that do not advance the plot or help you reach an ending. A mature understanding of the many ways there are of organising a society and a life may make us more tolerant of the people not like us, but it does not preclude the knowledge that, if we are to find meaning, depth and resonance in life, we must choose a language of deeds as we choose a language of words. Out of the many moralities available, there is one that is ours, and we do not have to denigrate the others to make that one our own.

21

Religion

So to the inevitable question: What about God? What about religion? Is some kind of faith essential to ethics?

Historically, religion has been the most authoritative and generative moral voice. But the liberal democratic West has been undergoing secularisation for some time. A 2017 British Social Attitudes survey found that 53 per cent of people, more than half of the population, describe themselves as having no religious affiliation whatsoever,[1] the first time since data collection began that they have represented a majority of the population. In the United States, 'nones', those of no religious affiliation, are the fastest-growing group in the population, having increased to 23.1 per cent according to a 2019 General Social Survey.[2] In a separate survey, the Pew Research Center found that, while only 17 per cent of baby boomers (born between 1946 and 1964) declared themselves religiously unaffiliated, 40 per cent of Millennials (born between 1981 and 1996) did so.[3] Is there a connection between religion and ethics? Can a purely secular society survive in the long run? Even if it can, is something lost to the moral life when it departs from its transcendental bearing?

These are hauntingly difficult questions to answer. Serious voices have expressed their doubts about the viability of morality in the absence of religious faith. Voltaire said he wanted his tailor, valet, cook and wife to believe in God because 'If they do, I shall be robbed less and cheated less.'[4] Dostoevsky, in *The Brothers Karamazov*, expressed a view often summarised as follows: if God did not exist, all would be permitted. (Though we should note that he did not use these precise words.)

The architects of the free societies of the West saw religion as the guardian of virtue, and virtue itself as essential to the future of freedom. George Washington spoke on this theme in his farewell address: 'Of all the dispositions and habits which lead to political prosperity, religion and morality are indispensable supports . . . And let us with caution indulge the supposition that morality can be maintained without religion . . . [R]eason and experience both forbid us to expect that national morality can prevail in exclusion of religious principle.'

We have already noted the significance assigned by Alexis de Tocqueville to religion as part of the frame and fabric of American democracy. He writes that 'liberty cannot be established without morality, nor morality without faith'.⁵ All the religions of America, he wrote, worship God in their own unique way, but 'all sects preach the same moral law in the name of God'.⁶ And that is all that is necessary for religion to secure the moral order. 'Liberty regards religion as its companion in all its battles and its triumphs, as the cradle of its infancy and the divine source of its claims. It considers religion as the safeguard of morality, and morality as the best security of law and the surest pledge of the duration of freedom.'⁷

John F. Kennedy, the first Catholic President of the United States, made an important political statement in the opening paragraph of his inaugural address: 'The same revolutionary beliefs for which our forebears fought are still at issue around the globe – the belief that the rights of man come not from the generosity of the state but from the hand of God.' This is an explicitly religious conception of human rights.

Will Durant, the historian, initially intended entering the Catholic priesthood, but became an atheist. Nonetheless, he writes: 'There is no significant example in history, before our time, of a society successfully maintaining moral life without the aid of religion.'⁸ This is how he analyses the breakdown of morality in the absence of religion: 'As education spreads, theologies lose credence, and receive an external conformity without influence upon conduct or hope. Life and ideas become increasingly secular . . . The moral code loses aura and force as its human origin is revealed, and as divine surveillance and sanctions are removed.'⁹

Each of these views, though they are certainly not identical, sees religion as a major shaping force in the moral texture of society. But the opposite case could surely be made. We saw something of this in the chapter asking 'Which Morality?' The two most fundamental sources of morality do not involve religion. They are pre-human. First is the instinct of compassion, of which the most basic is the regard of mother for child. More generally there is the factor of kin selection: our instinct to come to the aid of those with whom we are closely genetically connected. Hence morality is born within the family.

Then there is the logic of reciprocal altruism. I help the members of my group in the belief that when I need it, they will help me. This is the only way we defeat the lose–lose scenario of the Prisoner's Dilemma. Reciprocity allows us to function cooperatively as members of a team, and only as a team can we surmount the hazards that surround us. It creates the essential element called trust. Some such cooperative behaviour exists among all social animals.

In the case of humans, reciprocity leads in many societies to two principles. First there is the Golden Rule, which says: act towards others as you would wish them to act towards you. Then there is the corollary principle of Retributive Justice, that says: act towards others as they have acted to you. So to establish the values of compassion, altruism towards kin and reciprocity towards neighbours, you do not need religion. They tend to emerge in the course of time, through what we might call the social equivalent of natural selection. Cooperative groups survive; others fall by the wayside.

Unexpectedly, some such view seems to be implicit in the Hebrew Bible. God punishes Cain for murdering Abel despite not having told him, 'You shall not murder.' He punishes the citizens of Sodom, despite not having revealed a moral code to them. The Egyptian midwives who disobey Pharaoh and save the lives of the Israelite children – the first recorded act of civil disobedience in history – are described by the Bible as God-fearing. This is a general term that the Bible uses of everyone who acts morally. So the relationship is inverse: it is not that you need to fear God to be moral. Rather, being moral shows that you fear God. The Hebrew Bible, in these early stories, seems to assume that we have an innate moral sense. That is the voice of God within the human heart – which exists even prior to the rules and rituals, holy deeds and holy days that we call religion.

Why then is the moral sense not enough? Why do we need rules and rituals? Reciprocal altruism, as already noted, works with small groups where, by observation, memory and gossip, the members are able to know who to trust and who not. But this is impossible in a large group. In the eighteenth century, David Hume made this point:

> Two neighbours may agree to drain a meadow, which they possess in common; because it is easy for them to know each other's mind; and each must perceive, that the immediate consequence of his failing in his part, is the abandoning of the whole project. But it is very difficult, and indeed impossible, that a thousand persons should agree in any such action; it being difficult for them to concert so complicated a design, and still more difficult for them to execute it; while each seeks a pretext to free himself of the trouble and expense, and would lay the whole burden on others.[10]

The basic problem that had to be solved in order for complex civilisations to emerge was how to organise cooperation and establish relationships of trust on a large scale. Reciprocity is fine for small groups whose members know one another, but not for larger associations. The difficulty arose when, with the development of agriculture, people were then able to live in large numbers in close proximity. The creation of the first cities brought with it the question: *how do you build trust between strangers?* That is when the first great religions were born – not spirituality, which can be dated much earlier, but fully articulated systems of religion with priests, temples, myths, rituals, holy times, places and people. (I have written about this more fully in *The Great Partnership*.[11]) The birth of religion in this sense was the birth of civilisation.

Anthropologists calculate that for 99.9 per cent of our history, humans lived in small hunter-gatherer bands. One of the few surviving such groups, the Hadza in northern Tanzania, East Africa, has been studied by anthropologist Frank Marlowe. He writes that they do have spiritual beliefs, a cosmology, but it is not what we would think of as a religion. 'There are no churches, preachers, leaders, or religious guardians, no idols or images of gods, no regular organised meetings, no religious morality, no belief in an afterlife.'[12] Hunter-gatherers believed in spirits and gods, but thought that they had limited interest in the affairs of human beings.

As we trace the history of religion we find that when societies grow in size and complexity, we encounter increasingly elaborate religious rituals, formal priesthoods, monumental buildings, and the structuring of time around holy days. Religion and morality become more clearly associated with one another. As Ara Norenzayan puts it: 'Prosocial religions, with their Big Gods who watch, intervene, and demand hard-to-fake loyalty displays, facilitated the rise of cooperation in large groups of anonymous strangers.'[13] By creating the conditions for trust between strangers, religion allowed human beings to become the only species ever to have evolved from small, tight-knit groups to large, structured societies.

Religion, in its increasingly articulated and orchestrated forms, for the first time allowed large numbers of human beings to inhabit a single shared culture, encoded in sacred stories, rehearsed in choreographed rituals, supervised by priests, worshipped in sacrifice and prayer. What religion represented was a moral structure on a cosmic scale, in which the gods ensured the implementation of justice. The good would be rewarded and the bad punished, whether in this world or in the next. The world out there in the cosmos, and the world in here in the soul, came together to unite human beings in a single moral enterprise: the society-wide maintenance of order.

That, then, is the first point: by establishing moral communities on a large scale through shared beliefs and rituals rather than by frequent face-to-face interaction, religion solved the problem of establishing trust between strangers. Without this, it is doubtful that humanity would ever have left the hunter-gatherer stage.

*

That was the contribution of the first, polytheistic, religions. Then came monotheism, and the moral life was transformed again. If pre-monotheistic faiths consecrated the social structure, then monotheism consecrated the individual. For the first time in human consciousness, the single God confronted the singular person in an unmediated relationship. Unprecedentedly, in the Hebrew Bible the human person as such became God's 'significant other'. Each individual was 'in the image and likeness' of God. The intimacy of this relationship gave rise to a new kind of morality – based not on justice only but also on love: 'Love the Lord your God with all your heart, all your soul and all your might', 'Love your neighbour as yourself', and 'Love the stranger, because you know what it feels like to be a stranger.'

This led to a new understanding of the human person. If the free and creative God made humans in his image, then we too are capable of freedom and creativity. In contrast to the pre-Socratic Greeks, the Bible focuses less on character and fate than on will and choice. Its great early dramas – Adam and Eve in Eden, Cain and Abel, the patriarchs and matriarchs and the societies in which they live – are about the perennial choice between good and evil, righteousness and guilt. The human person is seen as both physical and spiritual, part body, part soul, dust of the earth, yet also the breath of God. As we have noted when considering human dignity, this view is at odds both with the Greek idea of fate and with the modern scientific idea of biological or neurological determinism.

From individual freedom flows social freedom. If human beings are free, they can change, and if we can do so as individuals then we can do likewise as societies. This led to the radical idea, first expressed in the Hebrew Bible, that time is an arena of change. This gave the West its dynamism. Virtually all other religious views saw time as cyclical, a succession of phases that always return to the same starting point. These yield essentially conservative societies, while the biblical view of time tends to restlessness and revolution, or at least evolution.

In biblical morality it is the individual, not the state, that is sacrosanct. The Bible is intensely critical of the world's first empires, Mesopotamia (the Tower of Babel) and Egypt of the book of Exodus, seeing them as oppressive powers prepared to sacrifice the individual for the sake of the system. For the Bible, a ruler is no holier than those he rules. Elsewhere, kings and pharaohs were seen as demigods and worshipped as such. This, for the Bible, is idolatry. Uniquely in the ancient world, the king in biblical Israel had no legislative power. John Milton made the point in *Paradise Lost*: 'Man over men / He made not lord; such title to Himself / Reserving, human left from human free.' Kingship and power are thus limited and secularised. The only ultimate sovereign is God himself.

If social order is not written into the structure of the cosmos, if individuals may not be sacrificed to the state, and if kings have no special access to godlike powers, it follows that society flourishes only when people behave well to one another. This vision gave rise to the unique world of the Hebrew prophets – figures like Elijah, Elisha, Amos, Hosea, Isaiah and Jeremiah – who spoke truth to power, criticised kings, and told the people endlessly to practise justice and compassion, righteousness and love. A good society prospers. A bad society fails. Isaiah 1 states the case simply and bluntly:

When you spread out your hands in prayer,
    I hide my eyes from you;
even when you offer many prayers,
    I am not listening ...
Learn to do right; seek justice.
Defend the oppressed.
Take up the cause of the fatherless;
    plead the case of the widow
        (Isaiah 1:15–17).

This distinctive morality is often called the Judeo-Christian ethic, and it played an important role in the emergence of the modern West, leading in the seventeenth and eighteenth centuries to the beginnings of democratic capitalism: the politics and economics of freedom.

The German sociologist Max Weber famously argued that 'the Protestant ethic' led to 'the spirit of capitalism', the economics of the free market. As for politics, covenant, the key concept of the Hebrew Bible, has been part of American political culture since the first Puritan settlers. Their first formal act was the Mayflower Pact of 1620: 'We whose names are underwritten ... solemnly and mutually in the presence of God, and of one another, covenant and combine our selves together in a civill body politick.' Aboard the *Arbella* in 1630, John Winthrop similarly declared, 'We are entered into covenant with Him [God] for this work.'

Covenant has been an underlying strand of American political thought ever since. Its most famous expression is the opening phrase of the preamble to the American Constitution: 'We, the people.' That phrase – used five times in Barak Obama's second inaugural address – is pure covenant terminology. It speaks of sovereignty lying in the hands not of a ruler or government but of the people themselves, conceived as a community of equals who have accepted collective responsibility for their common destiny and fate.

Politics and economics as we are familiar with them have a religious dimension at least in this sense: that religions shape cultures, and not all cultures give rise to market economics or democratic politics. Niall Ferguson, in his book *Civilization* (2011), tells how the Chinese Academy of Social Sciences was given the task of discovering how the West, having lagged behind China for centuries, eventually overtook it and established itself in a position of world pre-eminence. At first, said one scholar, we thought it was because you had more powerful guns than we had. Then we concluded it was because you had the best political system. Then we realised it was your economic system. He finished, 'But in the past 20 years, we have realised that the heart of your culture is your religion: Christianity. That is why the West has been so powerful. The Christian moral foundation of social and cultural life was what made possible the emergence of capitalism and then the successful transition to democratic politics. We don't have any doubt about this.'[14]

One key biblical idea played an important part in this development, namely the separation of powers. In the Hebrew Bible this takes the form of the division of authority between king, priest and prophet. In the New Testament, we find the injunction, 'Render unto Caesar the things that are Caesar's and to God the things that are God's.' These became influential precedents as Western societies moved to a formal and substantive separation of church and state. These three elements – individual dignity, equality and separation of powers – make possible the Locke–Jefferson conception of human rights and limited, constitutional government.

In the context of economics, we gain the important idea, emphasised particularly by Calvinism, of the dignity of labour: 'Six days shall you labour and do all your work, but the seventh day is a Sabbath to the Lord your God.' We serve God by work as well as by rest. This is in contrast to the ethics of ancient Greece in which leisure was the mark of nobility and labour the fate of the lower classes. This played an important part in the emergence of Western-style economics.

Not everyone would agree, but there is a strong case that the specifics of Judaism and Christianity, especially in its Calvinist expression, laid the foundations for the free societies of the West. In which case the key question is, can these societies survive in the long run without those foundations? Or is religion like a ladder that people climb but that, having reached a higher plane, they can then discard?

*

There are, I would argue, at least three areas where the contribution of religion to the moral basis of society is a continuing and essential one. The first relates to one of the most influential modern understandings of religion, put forward by the French sociologist Émile Durkheim (1858–1917). Durkheim believed that religion was best understood not in terms of beliefs but behaviours, and not as a supernatural phenomenon but as a natural one. This is how he defined it: 'A religion is a unified system of beliefs and practices relative to sacred things . . . which unite into one single moral community called a church, all those who adhere to them.'[15]

Religion creates community. That for Durkheim was its single most important function. Its symbols bind people together. Its rituals create what he called collective effervescence, a shared epiphany. It *binds and blinds*, to use Jonathan Haidt's terminology in *The Righteous Mind*; that is, it gives people a distinct identity and creates bonds between them while at the same time distancing them from those outside the group.[16] Religion, for Durkheim, is less about believing than belonging.

In *Darwin's Cathedral*, David Sloan Wilson mounts an evolutionary argument, combining a Darwinian and Durkheimian perspective. Religions have existed and survived, he says, because they helped groups come together, stay together, work together, and find strength through cooperation. The citizens of Calvin's Geneva so internalised his strict ethic of work, discipline, virtue and frugality that they were able to achieve exemplary success socially and economically. The intricate and demanding nature of Judaism allowed Jews to preserve their identity in exile and dispersion for two thousand years despite the fact that, wherever they found themselves, they were a cultural and religious minority.

Wilson's most spectacular example is of how the Balinese worship of the Goddess of the Waters allowed thousands of rice farmers, spread across hundreds of square kilometres, to manage the delicate process of sharing limited rainwater as it makes its way down the sides of a volcano, a marvellous feat of social co-ordination. All these things happened with little if any recourse to the coercive power of governments, solely because of the deeply internalised religious rules that give structure and substance to community.

Anthropologist Richard Sosis undertook a study of two hundred communes founded in the United States in the nine-teenth century.[17] He discovered that a mere 6 per cent of secular communes were still functioning twenty years after their founding, whereas 39 per cent of religious ones were. He also found that the more demanding the entrance requirements were in religious communes – the more sacrifices they asked of their members, such as giving up alcohol or tobacco – the more the members were willing to make sacrifices for one another, and the longer the commune lasted. This suggests not only that religious communities last longer than their secular equivalents, but that the stricter they are, the more resilient they become.

Coming to our own time, Harvard sociologist Robert Putnam, as mentioned earlier, has documented both the loss and the recovery of 'social capital', his phrase for interpersonal trust. Initially he became famous for the phrase he used to describe the progressive individualism afflicting Western democracies. Noting that more Americans than ever are going ten-pin bowling, but fewer are joining bowling clubs and leagues, he called it 'bowling alone'. It was a phrase that summed up an era.

The free market gave people unprecedented individual choices.

Liberal democracy left us freer than ever to decide how to structure our lives. Morality morphed into a seemingly infinite variety of lifestyles, to be put on and then discarded at will. Music, once a shared experience heard in concerts and recitals, began to be heard through a Walkman, then an iPod, on a strictly one-to-one basis.

Since Putnam's book was published in 2000, we have only travelled further along the same trajectory. Two generations ago, newspapers, radio and television were configured in such a way that an entire nation was receiving the news at much the same time in much the same way. Now news, and information generally, has been fragmented into myriad websites, YouTube videos, Tweets, Facebook postings and blogs from which you can choose those that resonate with your convictions, screening out all voices with which you disagree.

This proved bad news for those associations – marriages, families, congregations and communities – where we experience life as social animals. In the endless competition between our selfish genes and our group instincts, self has been winning, damaging our social ecology and weakening, in Robert Bellah's words, 'the subtle ties that bind human beings to one another, leaving them frightened and alone'.

A decade later, however, in a book entitled *American Grace* (2010), Putnam documented the good news. He discovered that a powerful store of social capital still existed in religious environments: the churches, synagogues and other places of worship that still bring people together in shared belonging and mutual responsibility. The evidence shows that religious people – defined by regular attendance at a place of worship – actually do make better neighbours.

An extensive survey carried out throughout the United States between 2004 and 2006 showed that frequent church- or synagogue-goers are more likely to give money to charity, regardless of whether the charity is religious or secular. They are also more likely to do voluntary work for a charity, give money to a homeless person, give excess change back to a shop assistant, donate blood, help a neighbour with housework, spend time with someone who is feeling depressed, allow other drivers to come out in front of them, offer a seat to a stranger, or help someone find a job.

For some minor acts of help, there was no difference between frequent and non-churchgoers. But there was no good deed among the fifteen on the survey more commonly practised by secular Americans than by their religious counterparts. Religious Americans are simply more likely to give of their time and money to others, not only within but also beyond their own communities.

Their altruism exceeds this. Frequent worshippers are also more active citizens. They are more likely to belong to community organisations, especially those concerned with young people, health, arts and leisure, neighbourhood and civic groups and professional associations. Within these organisations they are more likely to be officers or committee members. They take a more active part in local civic and political life, from local elections to town meetings to demonstrations. They are disproportionately represented among local activists for social and political reform. They get involved, turn up and lead. The margin of difference between them and the more secular is large.

Tested on attitudes, religiosity as measured by church or synagogue attendance turns out to be the best predictor of altruism and empathy: better than education, age, income, gender or race. On the basis of self-reported life satisfaction, religious people are also happier than their non-religious counterparts.

Interestingly, each of these attributes is related not to people's religious beliefs but to the frequency with which they attend a place of worship. Religion creates community, community creates altruism, and altruism turns us away from self and towards the common good. Putnam goes so far as to speculate that an atheist who went regularly to church (perhaps because of a spouse) would be more likely to volunteer in a soup kitchen than a believer who prays alone. Like Durkheim, he came to the conclusion that religion, as a moral force, is more about belonging than believing.

There is something about the tenor of relationships within a religious congregation that makes it the best tutorial in citizenship and good neighbourliness. Religions in liberal democratic societies are our ongoing tutorial in the 'art of association' that Alexis de Tocqueville saw as our apprenticeship in liberty. Religion creates communities, and communities create moral people.

*

Two other scholars, Ara Norenzayan in *Big Gods*, and Dominic Johnson in *God is Watching You*,[18] adopt a similar evolutionary perspective to that of David Sloan Wilson, but with a different emphasis. They focus not on religion's community-building function but on the moral impact of the idea that God sees what we do, even in private, that he rewards the good, and more significantly, that he punishes the guilty. It is specifically the punitive dimension of religious belief that is for them the fundamental difference that religion makes. Essentially, they agree with Voltaire, that those who believe in God rob and cheat less than those who don't.

For them, the fundamental problem to be overcome by any society is that of the free-rider. We all seek the benefits of cooperative endeavour, while being reluctant to pay the costs. That, as we noted above, was David Hume's point: 'each seeks a pretext to free himself of the trouble and expense [of a communal project], and would lay the whole burden on others'. Norenzayan's thesis is that 'social surveillance keeps people in line', or more simply, 'watched people are nice people'.[19]

The most powerful force in getting us to behave well is the knowledge, or belief, that we are being observed. Speeding drivers will slow down if they see a police car in their rear-view mirror. When charities do fundraising in public, people give more. In one ingenious experiment, a group of students at the University of Toronto were given six dollars and the opportunity to give any proportion of this to an anonymous stranger. Under a pretext, half of them were given clear eyeglasses to wear, and half, dark sunglasses. The ones wearing dark glasses gave on average $1.81. Those wearing clear glasses gave on average $2.71. The dark glasses gave students 'illusory anonymity', the false feeling that they were hidden from view. This was sufficient to move them from an equal-sharing to a more selfish mode of behaviour. Chenbo Zhong, Vanessa Bohns and Francesca Gino, who organised this experiment, also discovered that people in a dimly lit room were more likely to cheat than those in a brightly lit one. 'A good lamp is the best police,' they concluded.

Even subtle cues can make us more generous or law-abiding. Kevin Hayley and Dan Fessler found that if they exposed participants to drawings of human eyes, masquerading as an ordinary computer screensaver, they were 55 per cent more generous when they were subsequently given a sum of money and the choice of how much of it to give an anonymous stranger.[20] In another experiment, researchers placed a coffee machine in a university hallway, together with an 'honesty box'. People could take coffee as they wished, and leave money in the box. On some days, a poster with watchful eyes was hanging on the wall above the machine. On other days, there was a picture of a flower. On average, people left 2.76 times as much money on the days when the eyes were displayed.

It is not only the Bible that tells us God sees all we do. Norenzayan makes the point that divine eyes can also be found in representations of Horus in ancient Egypt, Buddha in villages in Tibet and Nepal, Viracocha in the Inca Empire, and many other portrayals of deities. What moves people to act in prosocial ways is not the idea of God as an abstract creative force, but rather the belief that He sees what we do – and not simply the belief but an active reminder of it.

In one experiment, people who were shown God-related words before a test were less likely to cheat than those who were not. In another, it was found that Christians give 300 per cent more to charity on Sundays than non-religious individuals, but on other days there is no difference. On Sundays, Christians expressed a stronger sense of being watched. It may therefore be that religion makes a difference because, through rituals, prayers and holy days, people are *reminded* that we are seen.

The power of religion, Norenzayan and Johnson argue, is precisely its negative aspect of divine punishment. Norenzayan assembles research evidence that shows, counterintuitively, that those who believe in a punitive God are more law-abiding and also more forgiving than those who believe in a forgiving God. His conclusion is that 'belief in divine punishment diminishes the motivation for earthly forms of costly punishment'.[21] Johnson regards the fear of divine punishment as, historically, a remarkably effective means of deterring free-riders and encouraging cooperation on a large scale.

What happens when people no longer believe in God, heavenly surveillance and divine punishment? The principle still applies: watched people are nice people. But what has emerged in the wake of the loss of religious belief is the phenomenon of being watched by CCTV, and the elaborate infrastructure of a surveillance society. Central agencies, commercial or governmental, now have immense and detailed knowledge of our emails and texts, purchases, bank transactions, viewing habits, even what we say to one another at home. Combined with advanced facial recognition techniques, this means that we can now be watched by others to an unprecedented degree, giving governments and other agencies potentially dangerous power to manipulate or control. It may have a similar effect to religious belief in some senses, but there is no guarantee that those who use this information will do so for our good as opposed to theirs.

*

Finally, there is the insight of Jean-Jacques Rousseau in *The Social Contract*. 'Perspectives which are general and goals remote are alike beyond the range of the common herd,' he said. People take short-term views. It is hard to engage them in a case for austerity now so that there may be prosperity in the long run. '[I]t is difficult for the individual, who has no taste for any scheme of government but that which serves his private interest, to appreciate the advantages to be derived from the lasting austerities which good laws impose.' Democratic politics is often condemned to operate within short time spans.

It follows, he says, that the lawgiver must 'have recourse to an authority of another order, one which can compel without violence and persuade without convincing'. This, he says, is why 'the founders of nations throughout history' have appealed to divine intervention and 'to attribute their own wisdom to the gods'.[22] The point remains relevant. How, in a culture of self-interest, do you persuade people to make sacrifices for long-term ends?

One example we have already mentioned is climate change. People have known about the damage we have been doing to the environment since the 1990s, yet the changes to our behaviour have been limited, except where change is relatively easy and un-costly, such as forgoing the use of plastic bags. Shifting to environmentally friendly modes of transportation has proven far more difficult.

How do you persuade people to make sacrifices now for the sake of benefits that may not be realised until long after they are dead? What obligations do we owe to people not yet born? It is quite difficult to answer such questions within conventional parameters of rational self-interest. Rousseau's concern about the short-term nature of normal political calculation should be ours also.

Before the 2009 United Nations Climate Change Conference in Copenhagen, the British Secretary of State for the Environment, Ed Miliband, expressed a wish to take with him a message from the religious communities of Britain. So, at Lambeth Palace under the aegis of the Archbishop of Canterbury Rowan Williams, leaders of all the major faiths spent a day with him, sharing their religious traditions about our relationship to and responsibility for the planet. It was a revealing moment since Ed, as far as I knew, was not personally religious. It was as if he sensed that this was an area in which faith had much to say to all of us, if only because its perspectives in time and space are so vast.

More directly relevant to the future of the liberal democratic nations of Europe is simply the question of birth rates. As Eric Kaufmann[23] has shown, as Europe has secularised, so birth rates have fallen. The birth rate in Britain in 2018 was the lowest since records began, having fallen 46 per cent from its peak in 1947.[24] A similar trajectory can be traced for almost all European countries. None has a replacement level rate. That means that Europe can only maintain a stable or growing population via immigration on an unprecedented scale. The sole sectors of the population that are growing are the religious ones: on average, the more religious, the larger the family. Again the logic is that of Rousseau. It takes a long-term perspective willingly to undergo the sacrifices involved in having and raising children.

So, religion has something to add to the conversation and to society regardless of its metaphysical foundations. It builds communities. It aids law-abidingness. And it helps us think long term. Most simply, the religious mindset awakens us to transcendence. It redeems our solitude. It breaks the carapace of selfhood and opens us to others and to the world.

PART FIVE
The Way Forward

22

Morality Matters

Gander, on the island of Newfoundland, Canada, was a small, quiet, relatively unknown town of ten thousand inhabitants far away from the urban centres of a hectic world, at least until 11 September 2001. That day, following the terrorist attacks on the World Trade Center and the Pentagon, the United States closed its airspace to incoming planes. Those destined for one of its airports were diverted elsewhere. Thirty-eight planes, carrying almost seven thousand passengers of ninety-seven different nationalities, were forced to land at Gander International Airport. A major humanitarian challenge had suddenly been thrust on the people of the town. The story of how they responded has since become the subject of several books, and more recently a musical, *Come From Away*.

The passengers were exhausted, disoriented and shocked. Some had been held on board planes for twenty-eight hours while extensive security checks were made on their luggage. Many of them had no idea where they were, or how to get in touch with relatives and friends to let them know they were safe. Yet almost immediately, they encountered an unusual sense of welcome. Greeting them was a feast prepared by the people of the town. Local bus drivers, who had been on strike, immediately set their grievances aside to take the newcomers to the various shelters that had been prepared for them around the town, in schools, Salvation Army centres and churches.

People invited them into their homes so they could shower and refresh themselves. They provided them with linen and toiletries. Local fast food outlets supplied them with chicken and pizza and sandwiches. Children were given toys. Those celebrating a birthday were given a party and presents. For those who did not know where they were, a volunteer had taped a map of the world on the wall of one of the shelters, with a big red arrow pointing to Gander and saying, 'You are here.'

Newtel, the Newfoundland telephone company, set up in front of its offices a bank of phones so that people could get in touch with relatives, free of charge. A local cable television provider set up screens in all the refuge centres so that the passengers could follow the news as it emerged. A centre was set up in one of the schools, providing access to emails and computers and television so that the passengers could maintain contact with their families and the world outside. When townspeople in their cars saw any of the 'plane people' in the street, they would stop and offer them a ride to wherever they were headed. Throughout their stay, which for some lasted almost a week, the passengers were given not just food and shelter, but psychological support and human warmth.

As the author of one of the books put it,

> for the better part of a week, nearly every man, woman, and child in Gander and the surrounding smaller towns stopped what they were doing so they could help. They placed their lives on hold for a group of strangers and asked for nothing in return. They affirmed the basic goodness of man at a time when it was easy to doubt such humanity still existed.[1]

*

It would be easy, after the analysis set out in this book, to be pessimistic about the future of Western liberal democracies. We have traced some of the dimensions of what has happened since the loss of the idea of society as a moral community. It began, as we saw, as the rarefied vision of intellectuals in the second half of the nineteenth century, followed from the 1930s onward by existentialists and emotivists who denied that there was a morality beyond the self. Then came the liberal revolution of the 1960s and the economic revolution – Thatcherism and Reaganomics – of the

1980s. They were followed by the fragmentation of culture and communication brought about by computers, the Internet, smart-phones and social media.

That is where we are today: often lonely, confused, disillusioned and mistrustful, living in societies divided into non-communicating groups, each of which believes that it is exploited, abused or threatened by others. From this comes a politics of anger that can easily lead to populism and the search for the strong leader who will somehow make the problems go away, but who often makes them worse. That is the dark mood that has settled in the minds of many of the liberal democracies of the West today.

What the story of the people of Gander tells us, however, is that pessimism is premature. It is not that we require a special effort to be moral. It is, in many respects, our default mode. We are made to compete, but we are also and equally made to cooperate. We need one another. We care about one another. Recall the opening sentence of Adam Smith's *Theory of Moral Sentiments*: 'How selfish soever man may be supposed, there are evidently some principles in his nature, which interest him in the fortunes of others, and render their happiness necessary to him, though he derives nothing from it, except the pleasure of seeing it.' The first theorist of market economics never forgot that we are not simply acquisitive. We are also, and fundamentally, moral.

The people of Gander were not alone. There were many instances of heroism, kindness and good neighbourliness in the wake of 11 September 2001. As often in history, the worst brings out the best in us. What made Gander exemplary, though, is that it is a small town in a remote location. As we have seen throughout, our moral sentiments begin in families and extend outward to communities. They depend on repeated face-to-face interactions. That is why the level of trust is usually far higher in such environments than in the relatively impersonal environments of large cities, where most of the faces around us belong to strangers, and our interactions are often of a one-off kind. That is where our self-regarding interests can sometimes grow unchecked. People can take advantage of one another. They become free-riders, seeking the benefits of collaborative endeavour without paying the price. As soon as this happens, levels of trust begin to decline.

Trust cannot be restored by the market or the state, because these are arenas of competition, not cooperation. It cannot be restored by smartphones and social media, precisely because these are not face to face. When I use social media, I am presenting myself, not encountering you in your full and distinctive otherness. When I use them to acquire information about the world, I have no immediate way of knowing whether the message I receive is true or false, objective or manipulative. When I use wealth or power to achieve my purposes, I am advancing my interests as an individual, not our interests as a moral community. This does not help the cause of trust. It further damages it.

The beautiful thing about morality, though, is that it begins with us. We do not need to wait for a great political leader, or an upturn in the economy, or a new mood in society, or an unexpected technological breakthrough, to begin to change the moral climate within which we live and move and have our being. In the opening chapter, I described our current situation as one in which we have outsourced morality to the market and the state. But morality in its truest sense cannot be outsourced. It is about taking responsibility, not handing it away. All it needs is for us to think about the 'We', not just the 'I', and immediately we change the tenor of our relationships.

When we behave towards others with care and concern, sensitivity and tact, honesty and integrity, generosity and grace, forbearance and forgiveness, we start to become a different person. And such is the nature of reciprocity – itself one of the deeply engraved instincts that is the basis of morality – that we begin to change the way others relate to us; not always, to be sure, but often. Slowly but surely, a new atmosphere begins to be felt, at least in the more intimate environments in which we function. Bad behaviour can easily become contagious, but so can good behaviour, and it usually wins out in the long run. We feel uplifted by people who care about other people.

This has now been shown to be a universal truth. In 2019, anthropologists at Oxford University published the results of a survey of moral attitudes in sixty cultures around the world. They discovered that there are seven basic moral rules that they all held in common: help your family, help your group, return favours, be brave, defer to superiors, divide resources fairly, and respect other people's property. In all the studied cultures, these seven behaviours were held to be morally good, and this was true across continents. They were not the sole preserve of the West. Dr Oliver Scott Curry, senior researcher at the Institute for Cognitive and Evolutionary Anthropology and one of the authors of the report, concluded: 'Everyone everywhere shares a common moral code. All agree that cooperating, promoting the common good, is the right thing to do.'[2] So for all the diversity I charted in the chapter on 'Which Morality?', there are moral universals, just as there is a basic depth grammar underlying the six thousand different languages spoken today.

And we all count. During the series of radio programmes I made for the BBC about morality, I asked Melinda Gates who, together with her husband Bill, has given billions of dollars in philanthropy, what she would say to teenagers today who have neither the wealth nor influence to do good on so large a scale. Her answer was a model of modesty and simplicity:

What I want to tell you is that when you look out over the arc of your life and what you want to do with your life and what you want it to stand for, the thing you are going to feel best about in life is that you are loved by your family and friends and that you have done something to change the world for the better in some way. And what I want to tell you in high school is that you already know that, and if you start now even in small ways, by little drops in the bucket, you will be amazed at how much that adds up over the course of your lifetime.

We change the world, she said, 'one act of kindness at a time'. And when we change the world, sometimes it changes us.

*

In July 2019 a video surfaced on Twitter. A Muslim-Israeli paramedic, Muawiya Kabha, a member of a response unit for an emergency medical service, was making a speech at a Jewish wedding in Israel at that time, telling the groom and guests a story about the bride, Shachar Kugelmas. He told them that he had first met her ten years earlier. He had arrived at the scene of a car crash and found her apparently dead. His was the second ambulance to arrive:

> The first ambulance arrived with a doctor. When I arrived there after those initial two minutes, the doctor informed me, 'This injured girl, don't touch her. I have already declared her dead. Let's treat the driver.' I told him, 'Okay, you treat the driver.' I stayed treating Shachar. From above, something told me that I needed to stay treating Shachar.
>
> When I got to Shachar, she was in cardiac arrest. In terms of strict protocol, the doctor was right. We needed to declare her dead. But what I felt from above was that I still needed to try to save her. I did CPR [cardiopulmonary resuscitation] on Shachar for forty minutes, when she was still stuck in the car. The police had already announced on the radio that there was one person dead in the car accident. Shachar's parents heard the bad news on their way from the North. We continued CPR on the way to the hospital and at the entrance to the hospital, she had a heart-beat. Her heart started to beat.
>
> That night, when I returned home, I didn't have hope. I put my head on the pillow and thought the Angel of Death might have beaten me. But I knew that I had done everything I could do to try to save her. In the end, I must have done what I needed to do, because look, Shachar is with us.

So I am here to tell Shachar, 'Thank you.' Usually the people we save tell *us* 'Thank you.' I want to tell *you* 'Thank you.' And I'll explain why.

People ask me all the time, 'How do you keep going after all the death you see in your work?' The answer is here. Shachar, I am able to continue my work because of you. Because *I saved your body. But you saved my soul*. Every time that I remember emergency calls that I have been to, I remember you and your smile. Thank you. Thank you. Mazal tov, congratulations, I love you both.[3]

Changing the world for others, changes us. To put it in Muawiya's terms, sometimes saving someone else's body is saving our own soul.

*

The contemporary world has given morality a rough ride. The word itself now evokes all we distrust most: the intrusion of impersonal standards into our private lives, the presence of judgement where judgement does not belong, the substitution of authority for choice. When a politician moralises, we suspect that he or she is searching for an excuse not to pay for something. When a religious leader moralises, we fear the imposition of certainties we no longer share, and we suspect that fundamentalism is not far behind. When a particularly newsworthy crime or social trend provokes ethical debate, it will not be long before voices are heard dismissing the conversation as 'moral panic'. We have come to share George Bernard Shaw's conviction that morality is one person's way of disrupting someone else's innocent enjoyment, or as H.G. Wells called it, 'jealousy with a halo'.

But this cannot be the whole picture. We do still care, and care passionately, about concerns that are essentially moral. We are disturbed by legal injustice and extreme economic inequality. We are distressed by our destruction of the environment in pursuit of economic growth. We are not indifferent to the suffering of others or to the harm we may be laying in store for future generations. We are as moral as any other generation. Perhaps more so, for television and the Internet have exposed us in the most vivid and immediate ways to sufferings that in a previous age we would hardly have known about, let alone seen. And our greater affluence and technological prowess have given us the resources to address ills – physical and economic – that an earlier generation might have seen as something about which nothing could be done, part of the sad but natural order of things. We are certainly not amoral. We remain sharply aware of the difference between what is and what ought to be.

There are already signs that Gen-Z – the cohort of those born on or after 1995 – is taking moral responsibility more seriously than its immediate predecessors. Since the turn of the millennium, according to a British government survey, there has been a decline in drug taking, teenage pregnancies, drinking, smoking and crime among young people.[4] Jean Twenge says that today's teenagers are 'less entitled and narcissistic than Millennials and have more moderate expectations'. They are 'not as overconfident and they have a stronger work ethic'.[5] David Brooks says that they are 'seething with moral passion, and rebelling against the privatisation of morality so prevalent in the Boomer and Gen-X generations'.[6] During the radio programmes on morality I made for the BBC, I found that the seventeen- and eighteen-year-olds who took part were as eloquent and insightful as the other participants, all of whom were world leaders in their field. These are very good signs.

Morality matters for the future no less than it did in the past. We were not made to live alone. To be sure, some have sung the praises of solitude, but for the most part our hopes, our happiness, our very identity are shaped by face-to-face interactions with others, which is where the moral sense is born, where we learn what it is to love and be loved, trust and be trusted, where we internalise those rules of conduct that allow us to engage in collaborative enterprise, where we gradually develop our instincts of empathy, sympathy, compassion, pity, kindness, generosity, hospitality, charity, and the rest. We are who we are through what we give to others.

The sages of antiquity never doubted this. Aristotle defined happiness as an activity of the soul in accordance with virtue. The prophets of ancient Israel never tired of insisting that the fate of society depended on the degree to which it practised justice and compassion, caring for the weak, the poor and the marginalised. Moral strength, they believed, was more important in the long run than military strength. Those republican and biblical principles were, in their slightly different ways, the source of the resilience of Britain and America and their passionate devotion to liberty.

Not only does morality shape the fate of nations. It forms the fabric of a life well lived. I had the privilege of studying with some of the greatest philosophers of our time, yet I learned more about morality in my years as a congregational rabbi than I did at Oxford and Cambridge, and I did so by conducting funerals. As a young rabbi in an ageing congregation, I often did not know the deceased personally, so I had to ask relatives and friends what they were like and what they would be remembered for. No one ever spoke about the clothes they wore or the cars they drove, the homes they lived in or the holidays they took. They spoke about their role in their family, their place in the congregation and its activities, the good deeds they did, the causes they supported, the voluntary work they undertook and the people they helped. It is not what we do for ourselves but what we give to others that is our epitaph and that ultimately floods life with meaning. We are moral animals.

Many reasons have been advanced as to why the concept of morality as a set of rules beyond the self has suffered an eclipse. We have become less religious, and religion was the classic source of our belief in a revealed morality, commandments engraved on tablets of stone. We have become more culturally diverse, and we now know that what seems wrong to one group may be permissible in a second and even admirable in a third.

We have inherited, however indirectly, a set of ideas from Marx and Nietzsche, that what passes for morality may be the mask over a hierarchy of power, a way of keeping people in their place. From psychoanalysis we have developed a suspicion that morality is a way of suppressing natural instinct, and as such is an enemy of self-expression. Perhaps, after the horror of two world wars, we simply reached the conclusion that previous generations had led us into the wilderness instead of the Promised Land, and the time had come to try another way. Each of these analyses has some truth to it, and there may be many more.

But there is a political dimension too. The twentieth century witnessed a vast expansion of the power and presence of the state. Things that were once the province of families, communities, religious congregations, voluntary organisations and cooperative groups were appropriated by governments. In part this was motivated by economic and political necessity. The modern nation-state needed an adaptable population, whose members shared a common culture and education. As women increasingly joined the workforce, care facilities had to be provided by the state. The standardisation required by industry and war spelled the break-up of more local traditions and associations. But there was also a deep moral dimension to the growth of the state, namely a terminal dissatisfaction with the inequalities of privilege. Why should some people but not others have access to the best schools and doctors? Could a decent society allow families to languish because of poverty and unemployment? These were, I believe, the right questions at a certain period in the development of Western democracies, and they led to the caring state.

But even the right decisions have long-term consequences, not all of which are benign. The growth of the state meant the atrophy of many of those local institutions, from the family outwards, where people learned the give-and-take of human relationships and the subtle codes of civility without which it is difficult for people to live closely together for very long. It also broke the connection between what we do and what happens to us, which is of the essence of moral responsibility. A child 'going wrong' in the past would be supported by family and friends, but they would deliver an unmistakable moral rebuke. Continued support came with conditions. The caring state can deliver no such message because a state is neither family nor friend. It is of its essence impersonal. It is there to help with few strings attached. It does not make moral judgements. It is beyond its competence and remit to make distinctions between the sufferings that befall us and those we bring upon ourselves. No one sought to have the state undermine moral responsibility. But inevitably that was its effect. It left it redundant and unemployed.

The displacement of the community by the state meant the replacement of morality by politics. That is why our moral agenda changed. Our concerns – with inequality and injustice, war and famine and ecology – go deep. But these are issues to be addressed by governments. We are willing to make sacrifices on behalf of such causes. We join protests, sign petitions, send donations. But these are large-scale and for the most part impersonal problems. They have relatively little to do with what morality has traditionally been about: the day-to-day conduct between neighbours and strangers, what Martin Buber called the 'I–Thou' dimension of our lives. Instead, in our personal relationships we believe in autonomy, the right to live our lives as we choose.

Today we live with the retreat of the state that began in the 1980s as Thatcherism in Britain, Reaganomics in the United States, and has continued since the crash of 2007/8 in the form of 'austerity measures' made necessary by the huge cost of the rescue operation to avoid a total collapse of the banking system, and thus of the economies of the interlinked modern world. We need to recover that capacity for collective self-help that was, and should be again, the distinguishing feature of a strong civil society.

We are not there yet. The tree of state has been removed, leaving the ivy of individual lives unsupported. As the state reduces its protective shelter, many people find themselves suddenly exposed. Single-parent families, the unemployed, inhabitants of inner-city ghettoes and others become the casualties. It is, and will continue to be, a traumatic experience, the pain of which only the most heartless can ignore.

The time has come for us to relearn many of the moral habits that came so naturally to our ancestors but have come to seem strange to us. We will have to rebuild families and communities and voluntary organisations. We will come to depend more on networks of kinship and friendship. And we will rapidly discover that their very existence depends on what we give as well as what we take, on our willingness to shoulder duties, responsibilities and commitments as well as claiming freedoms and rights. The 'I–It' relationship of taxation and benefit will increasingly be replaced by the 'I–Thou' of fellowship and community. And we may well come to see that the eclipse of personal morality that dominated the consciousness of a generation was a strange and passing phase in human affairs, and not the permanent revolution many thought it to be.

If so, I welcome the future. For it promises to restore to human relationships the compassion and grace, the mutuality and faithfulness, that the Hebrew Bible saw as a lasting ideal – more than that, as the way we bring the divine presence into our lives. The individualism of the past half-century has been one of unparalleled personal freedoms. But it has also been one of growing incivility and aggression, exploitation and manipulation, of temporary alliances rather than enduring loyalties, of quick pleasures over lasting happiness. It has been, quite simply, immature. So long as someone was there – the omnipresent state – to pick us up when we fell, it was overwhelmingly seductive. But it has become dysfunctional and cannot be sustained.

Morality matters. Not because we seek to be judgemental or self-righteous or pious. Not because we fondly recall a golden age that never was, when men were chivalrous, women decorous, sin discreet and all ranks of society knew their place. It matters, not because we are fundamentalists, convinced that we alone possess the moral certainties that form the architecture of virtue. Nor is it because we wish to relieve ourselves of responsibility for the pain, suffering and injustices of the world by blaming them on the victims who made the wrong choices. It matters not because we wish to impose a tidy-minded order on the chaos of human imagination and experiment, nor because we are ignorant of *autre temps, autre meures* and of the fact that ours is not the only way people have chosen to live.

Morality matters because we cherish relationships and believe that love, friendship, work and even the casual encounters of strangers are less fragile and abrasive when conducted against a shared code of civility and mutuality. It matters because we care for liberty and have come to understand that human dignity is better served by the restraints we impose on ourselves than by those forced upon us by external laws and punishment and police. It matters because we fear the impoverishment of significant groups within society when the only sources of value are material: success and wealth and physical attractiveness. In most societies – certainly ours – these are too unevenly distributed to be an adequate basis of self-worth.

Morality matters because we believe that there are other and more human ways of living than instinctual gratification tempered by regret. It matters because we believe that some essentials – love, marriage, parenthood – are so central to our being that we seek to endow them with as much permanence as is given to us in this unpredictable and transitory life. It matters because we must not abdicate our responsibility for those we brought into being by failing to provide them with a stable, caring environment within which to grow to maturity. It matters because we believe there are other routes out of the Hobbesian state of nature – the war of all against all – than by creating a Leviathan of a state. It matters because as long as humanity has thought about such things, we have recognised that there are achievements we cannot reach without the collaborative bonds of civil society and the virtues that alone make such a society possible.

Morality matters, finally, because despite all fashionable opinion to the contrary, we remain moved by altruism. We are touched by other people's pain. We feel enlarged by doing good, more so perhaps than by doing *well*, by material success. Decency, charity, compassion, integrity, faithfulness, courage, just being there for other people, matter to us. They matter to us despite the fact that we may now find it hard to say *why* they matter to us. They matter to us because we are human and because, in the words of Victorian philanthropist Sir Moses Montefiore, we are worth what we are willing to share with others.

These truths, undervalued for a generation, are the cultural climate change we now need. They are about to become vital again, and not a moment too soon.

23

From 'I' to 'We'

Can we restore what has been lost?

Are we destined to live with ever more divisive politics and ever more divided societies, growing inequalities and increasing loneliness, less public regard for truth and ever more determined efforts to ban and demonise the voices with which we disagree? Can we restore the trust and civility of public life and private relationships, or are the only institutions that matter the market and the state, the relentless pursuit of wealth and power? Can we change? My argument is that we can. There is one idea that whenever it has been applied has had the power to change the world. Cultures can shift from 'I' to 'We'.

We can change society for the future because people have done so in the past. James Q. Wilson argued, in *Crime and Human Nature*, that this is what happened in America in the first half of the nineteenth century.[1] People had long been moving from villages to towns to cities, but often whole families had moved together. They had a basis of social stability even in their new environment. In America in the 1820s and 1830s, however, there were large concentrations of single men, and a significant rise in drunkenness and crime. What followed by way of response was a massive re-moralisation of society, often led by religious groups, in a phenomenon known as the Second Great Awakening. A powerful set of moral concerns came to the fore – the abolition of slavery, the spread of temperance, the establishment of public schools and the drive to eliminate corporal and capital punishment. There was widespread public involvement in all these movements. Social dislocation was answered by social reintegration. An 'I' society became a 'We' society.

In our conversation for the BBC radio series on morality, Robert Putnam told me that something similar happened in the first half of the twentieth century. In the late eighteenth century, during the last Gilded Age, America was 'highly individualistic, starkly unequal, fiercely polarised, and deeply fragmented'. Following the Progressive Era at the beginning of the twentieth century, America became more equal, more cohesive, and more focused on responsibilities than rights. It moved from being an 'I' society to being a 'We' society.

In my book, *The Politics of Hope*, I argued that a parallel process took place in Britain in the nineteenth century. 'There is no community in England', wrote Benjamin Disraeli in 1845 in his novel *Sybil, or The Two Nations*. His concerns in the book sound uncannily contemporary. He was alarmed not only by the growing gap between rich and poor but also by the loneliness he sensed beneath the bustle of urban life. People, he wrote, 'are not in a state of cooperation, but of isolation'. The public response, already taking shape as he wrote those words, was an extraordinary proliferation of charitable groups, religiously based associations, public schools and Sunday schools, driven by, as well as educating for, social responsibility. Britain too moved from an 'I' to a 'We' society.[2]

It can be done in the future because it has been done in the past. And it begins with us, each of us as individuals. The moment we turn outward and concern ourselves with the welfare of others no less than with our own, we begin to change the world in the only way we can, one act at a time, one day at a time, one life at a time.

*

I have called the move from 'We' to 'I' cultural climate change. But there is a difference between this and environmental climate change. For us to make a significant difference to environmental climate change, billions of people must change the ways they act. That is because the environment is global. But culture is more local, especially when it concerns the tone and tenor of our relationships. To begin to make a difference, all we need to do is to change ourselves. To act morally. To be concerned with the welfare of others. To be someone people trust. To give. To volunteer. To listen. To smile. To be sensitive, generous, caring. To do any of these things is to make an immediate difference, not only to our own life but to those whose lives we touch. Morality is about us each of us in our own sphere of interaction, taking responsibility. We don't have to wait for the world to change for our lives to change.

In *The Road to Character*, David Brooks distinguishes between résumé virtues and eulogy virtues.[3] The former focus on achievement, the latter on character. The former tend to be about the self – the qualifications we acquired, the skills we have, our careers and successes. The latter are about the impact we have had on the lives of others. It is the eulogy virtues, the ones we are remembered for, that tend to invest a life with deeper meaning. To know that we have made things better for other people is a source of deep satisfaction. It seems that we have evolved to care about others, to have generous instincts and to come to the aid of those in need.

Doing good to others is, as I have already indicated, good for our health, physical and psychological. Giving makes us happier. In experiments in which people are given a sum of money, and half are told to spend it on themselves while the other half are told to give it to charity, those who gave it received more pleasure than those who spent it on themselves. A 2010 survey of people in 136 different countries found that in 122 of them, people who had donated money to charity in the previous month were happier than those who had not. The positive psychological impact of giving money to charity was, on average, equivalent to receiving a doubling of household income.[4]

We have also noted the health benefits of volunteering. The Greater Good Science Center at the University of California, Berkeley, continues to publish research findings on the health benefits of altruism.[5] A 2019 research study showed that acts of kindness of many different kinds, whether performed for family, friends or strangers, had positive effects for those who performed them, on both physical and emotional health.[6] Lifting others, we ourselves are lifted.

Taking pleasure in, and deriving strength from, altruism seems to be deeply embedded in our nature. Even children as young as eighteen months old show empathy for other children and adults in whom they see signs of distress. They will give a blanket to an adult who is cold or a toy to a child who is sad. Our capacity to feel and be moved by the pain of others is an undeniable fact of our nature. In short, as soon as we exercise our moral sense, in terms of helping others in particular, we gain enormous benefits, not just psychological but physical.

It is as if we realign ourselves with deeply engraved instincts that have somehow become underused in a world of self-esteem, self-satisfaction and self-preoccupation. The benefits are real, measurable and lasting. We have material needs and they are important. But we also have psychological, spiritual and moral needs, and they too are important. Once our basic needs for sustenance and security have been met, we are more enriched by what we give than by what we receive. There is something deep within us that yearns for connection with others, and that has been denied expression by much that has happened over the past half-century, and with particular acceleration in the past decade. In the liberal democracies of the West, there has been too much 'I', and too little 'We'. There has been too much individualism and too little of the moral bonds that lie at the heart of friendship, family and community.

Friendship, family and community exist in virtue of moral bonds. That is why they make us larger than we would be if we focused on self-interest alone. As I write these words, Elaine and I are looking forward to our golden wedding anniversary. In the TED Talk I gave in 2017, I spoke about our first meeting. It took place in Cambridge, England, where I was a philosophy student and Elaine was working at the hospital. I had read my Schopenhauer and Nietzsche, Sartre and Camus. I knew ontological loneliness, existential angst and epistemic doubt. I was self-preoccupied to a fault.

One day early in my final year I saw, across a college court-yard, a girl who was everything I was not. She smiled, she radiated sunshine, she was full of joy. It took me three weeks to put aside metaphysics and say, 'Let's get married.' Forty-nine years, three children and nine grandchildren later, I know it was the best decision of my life, because it's the people not like us who make us grow. Marriage is the supreme embodiment of openness to otherness.

Google's intelligent search, Facebook friends and reading the news via Twitter's narrowcasting effect rather than traditional broadcast media means that we are surrounded to a considerable extent by people like us whose opinions and prejudices are similar to ours. As I have mentioned, Cass Sunstein of Harvard has shown that if we surround ourselves with people with the same views as us, we get more extreme.[7] We need to renew those face-to-face encounters with the people not like us, to realise that we can disagree strongly and yet still stay friends. It's in those face-to-face encounters that we discover that the people not like us are just people, like us. Every time we hold out the hand of friendship to somebody not like us, whose class or creed or colour are different from ours, we heal one of the fractures of our wounded world.

*

At various points I have referred to a concept that has immense and transformative power. The concept is *covenant*, and I want here to explain why it is so significant.

Recall that one of the fundamental questions of the Enlightenment was how society could be preserved once dogmatic religious belief has been weakened. Could you keep society's mechanisms going on the basis of self-interest alone? That was when two powerful theories emerged, one about politics and the state, the other about economics and the market.

The political theory was formulated by Thomas Hobbes. In a state of nature, he said, where there were no laws, or at least none that could be enforced, there would be violence and constant fear of death. Life would be, in his memorable phrase, 'solitary, poor, nasty, brutish and short'. In such an environment, it would be in everyone's self-interest to hand over some of their powers to a central body, the Leviathan of the state, charged with maintaining the rule of law within and the defence of the realm from without. This was his version of the social contract, entered into on the basis of self-interest alone, namely the fear of violent death that would exist if there were no Leviathan to keep the peace.

Adam Smith made much the same argument about economics. As mentioned earlier, in one of the most famous sentences from *The Wealth of Nations*, he said, 'It is not from the benevolence of the butcher, the brewer, or the baker that we expect our dinner, but from their regard to their own interest.' An 'invisible hand' would turn the pursuit of self-interest into the actualisation of the common good. Self-interest, in other words, would sustain the market and the state.

Self-interest generates contracts. In a contract, two or more individuals, each pursuing their own advantage, come together to make an exchange for mutual benefit. I pay my garage mechanic to mend my car. I and others pay our taxes to ensure that we have the social services we need. So there is the commercial contract that creates the market, and the social contract that creates the state. But in both cases, the motivating factor is self-interest. Contracts are about 'I'.

A covenant generates a different kind of relationship altogether. Recall that what makes it different is that in covenant, two or more individuals, each respecting the dignity and integrity of the other, come together in a bond of love and trust, to share their interests, sometimes even to share their lives, by pledging their faithfulness to one another, to do together what neither can achieve alone. Unlike contracts, which are entered into for the sake of advantage, covenants are moral commitments sustained by loyalty and fidelity, even when they call for sacrifice. They are about you and I coming together to form a 'We'.

A contract is a *transaction*. A covenant is a *relationship*. A contract is about *interests*. A covenant is about *identity*. That is why contracts *benefit*, but covenants *transform*.

A covenant creates a moral community. It binds people together in a bond of mutual responsibility and care. It can be vast: there is, I believe, a covenant of human solidarity that binds all seven billion of us alive today to act responsibly towards the environment, human rights and the alleviation of poverty for the sake of generations not yet born. A covenant can also be small and personal: the simplest instance is a marriage when husband and wife pledge themselves to one another in an open-ended commitment to share a life.

What matters in a covenant is not how big or small is the group thereby included, but the commitment. It is the undertaking of responsibility for others, knowing that they too undertake responsibility for us. In a covenant, what matters is not wealth or power but the transformation that takes place when I embrace a world larger than the self. Covenants heal what markets and states sometimes harm.

*

How might covenantal thinking – the move from 'I' to 'We' – lead to a new approach to business, the market and economics? Contracts invite us to think about what we gain. Covenants ask us to think about the impact we have on others. In the case of business, this means not only shareholders and employees but also the wider society.

Something like a covenantal approach has recently been advocated by former Chief Economist of the International Monetary Fund and Governor of the Reserve Bank of India, Raghuram Rajan. In *The Third Pillar* (2019)[8] he argues that the state and the market have grown in the West at the cost of community, which is where many of our most important interactions take place. It has happened because of the disruptive effects of technological revolution since the 1970s. Great swathes of the population have lost their previous forms of employment, and this has had a devastating effect on them, their families and their communities. This is economically wasteful, politically dangerous and humanly tragic.

But communities can be rebuilt. Rajan gives the example of the Pilsen neighbourhood in Chicago. In the 1970s, it was an area of low education, low incomes, high unemployment, drugs, alcohol and crime. Then community activists, determined to reverse the slide, slowly but steadily cleaned up the neighbourhood, clamped down on crime, improved schools, gave job-training to former gang members, brought new businesses into the area and built affordable housing. This was a 'We' project *par excellence*: its success depended on active grassroots involvement. As one of the leading activists now tells newcomers when they buy a house, 'You are not buying a piece of property. You are buying a piece of the community.'[9]

Rajan's proposal is that economics must shift from *profit maximisation* to *value maximisation*; in other words, corporations should consider not only shareholders but also employees, and possibly other constituencies. Otherwise, he says, we are in great danger from populism and the disruptive politics of the far left or the far right. Ways must be found of harnessing the market and technology to strengthen communities, the essential 'third pillar' of a free society.

A not dissimilar approach has been advocated in Britain by Sir Ronald Cohen, one of Britain's first and most successful venture capitalists. In 2000, he was invited by the Treasury to become chairman of the Social Investment Task Force. In 2002 he helped found Bridges Ventures, an investment company that focused not on short-term profits but on long-term sustainability and social and environmental benefits. In 2011, at the request of the then Prime Minister Gordon Brown, he became the chairman of Big Society Capital, the first social investment bank in Britain.

Sir Ronald has recently spearheaded a movement towards what he calls *Impact Economics*, that is, the evaluation of a company's performance not only by its profits but also by its social and environmental impact, believing this to be as important as making money.[10] One way of doing so is through Social Impact Bonds, otherwise known as pay-for-success schemes, which invite organisations to deliver specific social outcomes in return for payment. Such funding has been used to reduce re-offending rates of prisoners in Peterborough, England, to educate girls in Rajasthan, to improve maternal and infant health in South Carolina, to help unemployed youth in the UK, to integrate the immigrant population in Massachusetts into the workforce, and to rehabilitate people affected by conflict in Africa. Impact economics reconceptualises the relationship between governments, entrepreneurs, philanthropists, for-profit and not-for-profit organisations. What makes it covenantal, not just contractual, economics is that it sees us all as part of a single moral community. It is about conceptualising business and investment not just for private gain, though this is important, but also for the common good.

Young people, Cohen says, are more likely to work for and invest in companies that have a positive impact on society. By choosing to invest in such companies, each of us, as shareholders, pension savers or holders of insurance policies, can have an influence on the way corporations act and make their decisions. The idea that there is a choice between making money and helping others is, he says, dangerous and wrong. You can do good and do well at the same time.

A third example comes from an entrepreneur, Daniel Lubetzky, founder of the health food company KIND. I came to know Daniel through his efforts for peace in the Middle East. Daniel entered business in the first place as a side project while engaged in research about legislative means to foster economic relationships between Israelis and Palestinians. While doing his research, he started a business, PeaceWorks, that brought together Israelis, Palestinians, Turks and Egyptians to make food based on local specialities, encouraging, through economic cooperation, friendships between groups of people who would not normally mix. Its success led him to go on to do something similar in Mexico, Sri Lanka, South Africa and Indonesia. He believed that when different ethnic and religious groups form businesses together, they are more likely to make peace because of the friendships and interdependencies joint enterprises create.[11]

Subsequently, his concern with obesity in the United States and the unhealthiness of many snacks led him to create a new business based on a series of snack bars with pure natural ingredients, under the label of KIND. What makes Daniel a new kind of entrepreneur is the way he conceptualises business as a force for social and moral transformation. In his head offices in New York, profit and not-for-profit enterprises work side by side in the same space. Among other initiatives, he has been working on ways of getting children to learn about the shared values that bring us together in common humanity. One of his initiatives, Simpatico, is a platform involving video conferencing and digital learning, connecting classrooms and helping children to make friends with others across the world.

He believes that a strong sense of mission gives a company and its workforce the resilience to survive difficult times, the focus to stay true to its core values, and the sense of team spirit that make people respect one another and create a strong corporate culture.

This is, admittedly, controversial territory. There are those who believe, with Milton Friedman and the 'Chicago school' of American economists, that the social responsibility of business is simply to make as much profit as possible. Business is one thing, they say, philanthropy another. But Raghuram Rajan today teaches at the University of Chicago: a sign that 'Chicago school' orthodoxy may be changing. Rajan, Cohen and Lubetzky – an economist, a venture capitalist and an entrepreneur, each a leader in their field – are showing us a new direction: an economics of 'We', not just of 'I'.

*

We have seen how covenant has had a significant role in the political culture of the United States. How might it be re-invoked in order to heal some of the deep divisions in the politics of contemporary America and Europe? Here we have a remarkable historical example of how covenantal thinking can help mend a shattered nation.

In September 1862 America was in the depths of its civil war, more bitterly divided than any Western democracy today. The Union forces had suffered a second defeat at Bull Run. Victory for the North seemed a remote possibility, and Union itself a distant and receding dream. It was then that Abraham Lincoln wrote a note in his diary, meant – one of his secretaries later said – for his eyes alone. He headed it, 'A Meditation on the Divine Will'. It contained the following paragraph:

> The will of God prevails. In great contests each party claims to act in accordance with the will of God. Both *may* be, and one *must* be wrong. God cannot be for and against the same thing at the same time. In the present Civil War it is quite possible that God's purpose is something different from the purpose of either part . . .

An exceptional idea was taking shape in the mind of one of the greatest leaders of the modern age. Convinced as he was that ending slavery was the right and morally necessary thing to do, nonetheless Lincoln in this note to himself refused to blame the other side for the war. None of us, he intimates, can fully understand the divine will or the purposes of history. Even if we are sure that our opponents are wrong, they may be serving some necessary role in the moral drama. Far from this leading him into indecisiveness, it moved him to something quite different: humility and a refusal to demonise his opponents.

Evidently the thought stayed with him, because on 3 October 1863, with the Civil War still at its height, Lincoln issued a Thanksgiving Proclamation. There had been Thanksgiving celebrations since the earliest settlers in the 1620s, but this was the first time a specific day had been set aside for the entire nation. Lincoln urged people to thank God because although the nation was at war with itself, there were still blessings for which both sides could express gratitude: a fruitful harvest, no foreign invasion, and so on. He also asked them to express 'humble penitence for our national perverseness and disobedience', and commend to God's tender care 'all those who have become widows, orphans, mourners or sufferers in the lamentable civil strife in which we are unavoidably engaged, and fervently implore the interposition of the Almighty Hand to heal the wounds of the nation and to restore it as soon as may be consistent with the divine purposes to the full enjoyment of peace, harmony, tranquillity and Union.'

Note the various elements of this proclamation. Lincoln does not urge his side against the other. He speaks of *national* perverseness, encouraging everyone to look within their own hearts and find there the strength to engage in self-criticism, atonement and humility. He asks all to think of the dead and the bereaved. He asks each to be thankful for what they have, and he asks divine help to heal the wounds of a lacerated nation. It was this that allowed Lincoln, in his second inaugural address, to deliver one of the great unifying political speeches of all time: 'With malice toward none, with charity for all, with firmness in the right as God gives us to see the right, let us strive on to finish the work we are in, to bind up the nation's wounds, to care for him who shall have borne the battle and for his widow and his orphan . . .'

It is possible to unite a divided nation. It takes time. Like some other peacemakers, Lincoln paid a heavy price, assassinated only a few weeks after this second inaugural. Yet he left an indelible lesson in what it is to speak to what he called 'the better angels of our nature'. He showed how to begin healing political wounds and rescuing a nation from division and confrontation.

Lincoln was driven throughout by his idea of the United States as a moral community. Although he did not explicitly use the word 'covenant', it clearly underlay his conception of the nation. This is how John Schaar sums up his political beliefs:

We are a nation formed by a covenant, by dedication to a set of principles and by an exchange of promises to uphold and advance certain commitments among ourselves and throughout the world. Those principles and commitments are the core of American identity, the soul of the body politic. They make the American nation unique, and uniquely valuable, among and to the other nations. But the other side of the conception contains a warning very like the warnings spoken by the prophets to Israel: if we fail in our promises to each other, and lose the principles of the covenant, then we lose everything, for they are we.[12]

Ultimately, Lincoln was driven by a moral conviction, inspired by the Judeo-Christian ethic and enshrined in the American Declaration of Independence. He restated it in the opening sentence of the Gettysburg Address when he spoke of 'a new nation, conceived in Liberty, and dedicated to the proposition that all men are created equal'.

Covenant is about what we have in common despite our differences. It speaks to us as active citizens sharing collective responsibility. It is not the politics of 'Us' against 'Them'; it is the politics of all-of-us-together. This cannot be the whole of politics, because much is inevitably about the clash of interests and the pursuit of power. But it can bring an underlying sense of moral community that holds a society together at times of stress, which is why Lincoln seems to have thought about it so deeply during the crisis years of the Civil War. For although he was deeply committed to the abolition of slavery, he was equally committed to the preservation of the Union. Only by shifting his thought to a higher plane could he reach an understanding of what it would take to achieve both, by speaking to the deepest moral commitments of Americans rather than by demonising the South.

*

We need to restore the covenant dimension to politics. Britain and America are today deeply divided societies, and the politics of recent years has played on those divisions. There are winners and losers from the new globalised economy. They live in different parts of the country. They have different attitudes to identity. They have significantly different approaches to family. They live in neighbourhoods with radically divergent levels of social capital. Many of those whose incomes have remained static for long periods, or declined, feel as if the political and economic elites are simply not interested in their welfare.

This is not, however, the first time that divides have opened up in societies on the basis of economic or geographical stratification. What makes the present moment different is the radical changes that have taken place in Western societies in recent years. Nations used to be held together by a single dominant religion or family of religions, and by a shared culture. That is not the case today. Partly it has to do with immigration. In part it is because of the abandonment, in the name of multiculturalism, of the idea of a national culture into which newcomers – like my father and grandparents, who were all immigrants to Britain – were expected to integrate. Partly also it has to do with the fragmentation of the media, so that people's attention is only occasionally focused on the same events at the same time. In a global age, the very idea of a national identity has become problematic.

We can no longer build national identity on religion or ethnicity or culture. But we can build it on covenant. A covenantal politics would speak of how, as a polity, an economy and culture, our fates are bound together. We benefit from each other. And because this is so, we should feel bound to benefit one another. It would speak about the best of our traditions, and how they are a heritage we are charged with honouring and handing on to future generations. It would be warmly inclusive. A nation is enlarged by its new arrivals who carry with them gifts from other places and other traditions. It would acknowledge that, yes, we have differences of opinion and interest, and sometimes that means favouring one side over another. But we will never do so without giving every side a voice and a respectful hearing. The politics of covenant does not demean or ridicule opponents. It honours the process of reasoning together. It gives special concern to those who most need help, and special honour to those who most give help.

A covenantal politics would emphasise our responsibilities to one another. Depressed areas need to be supported and local communities strengthened. Every individual has to be able to feel that he or she has a chance to fulfil their potential. Ways have to be found to encourage the successful to play their part in developing opportunities for those whom the modern economy has passed by. Covenant does not, in and of itself, suggest a larger or smaller state. It is not on the Right or Left of politics. It is, rather, a way of thinking about what politics actually represents.

Social contract theories see politics in terms of individual or collective self-interest. Covenant – the classic language of Milton and Locke, the early American settlers and the American Declaration of Independence – is not about interests but about responsibilities. It is about free individuals governing themselves for the sake of the common good, and about the free society as a moral project in which we all play our part, recognising that our destinies are interwoven.

That vision, which made Britain and America the great defenders of liberty in the twentieth century, has been out of fashion for a long time – for as long, indeed, as the 'We' has given way to the 'I'. Politics has regressed from covenant to contract: we pay our taxes, the government delivers services, and we search for the deal that is most advantageous to us. That is a diminished view of politics, which can work for a while, but which cannot hold together divided societies. We need to recover the covenant dimension of politics, to ensure that those who guide our destinies do so for the benefit of all.

Today's politics, which has seen a rise in populism, is often about division and confrontation. It is about dividing a nation into 'Us' and 'Them'. It is about resentment and fear and allocation of blame. It is about anger and a sense of betrayal. It is oppositional. It proposes handing power to the strong leader who assures his or her followers that, in return for their loyalty, he or she will fight their battles for them.

Covenantal politics, by contrast, is about 'We, the people', bound by a sense of shared belonging and collective responsibility; about strong local communities, active citizens and the devolution of responsibility. It is about reminding those who have more than they need of their responsibilities to those who have less than they need. It is about ensuring that everyone has a fair chance to make the most of their capacities and their lives.

One of the great historical lessons is that societies become strong when they care for the weak. They become rich when they care for the poor. They become invulnerable when they care for the vulnerable. That is the beating heart of the politics of covenant.

My firm belief is that the concept of covenant has the power to transform the world. It sees relationships in terms not of interests but of moral commitment. It changes everything it touches, from marriage to friendship to economics and politics, by turning self-interested individuals into a community in pursuit of the common good.

There is nothing inevitable about the division, fragmentation, extremism, isolation, the economics of inequality or the politics of anger that have been the mood of Britain and America in recent years. They have been the legacy of the misplaced belief that societies can function without a moral bond. They cannot, or at least not for long. That is why we are where we are.

But we can change. Societies have moved from 'I' to 'We' in the past. They did so in the nineteenth century. They did so in the twentieth century. They can do so in the future.

And it begins with us.

Notes

Preface and Acknowledgements

1. James Q. Wilson, *The Moral Sense*, Free Press, 1993, 8.
2. Philip Rieff, *The Triumph of the Therapeutic*, Chatto and Windus, 1966, 4.
3. Joan Didion, *The White Album*, Penguin, 1981, 134.
4. Alasdair MacIntyre, *After Virtue*, Duckworth, 1981.
5. I should mention that Roger Scruton has written a very good book, *The Uses of Pessimism and the Danger of False Hope*, Atlantic, 2012.
6. You can read a copy of my Templeton Prize acceptance speech here: http://rabbisacks.org/danger-outsourcing-morality-read-rabbi-sacks-speech-accepting-templeton-prize/.
7. You can watch my TED Talk at https://www.ted.com/talks/rabbi_lord_jonathan_sacks_how_we_can_face_the_future_without_fear_together.
8. You can download a podcast of the five-part BBC Radio 4 series on *Morality in the 21st Century*, together with my extended conversations with each of the participants, from the BBC website at https://www.bbc.co.uk/programmes/p06jxvm9/episodes/downloads.
9. My BBC Reith Lectures were published in a book entitled *The Persistence of Faith: Religion, Morality and Society in a Secular Age*, Bloomsbury, 1991, reprinted in 2005.

Introduction: Cultural Climate Change

1. *The Times*, 14 November 2019.
2. *Financial Times*, 27 June 2019.
3. *Guardian*, 3 December 2018.
4. *Guardian*, 25 January 2019.
5. *Wall Street Journal*, 28 March 2019.
6. 'Populism: The Phenomenon', Bridgewater Associates, 22 March 2017.

7. Bill Emmett, *The Fate of the West*, Profile, 2017, 207.
8. *The Times*, 29 December 2018.
9. 'Most U.S. Teens See Anxiety and Depression as a Major Problem Among Their Peers', Pew Research Center, 20 February 2019.
10. 'A Growing Number of American Teenagers – Particularly Girls – are Facing Depression', Pew Research Center, 12 July 2019.
11. 'The Good Childhood Report 2018', The Children's Society, August 2018.
12. Jean Twenge, *iGen: Why Today's Super-Connected Kids Are Growing Up Less Rebellious, More Tolerant, Less Happy – and Completely Unprepared for Adulthood*, Atria, 2017, 312.
13. *Sunday Times*, 28 April 2019.
14. 'CEO compensation surged in 2017', The Economic Policy Institute, August 2008.
15. *The Times*, 14 November 2019.
16. *Independent*, 13 February 2017.
17. Thomas Simpson and Eric Kaufmann, *Academic Freedom in the UK*, Policy Exchange, 2019.
18. Patrick Devlin, *The Enforcement of Morals*, Oxford University Press, 1965, 10.
19. Friedrich Hayek, *The Constitution of Liberty*, Routledge, 1960, 62.
20. Alasdair MacIntyre, *After Virtue*, Duckworth, 1981, 244–5.
21. Steven Pinker, *The Language Instinct*, Penguin, 1994, 32–5.

1: *Loneliness*

1. His findings will be published in Robert Putnam, *The Upswing*, Simon & Schuster, 2020.
2. DeWall, C.N., Pond, R.S., Campbell, W.K. and Twenge, J.M. (2011), 'Tuning in to Psychological Change: Linguistic Markers of Self-focus, Loneliness, Anger, Anti-social Behaviour, and Misery Increase Over Time in Popular US Song Lyrics', *Psychology of Aesthetics, Art, and Creativity*, 5, 200–207.
3. *Prospect*, 1 October 2019.
4. See Adrienne Lafrance, 'Me, myself and authenticity', *Atlantic*, 25 February 2015, for a dissenting interpretation.
5. 'Single-Person Households: Another Look at the Changing American Family', Deloitte Insights, November 2015.
6. 'The Cost of Living Alone', The Office of National Statistics, 4 April 2019.

7. Atul Gawande, 'Hellhole', *New Yorker*, 23 March 2009.
8. 'Loneliness: An Epidemic?', Harvard University, April 2018.
9. I thank my brother Alan for bringing this to my attention.
10. 'Combatting Loneliness One Conversation at a Time', Jo Cox Commission on Loneliness, December 2017.
11. 'Loneliness in America', Cigna, 1 May 2018.
12. Keming Yang and Christina Victor, 'Age and Loneliness in 25 European Nations', *Ageing and Society*, 31(8) (November 2011), 1368–88.
13. *The Hill*, 10 December 2017.
14. *Washington Post*, 21 March 2019.
15. 'What is the Average Length of a Marriage in the UK?', Raincourt, 2 October 2018.
16. Much of the following draws from Susan Pinker, *The Village Effect: Why Face-to-face Contact Matters*, Atlantic Books, 2015, 1–43; Neil Howe, 'Millennials and the loneliness epidemic', *Forbes*, 3 May 2019; 'Loneliness is a serious public health problem', *Economist*, 1 September 2018.
17. Dr Vivek Murthy, 'Work and the Loneliness Epidemic', *Harvard Business Review*, 2017.
18. J. Holt-Lunstad, T.B. Smith, M. Baker, T. Harris and D. Stephenson, 'Loneliness and Social Isolation as Risk Factors for Mortality: A Meta-analytic Review', *Perspectives on Psychological Science*, 10(2) (2015) 227–37.
19. 'The Potential Public Health Relevance of Social Isolation and Loneliness: Prevalence, Epidemiology and Risk Factors', *Public Policy & Aging Report* (Vol. 27, Issue 4, 2017), 2 January 2018.
20. C.M. Perissinotto, I. Stijacic Cenzer and K.E. Covinsky, 'Loneliness in Older Persons: A Predictor of Functional Decline and Death', *Arch Intern Med.* (2012).
21. 'Participating in Activities You Enjoy', National Institute on Aging, U.S. Department of Health & Human Services, 23 October 2017.
22. 'Social Networks, Social Support and Survival after Breast Cancer Diagnosis', *Journal of Clinical Oncology*, March 2006.
23. Sebastian Junger, *Tribe: On Homecoming and Belonging*, Fourth Estate, 2016, 93.
24. Susan Pinker, *The Village Effect*, 44–72.
25. Nicholas Christakis and James Fowler, *Connected: The Amazing Power of Social Networks and How They Shape Our Lives*, HarperPress, 2011.
26. M. Granovetter, 'The Strength of Weak Ties', *American Journal of Sociology*, 78 (1973), 1360–80.

27. Charles Taylor, *The Ethics of Authenticity*, Harvard University Press, 1991, 55.
28. Neal Howe, 'Millennials and the Loneliness Epidemic', *Forbes*, 3 May 2019; 'What Young People Fear the Most', Viceland UK Census, 21 September 2016.
29. Junger, *Tribe*, 109–10.
30. Robert Putnam, *American Grace*, Simon & Schuster, 2010.
31. Robert Bellah et al., *Habits of the Heart*, Hutchinson, 1988, 284.

2: *The Limits of Self-Help*

1. Will Storr, *Selfie: How the West Became So Self-obsessed and What It's Doing To Us*, Picador, 2018; Marianne Power, *Help Me*, Picador, 2018.
2. Abraham Maslow, *Motivation and Personality*, Harper, 1954; *Toward a Psychology of Being*, Wiley, 1998.
3. Carl Rogers, *Client-centred Therapy*, Constable, 1951; *On Becoming a Person*, Constable 1967.
4. Jean Twenge and Keith Campbell, *The Narcissism Epidemic*, Atria, 2009, 9.
5. Berakhot 5b.
6. *Daily Telegraph*, 9 April 2008.
7. Viktor Frankl, *The Unconscious God*, Simon & Schuster, 1975, 24.
8. Viktor Frankl, *The Unheard Cry for Meaning: Psychotherapy and Humanism*, Hodder & Stoughton, 1978, 35.
9. Iris Murdoch, *The Sovereignty of Good*, London, Routledge & Kegan Paul, 1970, 84.
10. See the important studies of ageing by George Vaillant: *Aging Well*, Warner, 2003; and *Triumphs of Experience*, Harvard University Press, 2012.

3: *Unsocial Media*

1. 'Global Social Media Research Summary 2019', Smart Insights, 12 February 2019.
2. BBC News, 14 August 2019.
3. 'How Teens and Parents Navigate Screen Time and Device Distractions', Pew Research Center, 22 August 2018.

4. 'Teens' Social Media Habits and Experiences', Pew Research Center, 28 November 2018.
5. Jean Twenge, *iGen: Why Today's Super-Connected Kids Are Growing Up Less Rebellious, More Tolerant, Less Happy – and Completely Unprepared for Adulthood*, Atria, 2017.
6. Ibid., 51.
7. Sherry Terkel, *Reclaiming Conversation*, Penguin Press, 2015, 42.
8. *The Times*, 30 October 2018.
9. *Guardian*, 4 January 2019.
10. The title of a book by Norman Mailer.
11. 'Smartphone Addiction Creates Imbalance in Brain', Radiological Society of North America, 30 November 2017.
12. 'Brain Drain: The Mere Presence of One's Own Smartphone Reduces Available Cognitive Capacity', *Journal of the Association for Consumer Research* (Vol. 2, Number 2), 3 April 2017.
13. *Guardian*, 17 April 2019.
14. Jenny S. Radesky, Jayna Schumacher, Barry Zuckerman, 'Mobile and Interactive Media Use by Young Children: The Good, the Bad, and the Unknown', *Pediatrics*, 135(1), January 2015.
15. *Daily Telegraph*, 1 February 2015.
16. *Guardian*, 29 August 2018.
17. On Internet-induced depression, see Twenge, 93–118.
18. *Guardian*, 8 April 2019.
19. See Turkle, especially 3–56.
20. Turkle, 33.
21. Adam Alter, *Irresistible*, Bodley Head, 2017, 1–10.
22. Bronislaw Malinowski, *The Sexual Life of Savages in North-Western Melanesia. An Ethnographic Account of Courtship, Marriage, and Family Life Among the Natives of the Trobriand Islands, British New Guinea*, London, 1929.
23. Robin Dunbar, *Grooming, Gossip and the Evolution of Language*, Faber & Faber, 2011.
24. *Independent*, 5 October 2018.
25. William Blake, *The Divine Image*.
26. Emmanuel Levinas, *Totality and Infinity*, Duquesne University Press, 1969, 198.
27. Ibid., 201.
28. Ibid., 206.

4: *The Fragile Family*

1. Alexis de Tocqueville, *Democracy in America*, The Modern Library, New York, 1981, 183.
2. James Q. Wilson, *The Moral Sense*, Free Press, 1993, 158.
3. Daniel Patrick Moynihan, *The Negro Family: The Case for National Action* (known as the Moynihan Report), 1965.
4. Ben Sasse, *The Vanishing American Adult*, St Martin's Press, 2017, 41.
5. 'Divorces in England and Wales: 2017', Office for National Statistics, 26 September 2018.
6. Ibid.
7. 'What is the Average Length of a Marriage in the UK?', Raincourt, 2 October 2018.
8. Robert Whelan, *Broken Homes and Battered Children*, London, Family Education Trust, 1993.
9. See James Q. Wilson, *The Marriage Problem*, HarperCollins, 2002, Chapter 2.
10. Charles Murray, *Coming Apart*, Crown Forum, 2012, 158.
11. On this, see William Tucker, *Marriage and Civilisation: How Monogamy Made us Human*, Regnery, 2014.
12. On this, see Simon May, *Love: A History*, Yale University Press, 2011.

5: *From 'We' to 'I'*

1. Larry Siedentop, *Inventing the Individual*, Allen Lane, 2014.
2. Paul Johnson, *The Birth of the Modern World Society 1815–1830*, HarperCollins, 1991.
3. Lionel Trilling, *Sincerity and Authenticity*, Harvard University Press, 1971, 24–5.
4. Christopher Hill, *The Century of Revolution: 1603–1741*, Nelson, 1961, 253.
5. Luther quotes 1 Peter 2:9 and Revelation 5:10. They are quoting Exodus 19:6.
6. Alasdair MacIntyre, *A Short History of Ethics*, Routledge & Kegan Paul, 1967, 126.
7. Exodus 3:14. I have pointed out elsewhere that this is a profound mistranslation. The Hebrew actually means, 'I will be what I will be.'
8. This idea is set out most fully in Friedrich Nietzsche, *The Antichrist*, Penguin Classics, 1990.

9. Alexis de Tocqueville, *Democracy in America*, The Modern Library, New York, 1981, 395.
10. Ibid., 583–4.
11. The suicide rate among males is higher than that for females, but the gap has been narrowing. The male-to-female suicide rate was 4.4 in 2000 and 3.6 in 2016. See the National Center for Health Statistics Data Brief No. 309, June 2018.
12. H. Hedegaard et al., *Suicide Rates in the United States Continue to Increase*, NCHS Data Brief No. 309, National Center for Health Statistics, 2018.
13. Robert Hall, *This Land of Strangers: The Relationship Crisis that Imperils Home, Work, Politics, and Faith*, Greenleaf, 2012.
14. Niobe Way, Alisha Ali and Carol Gilligan (eds.), *The Crisis of Connection: Roots, Consequences, and Solutions*, New York University Press, 2018.

6: Markets Without Morals

1. Report on Carillion, Work and Pensions Committee, UK Parliament, 16 May 2018.
2. Bethany Mclean and Peter Elkind, *The Smartest Guys in the Room: The Amazing Rise and Scandalous Fall of Enron*, Penguin, 2004.
3. 'Reforming Business for the 21st Century: A Framework for the Future of the Corporation', The British Academy, November 2018.
4. Anand Giridharadas, *Winners Take All: The Elite Charade of Changing the World*, Allen Lane, 2019.
5. Ferdinand Mount, *The New Few*, Simon & Schuster, 2012, 61.
6. Warren Buffett, Berkshire Hathaway Annual Letter, 2002.
7. 'CEO compensation surged in 2017', Economic Policy Institute, 16 August 2018.
8. *Guardian*, 19 March 2016.
9. 'Millennials and Gen Z have lost trust and loyalty with business', *Forbes*, 3 June 2018.
10. Paul Bloom, *Just Babies*, Bodley Head, 2013.
11. A recording of Frans de Waal's TED Talk can be found here: https://www.youtube.com/watch?v=meiU6TxysCg.
12. David Hume, *A Treatise of Human Nature*, Part II, 'Of justice and injustice'.
13. Bloom, op. cit., 59–100.
14. Ibid., 89–92.

7: *Consuming Happiness*

1. Richard Layard, *Happiness: Lessons from a New Science*, Allen Lane, 2005, 3.
2. Aristotle, *The Nicomachean Ethics*, Cambridge Texts in the History of Philosophy, Cambridge University Press, 2014.
3. John Locke, *Essay on Human Understanding*, Book 2, Chapter 21, para. 42.
4. See Charles Murray, *In Pursuit of Happiness and Good Government*, Simon & Schuster, 1988, 21–47.
5. UN World Happiness Report, 20 March 2019, https://worldhappi-ness.report/ed/2019/.
6. Richard Wilkinson and Kate Pickett, *The Spirit Level: Why More Equal Societies Almost Always Do Better*, Allen Lane, 2009, 3.
7. Juliet Schor, *The Overworked American: The Unexpected Decline of Leisure*, Basic Books, 1991, 120.
8. Layard, *Happiness*, 48–9.
9. Yuval Noah Harari, *Homo Deus*, Harvill Secker, 2015, 367–96.
10. Adam Alter, *Irresistible: Why We Can't Stop Checking, Scrolling, Clicking and Watching*, Bodley Head, 2017.
11. Spinoza, *Tractatus Theologico-Politicus*, Chapter III, 43.
12. John Maynard Keynes, *Essays in Persuasion*, The Collected Writings of John Maynard Keynes, Volume 9, Cambridge University Press, 1978, 321–32.
13. *Independent*, 17 November 2017.
14. 'The U.S. is the Most Overworked Developed Nation in the World', 20SomethingFinance, 2 January 2018.
15. Edward Skidelsky and Robert Skidelsky, *How Much is Enough: Money and the Good Life*, Penguin, 2012, Chapter 1.
16. James Kerr, *Legacy*, Constable, 2013.
17. Dan Ariely, *Predictably Irrational*, HarperCollins, 2008, 76–7.
18. Robert A. Emmons, *Thanks: How the New Science of Gratitude Can Make You Happier*, Houghton Mifflin, 2007, 66–70.
19. Sonja Lyubomirsky, *The How of Happiness*, Sphere, 2007, 89.
20. Lyubomirsky, op. cit., 91–4.
21. Stephen Post and Jill Neimark, *Why Good Things Happen to Good People*, Broadway Books, 2007, 8–10.
22. Doug Oman et al., 'Volunteerism and Mortality Among the Community-dwelling Elderly', *Journal of Health Psychology* (May 1999).
23. Post and Neimark, op. cit., 9.

24. Ibid.
25. Allen Luks, *The Healing Power of Doing Good: The Health and Spiritual Benefits of Helping Others*, Fawcett Columbine, 1992.
26. Lyubomirsky, op. cit., 125.
27. George Vaillant, *Aging Well*, Little, Brown, 2003; *Triumphs of Experience*, Harvard University Press, 2012.
28. Joshua Wolf Shenk, 'What Makes Us Happy?', *Atlantic*, June 2009.
29. *Harvard Gazette*, 11 April 2017.
30. David Brooks, *The Second Mountain: The Quest for a Moral Life*, Allen Lane, 2019, xxiv.
31. Lyubomirsky, op. cit., 90–1.
32. Lyubomirsky, op. cit., 126–8.
33. Tomáš Sedláček, *The Economics of Good and Evil: The Quest for Economic Meaning from Gilgamesh to Wall Street*, Oxford University Press, 2013, 244–5.
34. Ibid., Oxford University Press, 2011 (hardback), 86–90, 246–7.

8: *Democracy in Danger*

1. Peter Berger and Hansfried Kellner, *Sociology Reinterpreted*, Penguin, 1982, 143.
2. 'Public Trust in Government 1958–2017', Pew Research Center, 14 December 2017.
3. Yascha Mounk and Roberto Foa, 'The Democratic Disconnect', *Journal of Democracy* (July 2016). See also Yascha Mounk, *The People vs. Democracy: Why Our Freedom is in Danger and How to Save It*, Harvard University Press, 2018.
4. See Moses Naim, *The End of Power*, Basic Books, 2013.
5. J.L. Talmon, *The Origins of Totalitarian Democracy*, Secker & Warburg, 1952.
6. Mary Ann Glendon, *Rights Talk: The Impoverishment of Political Discourse*, Free Press, 1991, 119.
7. Ibid., 171.

9: *Identity Politics*

1. P.B. Shelley, *Prometheus Unbound* (1818).
2. Ernest Gellner, *Nations and Nationalism*, Cornell University Press, 1983.
3. Benedict Anderson, *Imagined Communities*, Verso, 1991.

4. Johann Gottfried Von Herder, *Outline of a Philosophy of the History of Man*, Franklin Classics, 2017, 400.
5. Jonathan Sacks, *The Home We Build Together*, Continuum, 2007.
6. Paul Sniderman and Louk Hagendoorn, *When Ways of Life Collide: Multiculturalism and Its Discontents in the Netherlands*, Princeton University Press, 2007, 134–5.
7. Ibid., 135.
8. Quoted in Douglas Murray, *The Madness of Crowds*, Bloomsbury Continuum, 2019, 240.
9. Mark Lilla, *The Once and Future Liberal*, Harper, 2017.
10. *Financial Times*, 10 December 2018.
11. 'Notes on Nationalism' was first published in 1945 in *Polemic* – a British magazine of philosophy, psychology and aesthetics published between 1945 and 1947. This was taken from George Orwell, *Notes on Nationalism*, Penguin Classics, 2018.

10: *Time and Consequence*

1. Patrick Devlin, 'Morals and the Criminal Law', in *The Enforcement of Morals*, Oxford University Press, 1965, 1–25.
2. Ibid., 10.
3. Ibid., 13.
4. H.L.A. Hart, *Law, Liberty and Morality*, Oxford University Press, 1963.
5. Karl Popper, *The Poverty of Historicism*, Routledge, 1991, 158.
6. Friedrich Hayek, *The Fatal Conceit*, Routledge, 1988.
7. Ibid., 136.
8. Centres for Disease Control and Prevention, July 2015, https://www.cdc.gov/vitalsigns/heroin/infographic.html.
9. 'For Opioid Use Disorder, Does Cannabis Produce Harm or Reduce Harm?', Recovery Research Institute, 26 January 2018.
10. 'Daily Use of High-Strength Cannabis Increases Risk of Psychosis', National Health Service, 20 March 2019.
11. 'Marijuana Use is Associated with Intimate Partner Violence Perpetration Among Men Arrested for Domestic Violence', Translational Issues in Psychological Science, Vol. 4(1), 1 March 2018.
12. *The Times*, 23 January 2019.
13. Centers for Disease Control and Prevention, July 2015, https://www.cdc.gov/vitalsigns/heroin/infographic.html.
14. *Daily Telegraph*, 18 May 2019.

15. *Independent*, 27 May 2018.
16. *Guardian*, 31 July 2018.
17. Mark Hertsgaard, *A Day in the Life: The Music and Artistry of the Beatles*, Delacorte, 1995, 193.
18. 'Oral Evidence: Clean Growth Strategy and International Climate Change Targets', Business, Energy and Industrial Strategy Committee, UK Parliament, 9 July 2019.
19. *New York Times*, 27 February 2015.

11: *Post-Truth*

1. James Ball, *Post-Truth*, Biteback Publishing, 2017; Matthew D'Ancona, *Post-Truth*, Ebury Press, 2017; Evan Davis, *Post-Truth*, Abacus, 2017.
2. D'Ancona, op. cit., 9.
3. A list of some of the more striking examples can be found in the *Independent*, 9 November 2016. See also David Greenberg, 'Are Clinton and Trump the biggest liars ever to run for President?', *Politico Magazine*, July/August 2016.
4. *The Times*, 17 December 2018.
5. Brookings Institution, Tech Tank, 23 October 2018.
6. 'Many Americans Say Made-Up News Is a Critical Problem That Needs to Be Fixed', Pew Research Center, 5 June 2019.
7. Remarks made at Global Conference for Media Freedom, London, 11 July 2019.
8. D'Ancona, op. cit., 4.
9. Ball, op. cit., 8. See also Tom Nichols, *The Death of Expertise*, Oxford University Press, 2018.
10. 'News Use Across Social Media Platforms 2018', Pew Research Center, 10 September 2018.
11. Ibid.
12. Paul Ricœur, *Freud and Philosophy*, Yale University Press, 1970.
13. T.S. Kuhn, *The Structure of Scientific Revolutions*, University of Chicago Press, 1970.
14. Alan Sokal and Jean Bricmont, *Intellectual Impostures*, Profile, 1998.
15. Nichols, op. cit., 69.
16. Friedrich Nietzsche, *The Gay Science*, translated with commentary by Walter Kaufmann, Vintage, 1974, 281.
17. Ibid., 283.

12: *Safe Space*

1. Bradley Campbell and Jason Manning, *The Rise of Victimhood Culture*, Palgrave Macmillan, 2018.
2. *New York Times*, 21 March 2015.
3. Greg Lukianoff and Jonathan Haidt, *The Coddling of the American Mind*, Penguin, 2018, 27–8.
4. I am grateful to Ian Metcalfe for this way of putting it.
5. A point made by Douglas Murray, *The Madness of Crowds*, Bloomsbury Continuum, 2019, 210–17.
6. *Sunday Times*, 14 July 2019.
7. *Daily Telegraph*, 13 May 2019.
8. *The Times*, 30 May 2019.
9. C.L. Stevenson, *Ethics and Language*, Oxford University Press, 1944; J.O. Urmson, *The Emotive Theory of Ethics*, Hutchinson, 1968.
10. Lukianoff and Haidt, op. cit., 2018.
11. 'How Does Cognitive Behavioral Therapy Work?', Medical News Today, 25 September 2018.
12. Julien Benda, *The Treason of the Intellectuals*, with a new introduction by Roger Kimball; trans. Richard Aldington, Transaction, 2007, 27.
13. See Jonathan Glover, *Humanity: A Moral History of the 20th Century*, 368–75.
14. *Guardian*, 13 March 2014.
15. Quoted in Glover, op. cit., 367.
16. 'The Experience of Jewish Students in 2016–17', NUS Connect, 3 April 2017.
17. *Independent*, 27 November 2015.
18. *Jewish News*, 29 May 2018.
19. *Jewish Chronicle*, 29 March 2019.
20. 'Learning Lessons: The Articulation of Antisemitism on Campus', *Renewal: A Journal of Social Democracy* (Vol. 27, No. 2), 2019.
21. Ed Husain, *The Islamist*, Penguin, 2007.
22. Lukianoff and Haidt, op. cit., 56–7.
23. Babylonian Talmud, *Baba Metzia* 84a.
24. George Orwell, *Orwell on Freedom*, Penguin Random House, 2018.

13: *Two Ways of Arguing*

1. BBC News, 30 October 2019.
2. The subtitle of an article by Ernest Owens, 'Obama's very boomer view of cancel culture', *New York Times*, 1 November 2019.
3. *The Times*, 2 November 2019.
4. In Akiba Solomon, *How We Fight White Supremacy*, Bold Type Books, 2019.
5. *New York Times*, 17 August 2019.
6. *The Times*, 2 November 2019.
7. *New York Times*, 7 June 2018.
8. Babylonian Talmud, *Eruvin* 13b.
9. The best recent treatment is Jan-Werner Muller's short book, *What is Populism?*, Penguin, 2017. See also the important paper, 'Populism: The Phenomenon', Bridgewater Associates, 22 March 2017.
10. See James Snyder, *On Tyranny: 20 Lessons from the 20th Century*, Bodley Head, 2017.
11. Ramban, *Commentary* to Num. 16:1.
12. Mishneh Avot 5:20.
13. Babylonian Talmud, *Pesachim* 22b.

14: *Victimhood*

1. Taken from the BBC Radio 4 series *Morality in the 21st Century*, Episode 5: Moral Heroes, 7 September 2018, https://www.bbc.co.uk/programmes/bobgtcrh. Used with permission from the BBC.
2. Michael Walzer, *Politics and Passion: Toward a More Egalitarian Liberalism*, Yale University Press, 2004, 37.
3. Edith Eger, *The Choice*, Rider, 2017, 9.

15: *The Return of Public Shaming*

1. Jon Ronson, *So You've Been Publicly Shamed*, Picador, 2015, 63ff.
2. Ibid., 268.
3. *New York Times*, 14 January 2019. Emily's story in her own words can be heard on the Invisibilia podcast, https://www.npr.org/2018/04/13/601971617/the-callout?t=1572963485786.
4. Ruth Benedict, *The Chrysanthemum and the Sword*, Houghton Mifflin, 2005.

5. Herbert Morris (ed.), *Guilt and Shame*, Wadsworth Publishing, 1971, 2.
6. Bernard Williams, *Shame and Necessity*, University of California Press, 1993, 89.
7. Robert Alter, *The Five Books of Moses: A Translation with Commentary*, W.W. Norton, 2004, 24–5.

16: *The Death of Civility*

1. Trevor Phillips and Hannah Stuart, *An Age of Incivility: Understanding the New Politics*, Policy Exchange, September 2018.
2. Ibid., 25–6.
3. 'Commission on Civility and Effective Governance', Center for the Study of the Presidency and Congress, January 2019, https://www. thepresidency.org/commission-on-civility-effective-governance.
4. Arthur C. Brooks, *Love Your Enemies*, Broadside, 2019, xiv.
5. Cass R. Sunstein, *Going to Extremes: How Like Minds Unite and Divide*, Oxford University Press, 2009.
6. David Goodhart, *The Road to Somewhere: The Populist Revolt and the Future of Politics*, Penguin, 2017.
7. Ibid., 4.
8. Stephen Carter, *Civility: Manners, Morals, and the Etiquette of Democracy*, Basic Books, 1998, 11.
9. Edward Shils, *The Virtue of Civility*, Liberty Fund, 1997, 4.
10. These are the dual principles of revelation and interpretation: the first is 'from heaven', the second is 'not in heaven'. Mishnah Sanhedrin 10:1; *Baba Metzia* 59b.
11. Rabbi A.I. Kook, *Orot*, Jerusalem, 1990, 152.
12. Mishnah Avot 4:1.

17: *Human Dignity*

1. I owe these quotes to Raymond Tallis, 'You chemical scum, you', in his *Reflections of a Metaphysical Flaneur*, Acumen, 2013.
2. Yuval Noah Harari, *Homo Deus*, Harvill Secker, 2016, 395.
3. Desmond Morris, *The Naked Ape*, Corgi, 1975.
4. A contemporary adaptation of the phrase attributed to Samuel Butler, that a chicken is an egg's way of making another egg. See Matt Ridley, *The Co-operative Gene*, Free Press, 2001, 9.
5. Sigmund Freud, *Totem and Taboo*, Routledge, 2001.

6. Sigmund Freud, *The Future of an Illusion*, Norton, 1975.
7. Michael T. Ghiselin, *The Economy of Nature and the Evolution of Sex*, University of California Press, 1974, 247.
8. Stephen Jay Gould, *Wonderful Life*, W.W. Norton & Co., 1989, 51.
9. Will Durant, *The Story of Civilization*, Vol. 1, 1935, 71.
10. *Hamlet*, Act 2, scene 2, 303–12.
11. Michael Rosen, *Dignity: Its History and Meaning*, Harvard University Press, 2012, 2.
12. Leon Kass, 'Human Dignity', in Kass, *Leading a Worthy Life*, Encounter Books, 2017, 159–78.
13. Quoted in Rosen, op. cit., 21.
14. Ibid., 24.
15. *Genealogy of Morality*, III, 25; Keith Ansell-Pearson and Carol Diethe (eds), Cambridge University Press, 1994, 115.
16. The term derives from the work of Paul Ricœur: see his *Freud and Philosophy: An Essay on Interpretation*, Yale University Press, 1970.
17. Friedrich Nietzsche, *The Gay Science*, translated with commentary by Walter Kaufmann, Vintage, 1974, 344.
18. Babylonian Talmud, *Eruvin* 100b.
19. Friedrich A. Von Hayek and William Warren Bartley, *The Fatal Conceit: The Errors of Socialism*, University of Chicago Press, 1989.
20. Yuval Noah Harari, *Homo Deus*, Harvill Secker, 2016. 368.
21. Ibid., 381.
22. Ibid., 397.
23. David Pears, *Predicting and Deciding*, Oxford University Press, 1964.
24. George Herbert Mead, *Mind, Self and Society*, Chicago University Press, 1934.
25. Planned Parenthood v. Casey, 505 U.S. 833 (29 June 1992) (joint opinion co-authored with Justices Souter and O'Connor).
26. Though see the works of Frans de Waal on the compassionate instinct that one does find in animals.

18: *Meaning*

1. 'Where Americans Find Meaning in Life', Pew Research Center, 20 November 2018.
2. *New York Times*, 4 July 2019.
3. John H. Pryor et al., 'The American Freshman: Forty Year Trends', Los Angeles: UCLA Higher Education Research Institute, 2007.

4. Quoted in David Brooks, *The Second Mountain*, Allen Lane, 2019, 47.
5. Bernard Williams, *Moral Luck*, Cambridge University Press, 1981.
6. Susan Wolf, *Meaning in Life and Why It Matters*, Princeton University Press, 2012.
7. Herbert Dreyfus and Sean Dorrance Kelly, *All Things Shining*, Free Press, 2011, 22–57.
8. Friedrich Nietzsche, *The Gay Science*, translated with commentary by Walter Kaufmann, Vintage, 1974, 181–2.
9. Yuval Noah Harari, *21 Lessons for the 21st Century*, Jonathan Cape, 2018, 269–308.
10. Philip Rieff, *My Life Among the Deathworks*, with an introduction by James Davison Hunter, University of Virginia Press, 2006.
11. Jerome Bruner, *Actual Minds, Possible Worlds*, Harvard University Press, 1986, 11–43.
12. Barbara Hardy, 'Towards a Poetics of Fiction: An Approach through Narrative', *Novel*, 2 (1968), 5–14.
13. Alasdair MacIntyre, *After Virtue*, Duckworth, 1981, 201.
14. Text of J.K. Rowling's Harvard University commencement speech, *Harvard Gazette*, 5 June 2008.
15. Dan McAdams, *The Redemptive Self*, Oxford University Press, 2006, 10.
16. *Einstein on Politics*, ed. David Rowe and Robert Shulmann, Princeton University Press, 2013, 227.

19: *Why Morality?*

1. Charles Darwin, *The Descent of Man*, Penguin Classics, 1989, 166.
2. Ibid., 113.
3. Alexis de Tocqueville, *Democracy in America*, The Modern Library, New York, 1981, Book 1, Chapter 16.
4. Ibid.
5. Ibid., Book 2, Ch. 5.
6. Ibid., Book 4, Ch. 6.
7. Ibid., Introduction.
8. *Democracy in America*, Vol. 2, Book 1, Ch. 2.

20: *Which Morality?*

1. Richard Nisbett, *The Geography of Thought*, Free Press, 2003.
2. Carol Gilligan, *In a Different Voice: Psychological Theory and Women's Development*, Harvard University Press, 1982.
3. Lawrence J. Walker, 'Sex Differences in the Development of Moral Reasoning: A Critical Review', *Child Development* 55(3) (1984), 677. Sara Jaffee and Janet Shibley Hyde, 'Gender Differences in Moral Orientation: A Meta-analysis', *Psychological Bulletin* 126(5) (2000), 703–26. Christina Hoff Sommers, *The War against Boys: How Misguided Feminism is Harming Our Young Men*, New York: Simon & Schuster, 2000.
4. Harry Redner, *Ethical Life: The Past and Present of Ethical Cultures*, Rowman & Littlefield, 2001.
5. Tamala Summers, *Why Honour Matters*, Basic Civitas Books, 2017, 22.
6. Peter Berger, 'On the Obsolescence of the Concept of Honour', *European Journal of Sociology* (1970), 339–47.
7. Redner, op. cit., 50.
8. Ibid., 60.
9. David Reisman, Nathan Glazer and Reuel Denney, *The Lonely Crowd: A Study of the Changing American Character*, Yale University Press, 1950.
10. Ibid., 11.
11. Berkeley Institute for the Future of Young Americans, 18 April 2019.

21: *Religion*

1. *Guardian*, 4 September 2017.
2. Religion News Service, 21 March 2019.
3. 'In U.S., Decline of Christianity Continues at Rapid Pace', Pew Research Center, 17 October 2019.
4. Owen Chadwick, *The Secularisation of the European Mind in the 19th Century*, Cambridge University Press, 1993, 10.
5. Alexis de Tocqueville, *Democracy in America*, The Modern Library, New York, 1981, 14.
6. Ibid., 182.
7. Ibid., 37.
8. Will and Ariel Durant, *The Lessons of History*, Simon & Schuster, 1996, 51.

9. Ibid., 92–3.
10. David Hume, *A Treatise of Human Nature*, edited, with an analytical index, by L.A. Selby-Bigge, Clarendon Press, 1978, 538.
11. Jonathan Sacks, *The Great Partnership: God, Science and the Search for Meaning*, Hodder & Stoughton, 2011.
12. Quoted in Ara Norenzayan, *Big Gods*, Princeton University Press, 2013, 122.
13. Ibid., 8.
14. Niall Ferguson, *Civilization: The West and the Rest*, Allen Lane, 2011, 287.
15. Émile Durkheim, *The Elementary Forms of Religious Life*, Free Press, 1995, 44.
16. Jonathan Haidt, *The Righteous Mind*, Pantheon, 2012, 193–317.
17. Sosis' work is discussed in both Norenzayan, *Big Gods*, op. cit., 94–117, and Jonathan Haidt, *The Righteous Mind*, op. cit., Chapter 11.
18. Dominic Johnson, *God is Watching You: How the Fear of God Makes Us Human*, Oxford University Press, 2016.
19. Norenzayan, op. cit., 19.
20. Kevin Hayley and Daniel Fessler, 'Nobody's Watching? Subtle Cues Affect Generosity in an Anonymous Economic Game', *Evolution and Human Behaviour*, 26 (2005), 245–56.
21. Nozenzayan, op. cit., 33–54.
22. Jean-Jacques Rousseau, *The Social Contract*, trans. Maurice Cranston, Penguin, 1968, 86–7.
23. Eric Kaufmann, *Shall the Righteous Inherit the Earth?*, Profile, 2010; *Whiteshift: Population, Immigration, and the Future of White Majorities*, Allen Lane, 2018.
24. Office for National Statistics, *Births in England and Wales, 2018*, 1 August 2019.

22: *Morality Matters*

1. Jim DeFede, *The Day the World Came to Town*, Regan Books, 2002, 7.
2. 'Seven Moral Rules Found All Around the World', The Institute of Cognitive & Evolutionary Anthropology, The University of Oxford, 11 February 2019.
3. *Jerusalem Post*, 12 July 2019.
4. HM Government Horizon Scanning Programme, *Social Attitudes of Young People*, December 2014.

5. Jean Twenge, *iGen: Why Today's Super-Connected Kids Are Growing Up Less Rebellious, More Tolerant, Less Happy – and Completely Unprepared for Adulthood*, Atria, 2017, 310.
6. *New York Times*, 4 July 2019.

23: *From 'I' to 'We'*

1. James Q. Wilson, *Crime and Human Nature*, Simon & Schuster, 1986, 430–8.
2. Jonathan Sacks, *The Politics of Hope*, Jonathan Cape, 1997, 245–58.
3. David Brooks, *The Road to Character*, Allen Lane, 2015, 3–15.
4. Lara Aknin et al., 'Prosocial Spending and Well-Being: Cross-Cultural Evidence for a Psychological Universal', *Harvard Business School Working Paper 11-038*, 2010.
5. 'Charter for Compassion', Greater Good Science Center, University of California Berkley, https://charterforcompassion.org/.
6. Lee Rowland and Oliver Scott Curry, 'A Range of Kindness Activities Boosts Happiness', *Journal of Social Psychology*, 159(3) (2019).
7. Cass Sunstein, *Going to Extremes*, Oxford University Press, 2011.
8. Raghuram Rajan, *The Third Pillar: The Revival of Community in a Polarised World*, William Collins, 2019.
9. Ibid., xxvi.
10. Ronald Cohen, *On Impact*, 2018; free downloadable PDF document available from www.onimpactnow.org.
11. Daniel Lubetzky, *Do the KIND Thing*, Ballantine Books, 2015.
12. Quoted in Philip Selznick, *The Moral Commonwealth*, University of California Press, 1994, 481.

Further Reading

Part One – The Solitary Self

1: Loneliness

Susan Pinker, *The Village Effect: How Face-to-face Contact Can Make Us Healthier, Happier, and Smarter*, New York, Spiegel & Grau, 2014.

John T. Cacioppo and William Patrick, *Loneliness: Human Nature and the Need for Social Connection*, New York, Norton, 2008.

Sebastian Junger, *Tribe: On Homecoming and Belonging*, New York, Twelve, 2016.

Niobe Way, Alisha Ali, Carol Gilligan and Pedro Noguera (eds), *The Crisis of Connection: Roots, Consequences, and Solutions*, New York, New York University Press, 2018.

2: The Limits of Self-Help

Will Storr, *Selfie: How We Became So Self-obsessed and What It's Doing to Us*, London, Picador, 2017.

Marianne Power, *Help Me: One Woman's Quest to Find Out if Self-help Really Can Change Her Life*, London, Picador, 2018.

Nicholas A. Christakis and James H. Fowler, *Connected: The Surprising Power of Our Social Networks and How They Shape Our Lives*, New York, Little, Brown and Co., 2009.

3: Unsocial Media

Jean M. Twenge, *iGen: Why Today's Super-Connected Kids Are Growing Up Less Rebellious, More Tolerant, Less Happy – and Completely Unprepared for Adulthood*, New York, Atria Books, 2018.

Sherry Turkle, *Alone Together: Why We Expect More from Technology and Less from Each Other*, New York, Basic Books, 2011.

Sherry Turkle, *Reclaiming Conversation: The Power of Talk in a Digital Age*, New York, Penguin Press, 2015.

Adam Alter, *Irresistible: The Rise of Addictive Technology and the Business of Keeping Us Hooked*, New York, Penguin Press, 2017.

Tim Wu, *The Attention Merchants: The Epic Scramble to Get Inside Our Heads*, New York, Alfred A. Knopf, 2016.

4: The Fragile Family

Charles Murray, *Coming Apart: The State of White America, 1960–2010*, New York, Crown Forum, 2012.

Robert D. Putnam, *Our Kids: The American Dream in Crisis*, New York, Simon & Schuster, 2015.

William Tucker, *Marriage and Civilization: How Monogamy Made Us Human*, Washington DC, Regnery Publishing, 2014.

Part Two – Consequences: The Market and the State

5: From 'We' to 'I'

Lionel Trilling, *Sincerity and Authenticity*, Cambridge, MA, Harvard University Press, 1972.

Alasdair MacIntyre, *A Short History of Ethics: A History of Moral Philosophy from the Homeric Age to the Twentieth Century*, London, Routledge & Kegan Paul, 1967.

Charles Taylor, *The Ethics of Authenticity*, Cambridge, MA, Harvard University Press, 1992.

Charles Taylor, *Sources of the Self: The Making of the Modern Identity*, Cambridge, MA, Harvard University Press, 1989.

Robert N. Bellah et al., *Habits of the Heart: Individualism and Commitment in American Life*, New York, Harper & Row, 1985.

6: Markets Without Morals

Robert Kuttner, *Can Democracy Survive Global Capitalism?*, New York, W.W. Norton & Company, 2018.

Adam Tooze, *Crashed: How a Decade of Financial Crises Changed the World*, New York, Penguin Books, 2019.

Alan S. Blinder, *After the Music Stopped: The Financial Crisis, the Response, and the Work Ahead*, New York, Penguin Press, 2013.

Michael Lewis, *The Big Short: Inside the Doomsday Machine*, New York, W.W. Norton, 2011.

Steven Pearlstein, *Can American Capitalism Survive? Why Greed Is Not Good, Opportunity Is Not Equal, and Fairness Won't Make Us Poor*, New York, St Martin's Press, 2018.

7: Consuming Happiness

Richard Layard, *Happiness: Lessons from a New Science*, London, Allen Lane, 2005.

Charles Murray, *In Pursuit of Happiness and Good Government*, New York, Simon & Schuster, 1988.

Richard Wilkinson and Kate Pickett, *The Spirit Level: Why More Equal Societies Almost Always Do Better*, London, Allen Lane, 2009.

Edward Skidelsky and Roberts Skidelsky, *How Much is Enough: Money and the Good Life*, London, Penguin, 2012.

Stephen Post and Jill Neimark, *Why Good Things Happen to Good People*, New York, Broadway Books, 2007.

Sonja Lyubomirsky, *The How of Happiness: A Practical Guide to Getting The Life You Want*, London, Sphere, 2007.

Robert A. Emmons, *Thanks: How the New Science of Gratitude Can Make You Happier*, Boston, Houghton Mifflin, 2007.

Tomáš Sedláček, *The Economics of Good and Evil: The Quest for Economic Meaning from Gilgamesh to Wall Street*, Oxford, Oxford University Press, 2013.

8: Democracy in Danger

Yascha Mounk, *The People vs. Democracy: Why Our Freedom is in Danger and How to Save It*, Cambridge, MA, Harvard University Press, 2018.

Moses Naim, *The End of Power*, New York, Basic Books, 2013.

Steven Levitsky and Daniel Ziblatt, *How Democracies Die: What History Reveals About Our Future*, New York, Crown, 2018.

Edward Luce, *The Retreat of Western Liberalism*, New York, Atlantic Monthly Press, 2017.

Mary Ann Glendon, *Rights Talk: The Impoverishment of Political Discourse*, New York, Free Press, 1991.

Yuval Levin, *The Fractured Republic: Renewing America's Social Contract in the Age of Individualism*, New York, Basic Books, 2016.

9: Identity Politics

Francis Fukuyama, *Identity: The Demand for Dignity and the Politics of Resentment*, New York, Farrar, Straus and Giroux, 2018.

Kwame Anthony Appiah, *The Lies That Bind: Rethinking Identity, Creed, Country, Color, Class, Culture*, New York, Liveright, 2018.

Mark Lilla, *The Once and Future Liberal: After Identity Politics*, New York, Harper, 2017.

Ben Cobley, *The Tribe: The Liberal-left and the System of Diversity*, Exeter, England, Societas, 2018.

Douglas Murray, *The Madness of Crowds: Gender, Race and Identity*, London, Bloomsbury Continuum, 2019.

10: Time and Consequence

Patrick Devlin, *The Enforcement of Morals*, London, Oxford University Press, 1965.

H.L.A. Hart, *Law, Liberty and Morality*, Oxford, Oxford University Press, 1963.

Friedrich Hayek, *The Fatal Conceit: The Errors of Socialism*, London, Routledge, 1988.

Hans Jonas, *The Imperative of Responsibility: In Search of an Ethics for the Technological Age*, Chicago, University of Chicago Press, 1984.

Part Three – Can We Still Reason Together?

11: Post-Truth

James Ball, *Post-Truth: How Bullshit Conquered the World*, London, Biteback Publishing, 2017.

Matthew d'Ancona, *Post-Truth: The New War on Truth and How to Fight Back*, London, Ebury Press, 2017.

Evan Davis, *Post-Truth: Why We Have Reached Peak Bullshit and What We Can Do About It*, London, Little, Brown, 2017.

Tom Nichols, *The Death of Expertise: The Campaign Against Established Knowledge and Why It Matters*, New York, Oxford University Press, 2017.

12: Safe Space

Greg Lukianoff and Jonathan Haidt, *The Coddling of the American Mind: How Good Intentions and Bad Ideas Are Setting Up a Generation for Failure*, New York, Penguin Books, 2019.

Bradley Campbell and Jason Manning, *The Rise of Victimhood Culture: Microaggressions, Safe Spaces, and the New Culture Wars*, Cham, Switzerland, Palgrave Macmillan, 2018

Heather Mac Donald, *The Diversity Delusion: How Race and Gender Pandering Corrupt the University and Undermine Our Culture*, New York, St Martin's Press, 2018.

13: Two Ways of Arguing

On woke, see the brilliantly funny Titania McGrath, *Woke: A Guide to Social Justice*, London, Constable, 2019.

On populism, see Jan-Werner Muller, *What is Populism?*, London, Penguin, 2017.

Timothy Snyder, *On Tyranny: 20 Lessons from the 20th Century*, London, Bodley Head, 2017.
Roger Eatwell and Matthew Goodwin, *National Populism: The Revolt Against Liberal Democracy*, London, Pelican, 2018.

14: Victimhood
Bradley Campbell and Jason Manning, *The Rise of Victimhood Culture: Microaggressions, Safe Spaces, and the New Culture Wars*, Cham, Switzerland, Palgrave Macmillan, 2018.
David Green, *We're Nearly All Victims Now! How the Politics of Victimhood is Undermining Our Liberal Culture*, London, Civitas, second revised edition, 2019.
Edith Eger, *The Choice: A True Story of Hope*, London, Rider Books, 2018.

15: The Return of Public Shaming
Jon Ronson, *So You've Been Publicly Shamed*, London, Picador, 2015.
Jennifer Jacquet, *Is Shame Necessary? New Uses for an Old Tool*, New York, Pantheon Books, 2015.
Ágnes Heller, *The Power of Shame: A Rational Perspective*, London, Routledge & Kegan Paul, 1985.
Herbert Morris (ed.), *Guilt and Shame*, Belmont, CA, Wadsworth Publishing, 1971.

16: The Death of Civility
Stephen Carter, *Civility: Manners, Morals, and the Etiquette of Democracy*, New York, Basic Books, 1998.
Edward Shils, *The Virtue of Civility*, Indianapolis, Liberty Fund, 1997.
Trevor Phillips and Hannah Stuart, *An Age of Incivility: Understanding the New Politics*, London, Policy Exchange, September 2018.

Part Four – Being Human

17: **Human Dignity**
Yuval Harari, *Homo Deus*, London, Vintage, 2017.
Michael Rosen, *Dignity: Its History and Meaning*, Cambridge, MA, Harvard University Press, 2012.
Leon Kass, *Life, Liberty, and the Defense of Dignity: The Challenge for Bioethics*, San Francisco, CA, Encounter Books, 2002.
Leon Kass, *Leading a Worthy Life*, New York, Encounter Books, 2017.

18: **Meaning**
Dan McAdams, *The Redemptive Self: Stories Americans Live By*, New York, Oxford University Press, 2006.
Hubert Dreyfus and Sean Dorrance Kelly, *All Things Shining: Reading the Western Classics to Find Meaning in a Secular Age*, New York, Free Press, 2011.
Emily Esfahani Smith, *The Power of Meaning: Crafting a Life That Matters*, New York, Crown, 2017.
Viktor E. Frankl, *Man's Search for Meaning: An Introduction to Logotherapy*, translated by Ilse Lasch, Boston, Beacon Press, 1962.
Viktor E. Frankl, *The Unheard Cry for Meaning: Psychotherapy and Humanism*, New York, Simon & Schuster, 1978.

19: **Why Morality?**
Matt Ridley, *The Origins of Virtue*, London, Viking, 1996.
Robert Wright, *The Moral Animal: The New Science of Evolutionary Psychology*, New York, Pantheon Books, 1994.
Christopher Boehm, *Moral Origins: The Evolution of Virtue, Altruism, and Shame*, New York, Basic Books, 2012.
Dacher Keltner, Jason Marsh and Jeremy Adam Smith (eds), *The Compassionate Instinct: The Science of Human Goodness*, New York, W.W. Norton & Co., 2010.

Joseph Henrich, *The Secret of Our Success: How Culture is Driving Human Evolution, Domesticating Our Species, and Making Us Smarter*, Princeton, Princeton University Press, 2016.

Robert M. Sapolsky, *Behave: The Biology of Humans at Our Best and Worst*, London, Bodley Head, 2017.

20: Which Morality?

Kenan Malik, *The Quest for a Moral Compass: A Global History of Ethics*, London, Atlantic Books, 2014.

Harry Redner, *Ethical Life: The Past and Present of Ethical Cultures*, New York, Rowman and Littlefield, 2001.

David Reisman, Nathan Glazer and Reuel Denney, *The Lonely Crowd: A Study of the Changing American Character*, New Haven, Yale University Press, 1950.

21: Religion

Ara Norenzayan, *Big Gods: How Religion Transformed Cooperation and Conflict*, Princeton, Princeton University Press, 2013.

Dominic Johnson, *God is Watching You: How the Fear of God Makes us Human*, New York, Oxford University Press, 2016.

David Sloan Wilson, *Darwin's Cathedral: Evolution, Religion, and the Nature of Society*, Chicago, University of Chicago Press, 2002.

Part Five – The Way Forward

22: Morality Matters

Jim DeFede, *The Day the World Came to Town: 9/11 in Gander, Newfoundland*, New York, Regan Books, 2002.

David Brooks, *The Road to Character*, New York, Random House, 2016.

23: From 'I' to 'We'

Raghuram Rajan, *The Third Pillar: The Revival of Community in a Polarised World*, London, William Collins, 2019.

Philip Selznick, *The Moral Commonwealth: Social Theory and the Promise of Community*, Berkeley, CA, University of California Press, 1994.

Jonathan Sacks, *The Politics of Hope*, London, Vintage, 2000.

Jonathan Sacks, *The Home We Build Together: Recreating Society*, London, Continuum, 2007.

Daniel Lubetzky, *Do the KIND Thing: Think Boundlessly, Work Purposefully, Live Passionately*, New York, Ballantine Books, 2015.